Modern Presidents
and the Presidency

Modern Presidents and the Presidency

Edited by

Marc Landy
Boston College

Proceedings of the Second
Thomas P. O'Neill, Jr., Symposium
on American Politics
Department of Political Science
Boston College

Lexington Books
D.C. Heath and Company/Lexington, Massachusetts/Toronto

Library of Congress Cataloging in Publication Data

Main entry under title:
  Modern presidents and the presidency.

  Revised papers and comments originally presented at the Second Thomas P. O'Neill, Jr.
Symposium on American Politics, held at Boston College in Oct. 1983, sponsored by the Boston
College Political Science Dept.
  Includes index.
  1. Presidents—United States—Congresses.   2. United States—Politics and government—
20th century—Congresses.   I. Landy, Marc, 1946-   .   II. Thomas P. O'Neill, Jr. Symposium
on American Politics (2nd : 1983 : Boston College)   III. Boston College. Political Science Dept.

JK516.M56 1985   353.03'1   84-47857
ISBN 0-669-08683-5 (alk. paper)
ISBN 0-669-09468-4 (pbk.: alk. paper)

Published simultaneously in Canada
Printed in the United States of America on acid-free paper
Casebound International Standard Book Number: 0-669-08683-5
Paperbound International Standard Book Number: 0-669-09468-4
Library of Congress Catalog Card Number: 84-47857

Contents

Preface

This book consists of revised and edited papers and comments, the original versions of which were presented at the Second Thomas P. O'Neill, Jr., Symposium on American Politics held at Boston College in October 1983. The symposium was organized by the Boston College Political Science Department with financial support from the university's Thomas P. O'Neill, Jr., Chair in American Politics. Speaker O'Neill graduated from Boston College in 1936 and was awarded an honorary doctorate of laws by the university in 1973. The first two holders of the O'Neill Chair, Professor Samuel H. Beer and Congressman Richard Bolling, participated in the symposium and their comments appear in this volume. The O'Neill Symposium is a biennial event devoted to the examination of American political institutions. The first symposium was devoted to the U.S. Congress. The third symposium, to be held in fall 1985, will examine American elections.

The grandeur of the presidency can serve to obscure the great debt which the president owes to the other institutions and people with whom he shares responsibility for governance and for political leadership. Tip O'Neill has served with distinction as the presiding officer of both the Massachusetts House of Representatives and the U.S. House of Representatives. He has been the unofficial leader of the opposition party and is the coiner of that epic phrase, "All politics is local." He is the perfect embodiment of those political forces which work to keep the president rooted in the realities of republican government and attuned to the aspirations of a democratic people.

Acknowledgments

The symposium on which this book was based was planned by a committee of the Boston College Political Science Department composed of Gary Brazier, Dennis Hale, Marc Landy, David Manwaring, Kay Schlozman, Robert Scigliano, and John Tierney. Robert Faulkner, chairman of the department, was of great assistance in organizing the conference and in the preparation of this volume. Denise Trapani of the Boston College Development Office provided expert administrative coordination. Father J. Donald Monan, S.J., President of Boston College, gave the full support of his office to this project. University Vice President Margaret Dwyer provided many valuable forms of guidance and assistance. The secretarial staff of the Political Science Department—Yvette Forget, Claire Sullivan, Joni Leone—with the assistance of Frances Fagan, were of invaluable help in the preparation and editing of the manuscripts. Daniel McGroarty prepared the selected bibliography and the index.

I also wish to thank the contributors to this volume, who responded to editorially imposed deadlines with alacrity and good humor.

Introduction

The presidency is so big it is hard to see. The president has become our relative: loved, hated, obsessively scrutinized, and too close to think clearly about. For some analysts he comes to permeate the atmosphere like a primitive god, requiring either propitiation or exorcism. Others, seeking to establish greater emotional distance, try to depersonalize the office, pretending that the personality of its occupant, and of his close aides and advisors as well, can be safely ignored in favor of a rigorous scrutiny of organization charts, paper flows, and whatever else can be listed and counted. These modern forms of scholasticism and animism vie with one another as means for evading the real problems of theory and analysis which the contemporary presidency poses.

Though a relative, the president is not our peer. Our intimacy with him is not achieved face to face. It comes via the electronic media, ensuring that communication is all one way. No monarch ever enjoyed such an opportunity to confront his or her subjects without backtalk. One has only to compare the image of the medieval king holding court in the midst of his people to that of the president filling all twenty-three inches of the television screen as he talks directly to each of us from the Oval Office to recognize what a vast increase in power has accrued to this modern executive.[1] For a nation whose very existence is owed to a rebellion against a king, these supramonarchical attributes are disturbing. In a republic, political actors share the limelight. In our politics, the president increasingly dominates center stage.

Yet he is no autocrat. His powers pale before those of totalitarian rulers or even petty despots. In other Western countries, prime ministers need only obtain the passive acquiescence of their cabinet-rank party allies in order to turn their wishes into law. Parliament is a rubber stamp. The president faces two houses of Congress—hostile at worst, truculent at best—who cling to the notion that they have the right to revise and to deny presidential initiatives. As President Nixon discovered to his chagrin, the division of powers provided for in the Constitution serves to arm both Court and Congress with potent weapons for bringing a president to heel.

While the Constitution serves to keep the president from becoming a king, it does not prevent him from laying claim to one of the chief sources of monarchical authority, the claim of stewardship. Despite the existence of the electoral college, modern presidents assert that they are the only elected officials chosen by all the people. From this they derive both a duty and a right: a duty to protect the interests of those least able to protect themselves, and a right to serve as the primary initiator and animator of public policy. By aping the monarch's claim to a privileged relationship with the common people, the president has succeeded in becoming the very symbol of the American commitment to democracy and equality.

To add to the confusion, the president is not just a person but an institution. In addition to the cabinet departments whose leaders the president appoints, the chief executive presides over a complex web of agencies and councils which have grown up within the executive office of the president. As James Fallows points out, one of the most difficult tasks facing a president is to provide a sense of direction to this vast array of people and organizations which are ostensibly there to serve him.[2] If he cannot provide such leadership, staffers and bureaucrats will find many other competing political forces—unions, industries, public interest groups, and more—eager to provide it.

To some extent these developments are the result of forces beyond anyone's control. Expansion of centralized power and the identification of the head of government with "the people" are both phenomena common to nations around the globe. However, as we have already seen, the U.S. president is not just another chief executive of a large state. To understand and appreciate this singularity one must not only look to the Constitution but also to the contributions which specific incumbents have made to the office. They have created images of what the president is like and they have stamped those impressions upon the public's memory.

The ability of presidents to shape public expectations about the presidency began at the beginning and has continued ever since. George Washington's embodiment of personal nobility and republican commitment fixed the notion in the public mind that the president would neither aggrandize the office via monarchical pretension nor trivialize it via petty partisanship. Andrew Jackson's appeal for popular support and his use of the Democratic party as a vehicle for mobilizing it added the roles of partisan leader and egalitarian symbol to the presidential repertoire. Lincoln's successful prosecution of the Civil War in the name of the Union resolved the ambivalence surrounding American nationhood and determined that the president would serve as the very embodiment of this triumphant nationalism. Woodrow Wilson expanded upon Theodore Roosevelt's notion of stewardship to make it the crux of a vision of the presidential office, a vision borrowed wholly and wholeheartedly by Franklin Delano Roosevelt. The specific influences which FDR, Eisenhower, Johnson, and Nixon have had on the modern presidency are explored in the chapters which this book devotes to them.

History favors winners. Yet some of the most important contributions to the evolution of the presidency have been made by losers. William Jennings Bryan created the modern presidential campaign by abandoning his front porch and traveling the length and breadth of the country in a quest for votes. Al Smith, the first Roman Catholic and the first Irish-American to gain the endorsement of a major party, did much to wipe away the tarnish of religious exclusivity and ethnic bigotry which had tainted the presidential office. And, the presence of Geraldine Ferraro on the 1984 Democratic ticket decisively undercut the traditional assumption that presidential politics is an exclusively male preserve.

The enormous impact of individuals upon the office means that a study of the presidency requires a study of the character of individual presidents. As several studies in this book show, the president's actions are decisively shaped by his family upbringing, by the influence of key individuals, and by his own personal understanding of history, of America, of other nations, and, not least, of the responsibilities of office. As important as character is, it does not capture all that one needs to know to evaluate a president's leadership. Leadership is not simply a personal attribute like intelligence, creativity, or goodness. It is relational and requires a particular marriage of qualities and understandings between leader and led. Despite their impressive leadership skills, one could no more imagine the late George Meany leading a citizen's protest against air pollution than one could envisage Ralph Nader presiding over a meeting of the AFL-CIO Executive Council. Most successful leaders deal with a constituency that is relatively homogeneous. The president faces one as diverse as the nation itself. Some presidents have been able to educate, cajole, inspire, and even ennoble the citizenry at crucial junctures in our history. To understand the nature and the sources of such leadership is perhaps the most difficult and the most important task facing students of the presidency.

To confront the task of seeing the presidency, this book brings together a diverse group of professors, journalists, and professional politicians. They display a refreshing unwillingness to limit themselves to what one might expect either of academics, "pols," or "the media." For example, Congressman Barney Frank displays his theoretical prowess by proposing a scheme for reconceptualizing the executive office of the president, while Professor Sam Beer artfully weaves his practical experience as a Roosevelt administration speech writer into his scholarly interpretation of the meaning and measure of FDR's New Deal accomplishments. Nonetheless, the calculated effort to view the presidency through three different lenses—those of the scholar, the reporter, and the political practitioner—has its intended effect. The academics provide a broad frame of reference and standards of evaluation for the specific discussions. Often, they are able to provide means for reconsidering the topic at hand in unconventional and stimulating ways. The journalists subject these conceptualizations to rigorous immersion in the evidence, and the politicians provide a keen sense of what the political constraints facing the executive actually are, bolstering their arguments with a rich supply of evocative and provocative anecdotes.

The contents of this book, like its contributors, are diverse—and for the same reason. Diversity is of the essence of the subject at hand. Since the presidency is both an institution and a person, both require study. Thus, part of the book is devoted to general themes of relevance to the contemporary office, while the rest is devoted to the activities of a select sample of the men who have held it in modern times.

The great advantage which this book offers to teachers of undergraduate courses about the presidency is its blend of contributors and content. The inclusion of journalists and politicians provides readers with a sense of immediacy, of the richness of political life, often lacking in academic texts. The contributors disagree about many important things: whether the executive office of the president is overly politicized; whether the president has made excessive use of his capacity to dominate public debate; whether particular presidents really were successful political leaders; and so forth. These debates are stimulating in their own right and they also inform the student that great questions about executive governance and political leadership are far from settled, and that he or she is in fact participating in a serious and continuing intellectual quest. The interest of the student is held by the highly readable, jargon-free prose in which the chapters are written. From the perspective of undergraduate teaching, this book fills a very significant gap in the existing presidency literature. Currently, the literature is dominated by three sorts of writings: texts, biographies, and memoirs. Each of these forms possesses inherent defects. Texts must either be encyclopedic or superficial. In either case they have a difficult time capturing the drama and excitement of presidential politics. Memoirs are valuable but are often more concerned with enhancing the reputation of the author than with providing useful political analysis. Biographies—at most one or two—can be assigned in a one-semester course.

This book offers the advantages of each of these forms while minimizing their defects. It concentrates on three central analytic questions about modern presidents: the impact of their character on their performance; their role as public educators and molders of opinion; and their role as managers of the executive branch. It provides detailed yet succinct examinations of four of the most influential modern presidents: two Democrats and two Republicans. In each case, insightful reminiscences are complemented by detached academic scrutiny.

The four presidents chosen include the two most politically successful of modern presidents—Franklin Roosevelt and Dwight Eisenhower—and two of the most controversial—Lyndon Johnson and Richard Nixon. No discussion of modern presidents can ignore Franklin Roosevelt. Not only did he win election to the office four times, but he placed his stamp upon both the political and administrative dimensions of the office to an unparalleled extent. As William

Leuchtenburg has persuasively argued, subsequent presidents have, in one way or another, labored in his shadow.[3] Dwight Eisenhower is the most recent president to actually complete two terms in office. His tenure was marked by extraordinary popular acclaim, and academic disdain. The failure of his successors to maintain public support reopens the question as to who was more correct about him: the people or the experts. The controversy which continues to surround Lyndon Johnson and Richard Nixon stems both from their aggressive use of presidential power and from questions about their character. As the emotional impact of the Vietnam War and Watergate recedes, it becomes both possible and useful to reexamine these two enigmatic leaders and to reevaluate their performance in office.

The book begins with a discussion of presidential character. Both Richard Neustadt and Lou Cannon dwell upon the ways in which the president's personal views and experiences influence his behavior in office. For example, Cannon discerns that Reagan's commitment to reduced taxation results not from his reading of supply-side economics but from his own costly confrontation with the Internal Revenue Service just after World War II. He traces Reagan's extraordinary ability to inspire trust and affection among common people to the fact that he was born and raised a Democrat. Reagan's partisan roots are revealed by his habit of referring to the opposition party as the Democratic party rather than as the Democrat party, the approved Republican term.

Neustadt is likewise fascinated by the influence of the president's own personal mindset upon the way he actually behaves in office. He makes use of his own extensive firsthand knowledge of the Truman presidency to probe the various ways in which a president's view of history, of America, of other nations, and of the responsibilities of his office influence his actions. For example, Truman considered Francisco Franco to be a fascist and a bigot. Therefore he vigorously resisted the sage advice of his foreign policy advisors to provide military aid to Spain.

The "Rhetorical Presidency" is the face of the president that gazes outward toward the public. Such a topic is particularly worthy of consideration during the presidency of a man who has acquired the nickname of "Great Communicator." What should the rhetorical function of the president be? Professor James Ceaser fears that proponents of what he terms the "rhetorical model" have created a dangerously inflated conception of the president as persuader. Thus, they promote unrealistic expectations concerning the capacity of government and risk undermining the subtle system of checks and balances needed for stable republican government. By misinterpreting the arguments of the nation's Founders concerning the nature of the presidency and by criticizing the constitutional limitations on the office, they have, paradoxically, laid the groundwork for the strong contemporary attacks upon presidential power.

George Reedy, a former presidential press secretary, also uses the Constitution as his point of departure for examining presidential rhetoric. He notes the lack of a distinction in the American constitutional system between head of state and head of government. The president is both, and therefore he performs the often contradictory rhetorical tasks associated with each. As head of state, he must symbolize national unity and cohesion. As head of government he must implement his program, a task that often calls for combat and partisanship. Reedy examines the actual use of presidential rhetoric in terms of how it succeeds or fails to bridge this seemingly unbridgeable gap.

Pollster Irwin Harrison looks at the limits upon the success of presidential rhetoric imposed by the media. He is impressed by the media's ability to undermine presidential claims of positive accomplishments and he is concerned that its very short attention span causes it to "turn" on a president after a couple of years in office, regardless of how good a job he has been doing. James Fallows, a journalist and former presidential speech writer, disputes Ceaser's emphasis upon the overuse of presidential rhetoric. He sees a clear need for the forceful use of speech to enable a president to build public support for his program and, equally important, to convey a sense of purpose and direction to his own allies and subordinates.

The "Institutionalized Presidency" is the face of the president that looks inward toward the complex web of agencies, offices, and staff that surround him. Does this enormous apparatus represent a vital instrument of executive leadership and policy coordination and continuity, a bureaucratic morass that saps leadership resources, or a despotic instrument usurping authority which appropriately belongs either to cabinet departments or the Congress? Hugh Heclo takes a historical approach to these questions by examining the origins of the executive office of the president and tracing its subsequent development, as well as the checkered history of efforts to rethink and reform it. He is particularly concerned with finding means for establishing the appropriate staffing balance within the executive office between temporary political appointees loyal to the president and career civil servants loyal to the presidency.

Professor Thomas Cronin examines the organizational arrangements surrounding the president to assess how well they enable the president to obtain the information he needs to exercise effective leadership. He finds that a disturbing gap has developed between the largely nongovernmental "brains" of the society and the formal mechanisms which provide information for the state. Barney Frank draws upon his experience as a member of the House of Representatives to consider the impact of the expansion of the executive office of the president on the ability of the Congress to perform its executive oversight duties. Frank suggests ways for reorganizing the office to enable the Congress to carry out its constitutionally prescribed task more effectively. Former White House correspondent Katharine Ferguson disputes the idea that the president has become a prisoner of his erstwhile subordinates. She provides important examples in which the president proved himself quite able to slip loose from his organizational harness and take actions reflecting his own personal judgments and preferences. She also takes issue with Professor Heclo's proposal for increasing the prominence of civil servants as opposed to partisan loyalists within the executive office.

The chapter on Franklin Delano Roosevelt examines FDR the democrat and FDR the Democrat. How did a man who grew up in splendid isolation among the landed gentry become the champion of the common man? What principles of design and construction governed his approach to rebuilding the Democratic party? In order to gain a fresh vantage point to explore these difficult questions both Geoffrey Ward and I examine FDR in light of his relationship with mentors and rivals. Ward considers the development of FDR's political ambition and political character by investigating the influence exerted upon him by his cousin, Theodore Roosevelt. I consider FDR's behavior toward his most powerful and dangerous intraparty competitor, John L. Lewis, in order to understand how he sought to both conciliate and subordinate a crucial constituent element of his renewed party, the labor movement.

The pursuit of FDR, democrat and Democrat, is joined by Samuel Beer and Edward Prichard, who, in addition to their other scholarly and political accomplishments, both worked for Roosevelt. Beer examines the way in which FDR groped toward the development of an ideology that was compatible with the political coalition he had forged. Prichard offers compelling explanations of why FDR chose the Democratic route, rather than the Republican path favored by his Cousin Theodore, to pursue his democratic ideals. He also touches up the somewhat rosy portrait of John L. Lewis which I painted by adding the darker hues of nepotism and autocracy to the picture. His comments retain their wit and trenchancy when reduced to written form, but one cannot but pity those who did not hear them delivered orally. The imitation of John L. Lewis, replete with stentorian tones and self-propelled eyebrows, has lost none of the vividness for which it was famous during the New Deal period.

In recent years, Dwight Eisenhower's reputation among scholars of the presidency has risen markedly. Perhaps the most important cause of this reassessment has been Fred Greenstein's biography of Eisenhower, subtitled "The Hidden-Hand Presidency." Here, Greenstein defends his thesis that Eisenhower's skills as a president have been vastly underestimated and that this underestimation is itself a backhanded tribute to the deftness with which Eisenhower concealed his actions and intentions. Greenstein's defense met with skepticism from Congressman Richard Bolling, who was an active member of the congressional opposition to Eisenhower, and from Robert Donovan, a journalist who covered Eisenhower and who is himself an Eisenhower biographer. Kenneth Davis's account of Eisenhower's transition from soldier to president provides facts and insights which illustrate both Eisenhower's talents and his limitations.

Lyndon Johnson continues to be the subject of critical assault. The most recent barrage was launched by *The Path to Power*, the first volume of Robert Caro's projected three-volume biography, which dwells upon Johnson's financial dealings and backdoor political maneuvers.[4] Here, Wilson C. McWilliams provides a spirited counterattack. He titles his chapter "Lyndon B. Johnson: The Last of the Great Presidents," and proceeds to explore the meaning of presidential greatness and to explain why LBJ was great. McWilliams's contention is substantiated and elaborated by two men who served LBJ, Harry McPherson and John Roche. They provide memorable examples of LBJ's personal weaknesses and political failings as well as of the political courage and principled commitments that constitute his valid claim to greatness.

Discussion of the Nixon presidency has been dominated by Watergate to such an extent that other important aspects of it have not received adequate attention. Although the shadow of Watergate is not entirely absent here, a strong effort is made by all the participants to examine and interpret Nixon's leadership with regard to the full range of foreign and domestic issues which arose during his tenure in office. Congressman John J. Rhodes, minority leader of the House of Representatives during the Nixon presidency, presents a detailed job description for the president and then measures Nixon's accomplishments against it. Hedley Donovan, former editor in chief of Time, Inc., examines some of the traits of character that led to what he terms Nixon's "broken" presidency. He offers reasons to expect that Nixon's reputation will improve somewhat during the coming decades. Professor Robert Scigliano discusses the degree to which responsibility for Nixon's broken presidency must be shared by his critics. Professor David Manwaring comments upon the degree to which Nixon's power as president derived not from his skills as a partisan or popular leader but rather from his willingness to make the fullest possible use of the grants of discretionary authority yielded to him by the Constitution and the Congress. He then considers the impact of Nixon's exploitation of institutional power upon the current state of the presidency.

This brief overview cannot possibly convey the deliberative quality of the chapters taken as a whole or the ability of the commentators to take into account what the authors have to say and to elaborate, modify, or dispute the propositions offered. The actual manner in which theory, observation, and political judgment mesh together is subtle and pleasing in ways that no summary can adequately capture. At this juncture readers should be left to their own resources to discover the many insights which this deliberative forum has to reveal.

Notes

1. The best depiction of this evolution of executive authority is in Bertrand de Jouvenel's *On Power* (Boston: Beacon Press, 1948).

2. See his comments on "the rhetorical presidency" in this book, on page 43.

3. For a discussion of the impact of FDR on subsequent presidents see William Leuchtenburg, *In the Shadow of FDR: Harry Truman to Ronald Reagan* (Ithaca, N.Y.: Cornell University Press, 1983).

4. Robert Caro, *The Years of Lyndon Johnson: The Path to Power* (New York: Alfred A. Knopf, 1982).

Part I
Presidential Character

1
Truman in Action: A Retrospect

Richard E. Neustadt

Harry S Truman is the only two-term president since Wilson not granted an entire part in this book. I understand why Truman is not given more than a chapter: Truman has not made an indelible impression on historians. He did, however, make an indelible impression on me. And I once became quite famous for quoting just one Truman aphorism, which has to do with Eisenhower entering the presidency: "Poor Ike, it won't be a bit like the army. He'll sit here and say 'do this', 'do that' and nothing will happen." My success with that one leads me to think that if I reach into my little store of Truman stories I can give you a few that pose questions applicable to the other presidents covered in this book, and even applicable to the current occupant of the White House.

Let me begin with Mr. Truman's feelings, often voiced, about two of his predecessors, Theodore Roosevelt and Woodrow Wilson. The simple term that Mr. Truman used for Teddy Roosevelt was "four-flusher." "TR talked a big game, but when did he ever go up on the Hill and try to do anything about anti-trust legislation? He was always pussyfooting around the Speaker, always stumbling all over himself to be polite and stay out of the way." On the other hand, Mr. Truman had an enormous respect for Woodrow Wilson. What he mentioned when I heard him reminisce was not the Wilson of the War in 1918 and the League fight and the final tragedy. Rather it was the Wilson of 1913–14; getting an innovative program through Congress; going personally before the Senate and the House for the first time since John Adams; and doing his best, quite successfully, to make things happen up there. Now, at the time that Wilson was doing those things, Mr. Truman was farming in western Missouri. How he had such feel for the innovative president pushing a liberal program despite the lack of radio or television, or any of the media we now think "revolutionized" communication, I don't know. But after a day of farming, Truman did *something;* he read *something;* he heard *something* that made an enormous impact on him. His memories of Wilson were memories of history forward, not backward. He did not remember Wilson the way those of my students who have studied him recall him, League of Nations first. Truman remembered Wilson from the other direction, from the outset of his presidency. What made a great impression on him was the early Wilson. Had we stopped to think about this phenomenon of remembering forward it might have helped us understand how Ronald Reagan thinks about Franklin Roosevelt. It is not the Roosevelt of Yalta; and, before that, the Second New Deal—Social Security and so forth. Instead, to judge from Reagan's comments it is, rather, the FDR of the Hundred Days, the First New Deal.

With regard to every president, it is worth asking: What does he remember and in what order? What comes first? Getting that straight may tell you quite a lot about his underlying attitudes toward his office.

Now for a second Truman story—this one leaps from Woodrow Wilson all the way to nuclear weapons. In 1957 I was talking with Truman while doing some research at his library, and I asked him about the impact of the Soviet fusion bomb: How did the Soviet success in exploding a thermonuclear device only months after our first hydrogen explosion, affect the political balance of the world? Mr. Truman talked about that a little while, and then he said, "You know, I don't believe they have it. Oh, they may have something as big as a house or a freight car. But it's not something you can put in a plane or actually use." That was 1957. That first Soviet explosion had occurred in 1953. Truman added, "After all, they're Russians. They're basically peasants. They're not Americans. They can't hope to achieve the technology we've achieved." Now that wasn't said with any sense of Cold War competitiveness. It reflected, rather, a deep sense of America as God's country, first in all things, onward and upward, through his pores so to speak, learned on the middle border of the Middle West before the First World War.

I went East in something of a trance after that. On the way I stopped in Washington and told this story to a former colleague of mine at the Truman White House. He said, "Oh, that's nothing; in 1951, the president said the same thing to me about the A-bomb." (The first Soviet fission explosion had come two years earlier.) My friend went on to say that he had reported Truman's remark to Admiral Dennison, and naval aide, then the liaison on such matters, and Dennison grew so concerned that he arranged to rebrief Mr. Truman on the aerial intelligence mechanisms by which we were able to tell, definitely, what it was that the Soviets had exploded. Mr. Truman gave permission for another briefing and was very polite about it. According to my friend, he listened attentively to the whole thing and then he said,

> Gentlemen, I understand perfectly well. I understand you this time and I understood you last time. Given the technology built into our mechanisms for surveillance, we have to go on the assumption that the Soviets have developed nuclear capability and have tested it so and so many times, and that they've packaged it in ways which force us to assume they have usable weapons. I understand that. Given the technology and the intelligence reports, we have, that has to be our assumption. All right. I'm prepared to make that assumption. Fine. Thank you very much.

Then, as my colleague rose to leave the room, Mr. Truman reached up, pulled him by the sleeve and with a twinkle in his eyes said,

But I don't really believe it.

Where do presidents draw the line between belief and the assumptions they will use for action? How willing are they to draw any line? Often in these last three years, I have asked myself this question with respect to the president. I don't have any notion what the answer may be in his case. I am not trying to impute anything. But it is a very interesting question—and important for the course of policy.

Mr. Truman for his part, was not easily or automatically deflected from a personal belief to an assumption that belied it as his basis for a policy. To take another instance, he believed high interest rates were bad for the United States. From 1945 to 1951 the interest rate on government bonds remained at 2½ percent, no higher, because that is what he believed. Finally, during the Korean War, as an anti-inflation measure, the secretary of the treasury, the chief White House economist, and the chairman of the Federal Reserve Board prevailed on him to let them put higher rates on Treasury bonds. But he did not yield easily.

Or take another instance, Franco's Spain. For a year and a half, Truman held Dean Acheson back on military aid to build air bases there because, as a matter of personal belief, the president did not want to help fascists. What's more he didn't want to help bigots, which by his lights the Franco people were. "Do you know," Mr. Truman would say, "they won't let Protestants be buried underground?" Well, he yielded on that one too. He didn't yield easily. In the end, however, he accepted the assumption that our airborne nuclear deterrent, as it then was, and European defense required bases in Spain. He acted on that assumption, based policy on it, but he went right on believing Spain's leaders were bigots. Given overwhelming reasons, he eventually unhinged his policy from his belief. Given technologic grounds in the Soviet instance, he moved faster. Where would other presidents have drawn the line? On what and when?

Now for another story. In 1949, soon after we first learned of the initial Soviet fission explosion, there was a big row inside the U.S. government on whether to divert research funds from new kinds of fission weapons, atomic weapons so-called, to a crash program to attempt to develop a fusion weapon, a hydrogen weapon. The outlook was not favorable. And a great many scientists, including Robert Oppenheimer, insisted that since the outlook was unfavorable, it was better to keep the research and development money going into *atomic* weapons and not do a crash program in this other direction. Indeed, that was Mr. Oppenheimer's fatal piece of advocacy, the real reason he was driven out of government some four years later.

I once asked Mr. Truman while he was still in office about his decision to go the other way. Because, after advice from a committee headed by Dean Acheson, his decision was to go with the crash program even though the science was not favorable. I asked him whether that was a hard decision. Scientists ever since have been telling us that it was a terrible decision, fraught with the future of humanity. "No," said Mr. Truman, "that wasn't a hard decision: that was an easy decision." He continued, as I recall,

> I asked them three questions. Might we be able to make it if we persevered with our research? They said "yes." Might the Russians be able to make it if they persevered with their research? They answered "yes." Then I asked, might they be able to make it even if we don't make it? And they answered "yes." So I had no choice: we had to try; *I couldn't bind my successor.*

If there were options to be had, Mr. Truman felt his successor must have them. He must see to it. He felt himself to be, then, the trustee for the next president. To a remarkable degree Mr. Truman distinguished the presidency from himself. He saw the office as a living chain of presidents, stretching from George Washington on into the future, each a trustee for those following after. He saw himself as merely—accidentally to begin with—a temporary link in that immortal chain, lucky to be there (he enjoyed it immensely), and grateful for the chance to do his duty by the office. He revered the office. He often talked about "the president" in the third person; rarely, did he confuse that august and immortal personage with himself, Harry Truman.

On the other hand, I recall one occasion where this president deliberately stepped across the line and identified the presidency with himself, with Truman personally. He had first been proposed for the Senate by the then political boss of Kansas City, Tom Pendergast, who later went to jail for tax evasion and subsequently died a broken man. Years later, Dean Acheson, the secretary of state, got angry at a press conference, set off a great press uproar, and felt he had improperly embarrassed the administration. So he went to the White House and tendered his resignation. Truman refused it. His words are of interest. Both men recounted them to me, quite independently, so I believe I have them straight. They make the punch line for my final story.

The incident had been occasioned by the conviction of Alger Hiss in his second trial for perjury (inferentially treason). Hiss had once been a State Department colleague of Acheson's; his brother had worked in Acheson's law firm. Eastern establishmentarians in general had rallied to Hiss and Acheson, who were quintessentially Eastern Establishment. So at the next press conference the reporters ignored foreign policy and shouted out questions about whether he would not repudiate his acquaintance with the newly convicted perjurer. Acheson thought it a squalid and irrelevant concern. He and Hiss had not been close; they had, however, been friendly, and his son-in-law was close to Hiss's brother. He got his dander up, his moustache bristled, he quoted the biblical passage, and he snapped "I shall not turn my back on Alger Hiss." This statement created the uproar which led to his decision to resign.

When Acheson came in to do that, Truman listened quietly but with increasing seriousness, then responded:

Dean, of course you can't resign. I won't let you. Forget it. And I don't ever want to hear you talk like that again. Don't you realize that as president of the United States I followed a criminal to his grave—and I knew exactly what I was doing.

In 1947, when Pendergast died, Truman had gone to the funeral.

"I knew exactly what I was doing." Those words say that there were times when Truman occasionally subordinated his office to himself, to Harry S Truman the person. They further say that these were times worked out by calls on loyalty. Loyalty was for Truman a prime virtue and there thus could be occasions—here indeed are two—when it took precedence over his obligation to the presidency. Neither official dignity nor political advantage could outweigh the claims of loyalty in these circumstances.

Whether Truman was right in either instance is arguable. If "right" is tantamount to reasons of state, to public credibility, to prudence, to husbanding each ounce of potential influence for future use, then very likely he was wrong. If "right" is seen in terms more personal, as decency toward other humans, taken one by one, then he assuredly did right. For this is a heartwarming story. If I didn't have it to tell, we might judge him a greater politician than we do, but not a better man.

How do other presidents treat loyalty? When do they elevate its claims, when do they put it down, on what premises, with what results for policy? No question is more significant in studying the conduct of the presidency.

What these little stories add up to will, I hope, be obvious, and being so will be of use to the study of presidents. How the man in office remembers history, what history, and in what order is important. How he regards America—as an idea, as a trend, and as a fate—is important. Mr. Truman could no more imagine anything fundamentally bad happening to this country than he could imagine flying self-propelled to Mars. He had an unshakable faith that America's course was indeed onward and upward. How the president views other nations is important. If he thinks them peasants, that is consequential. So also if he thinks them an evil empire, assuming that is what he really thinks. It matters how he sees himself in office and how he sees the office in relation to himself. To a large extent the presidency has been institutionalized. But institutionalized or not, these things affect the history of presidencies and the choice-making of presidents.

2
The Real Reagan

Lou Cannon

When I wrote my recent biography, *Reagan,* I was operating under the delusion that I did not have to write about Reagan's formative years because I had already done that in an earlier biography. Those who are cursed with reading every political biography that comes along, as I am, know that most of the authors of political biographies like to get through the "log cabin phase" with dispatch. Every president, it turns out, had a father and a mother. Most of them grew up in circumstances in which one of the parents at least, usually the mother, propelled them to greatness; otherwise they would not have become presidents. It is remarkable how the opening chapters of political biographies blend into other opening chapters of other political biographies and how little they tell you. So I thought, having already performed my obligatory service, I could start where I had left off with the previous book, which was really at the end of Reagan's first term as governor of California, I would write about what I was really interested in, which is how he had performed as governor in the second term (surprisingly well); how he had campaigned against Ford; how he had won the nomination in 1980; and so on (this being right after he had been elected and was in the first year of his presidency). As it turned out, I did not understand Ronald Reagan at all. To try to understand all of the things that happened in the years that intervened, I found I had to understand Reagan better, I had to spend time on his childhood, more time on his formative years.

If you want to understand why Ronald Reagan favors tax reduction at a time that we are running record deficits, you do not understand it by trying to wade through tracts by Jack Kemp or Jude Wanniski, and wonder how these particular theologians waylaid him on the way to the White House and poured this stuff on his head. You have to understand what happened in Ronald Reagan's own life. What happened in Ronald Reagan's own life on taxes was this: He made a movie called King's Row that was released in the early 1940s. At the time it was released, he was already in the army, where he spent time making training films. But this movie, which was considered Reagan's best movie (a view with which I happen to disagree; I think he made a number of better movies) won him a very good contract, which his agent had negotiated. When he got out of the service in the mid-40s, his career was foundering. He was one of the group of not-quite-stars who people forgot about when they went away in the army, and there was a whole new group of movie fans who had never heard of Ronald Reagan and the others who were just at the brink of stardom before the war. Nonetheless, he had this wonderful contract and was making a lot of money.

This happened during a window in U.S. history when marginal tax rates were at 90 percent and individuals could not income average. Corporations could, but individuals could not. This was an inequity which any economist, liberal or conservative, would agree was unfair to the ballplayer, the actor, or the novelist who had a lot of income one year and none the next. This inequity was corrected by Congress within the space of a few years. But it hurt Reagan. He had no idea, having grown up poor, that people could earn a lot of money and hav. most of it taken from them in taxation. He would go to other actors and actresses whom he knew in Hollywood at that time when he was a Democratic liberal—and suggest the idea of a human depletion allowance, like the oil depletion allowance. It never caught on, but nonetheless, Ronald Reagan kept this view that personal income taxes were too high and ought to be reduced. And, in the face of the collective advice of his entire, rather bewildering array of advisors, Ronald Reagan hung tough on the third year of the tax cut, even though probably from an economic point of view he should not have.

This is an illustration of what is needed to understand Ronald Reagan's view of anything; it is just as true with regard to foreign policy. He first formed his views about the Soviet system when Communism was a monolith and the Soviets called the tune. He has retained this view for decades after the Communist world has fragmented. I think he has a realistic view of the Soviets. What he does not understand is that the Soviets are not the only Communist force in the world. President Ronald Reagan has had a very difficult time, it's taken three and a half years, realizing that for better or worse, the government of the People's Republic of China in fact represents China, and that that's where he's got to go rather than Taiwan. I don't say that glibly, because I think that in his basic view of the Soviets he is much more realistic than President Carter, who discovered after Afghanistan that he had had the wrong view, as he told everybody.

John Glenn, who had the greatest record of support for Carter of any senator, now calls him a failed president. It's one of the few times I ever felt sympathetic to Jimmy Carter. But if that's true, Ronald Reagan was, like a lot of us, a failed Democrat. He grew up a Democrat. His metaphors, his language, and tone—the way he addresses people—are in a Democratic mode. He still talks about the Democratic party. Modern Sunbelt Republicans talk about the Democrat party; those of us who grew up Democrats never called it the Democrat party. The resonance is right, the voice is right, because the experiences were authentic. What happened to Ronald Reagan happened to a lot of people in this country. They grew up poor; they achieved success, usually not as much success as he did; and they became Republicans. I once said, and I was torn apart by my conservative audience, that Ronald Reagan became Republican because he became rich. That was too flip and is the kind of oversimplification of which Reagan himself would be proud.

A friend of mine in the White House asked why I called the book just *Reagan,* without a subtitle, "Study in Power," or the like. The friend said "Good—the title's so simple even he'll remember it." That is not as much a shot at Reagan as it sounds, but rather like the Mark Twain remark about Wagner's music being better than it sounds. Reagan fudges the facts; he gets things wrong. (I once wrote of him he never met a statistic he didn't like.) But there is an essential honesty about Reagan in terms of his own origins. He knows who he was. He knows where he came from, he knows that he grew up a Democrat. He knows why he changed. He is addressing a country in which that happened to an awful lot of people. When Ronald Reagan speaks to people there is a resonance.

Ronald Reagan has made mincemeat of the very silly notion that television gives you the guy with the good looks and the teeth, "the pretty blonde," the anchorman whom one of my colleagus satirizes as Terry Splendid, who has the biggest teeth of anybody in the world except John Tunney. Ronald Reagan has used television to talk issues. Ronald Reagan would not be in the White House, and nobody would be talking about him, except that in 1976 in North Carolina after he had lost five primaries, he showed half-hour TV programs telling how he felt about the Panama Canal and the Soviets. Everybody in his campaign thought this was the stupidist thing they had ever heard of. Nobody is going to watch a half hour of Ronald Reagan on TV. Nobody is concerned about issues. But the fact of the matter is, he won the North Carolina primary. He came within a hundred votes of becoming the Republican nominee that year, and he would not have been the Republican presidential nominee in 1980, and he would not now be the president if he had not done that.

Ronald Reagan is the president whether we like it or not. I like some things he does very much; I think that other things he's done are deplorable; and there is a whole middle range where I cannot figure out what he has done. But, like it or not, Ronald Reagan stands for something. He has a set of values; he brings them to the presidency as his hero, Franklin Roosevelt, brought them to the presidency; and this means a lot to people. Ronald Reagan speaks to people in an authentic voice, and the people who dislike and oppose him who find his presidency harmful, view him as an important and significant president.

There is a great danger in assessing a presidency during its existence and probably in assessing it in the lifetime of the people who are doing the assessing. Hedley Donovan wrote a brilliant essay about fashions in the presidency, describing how in our lifetime we have changed our views of how good a president Eisenhower was, or Truman was. Truman left office at a lower level of popular esteem even than Richard Nixon, who left office rather than be impeached. Jefferson, whom many of us celebrate as a hero, was almost forgotten before Roosevelt rescued his reputation.

We do not know whether Ronald Reagan will achieve an arms control agreement with the Soviets, which is to me the most important issue of our time and certainly of our children's time. I asked a Soviet diplomat, "Would you rather deal with the devil you know or the devil you do not know?" And his answer was that they would always prefer to deal with the devil they know. If you look at the history of the Soviet Union and their dealings with conservatives compared to liberals and social democrats, they do tend to be more comfortable in dealing with people who fit their ideological preconceptions. Because of the Soviet needs, not because of any goodness of anybody's heart, but because they have real economic needs and problems, there is some economic imperative on them to limit at least the levels of these terrible death-dealing weapons that we are both building.

Without knowing whether he will achieve an arms control agreement, however, I would say Ronald Reagan has had an enormous impact on this country. He has defined the dialogue. He has been a defining president in the way that Roosevelt was. You see this in the Democratic budget alternatives that call for increases in defense spending and cuts in entitlements. They do not call for the kind of increases that Ronald Reagan wants or the cuts that Ronald Reagan wants, but he has defined the dialogue and I think that we have reached a period of pause in America, a period of re-evaluation. Ben Wattenberg once asked Ronald Reagan on television whether what he wanted to do was to reverse the New Deal or call a halt to it. Ronald Reagan did not answer the question. But it is quite clear to me that what he has done is certainly not reverse it. Social Security and all these things are irreversible. He has called, if not a halt, a great pause to it. How far do social democratic programs go? How far do welfare programs go? How much do we commit to a defense budget and how much do we commit to social program? I think that whatever happens in 1984 that history is likely to write that Ronald Reagan changed the direction in which the government was going, and I will leave it to all of you to decide whether that is good or wise.

Part II
The Rhetorical Presidency

3

The Rhetorical Presidency Revisited

James W. Ceaser

The term "the rhetorical presidency" has a decidedly rhetorical ring to it. It sounds engaging, important—indeed perfectly suited as a topic not just for an academic panel, but even for a "serious" discussion on the MacNeil-Lehrer Report. Yet like so many such terms, it suffers the defect of its virtue. It is catchy, but what if anything does it mean? Does it describe the whole of the presidency, or just one part (the mouth)? And, whether whole or part, does it refer to a "neutral" property, to something beneficial, or to a malady afflicting the body politic?

There are, as I see it, two possible conceptions of "the rhetorical presidency," one quite literal and the other more theoretical. The literal conception refers to the concrete and largely observable activity by presidents and their aides to inform, impress, or persuade the public by means of official speeches and public comments, deliberately divulged information, and special staged events like a town meeting. Two comments are in order about this definition. First, by limiting it to messages intended for public audiences, such as the Congress or the nation, it excludes efforts at persuasion made in private unless the substance of these exchanges is intended to be made public. Second, rhetorical techniques are not the only means, nor even necessarily the most effective means, by which presidents seek to inform, impress, or persuade public audiences. Actions, the old adage goes, speak louder than words, and a decision like President Reagan's dismissal of the nation's striking air traffic controllers in 1981 can say more than a hundred speeches about a president's firmness and resolve.

An attempt to study the rhetorical presidency in this literal sense would focus first on the president's words as uttered in speeches, press conferences, and written reports issued under his name. Expanding this somewhat—in line with Aristotle's observation that a speaker's ability to persuade is influenced greatly by the audience's perception of his or her character—we can say that a study of the rhetorical presidency would also include the conscious attempts by the president and his aides to present a certain "image" of the president's character. Thus one can count as part of the aspects of the rhetorical dimension of the presidency the efforts to make Ronald Reagan look compassionate by having him visit poor neighborhoods or the strategy outlined by Patrick Caddell in his memo to President Carter in early 1977. Caddell warned that candidates risk defeat if they rely too much on substance rather than style. He advised increased use of symbolic actions, "perhaps by ostentatious use of guests such as Bob Dylan and Martin Luther King, Sr."[1]

Finally, keeping in mind that the subject is the rhetorical presidency and not just the rhetorical president, we should also include as rhetoric information that presidential aides give to the press in regard to what the president is said to be thinking about matters of general interest. Information of this kind usually finds its way into the press and therefore is, presumably, given, except where aides cannot resist unburdening themselves to journalistic "friends," with a view to its effect on some audience. The public picture of the presidency emerges as much from news reports as it does from direct communications between the president and the public.

To locate the rhetorical presidency in its physical or institutional aspect, one would look at the White House speech-writing process and at a large part of its "public relations" decision-making process. Attention would be given to the speech writers, the pollsters and media advisors, the press secretary, and all the other aides occasionally or intimately involved in carrying out rhetorical activities. And of course one could not ignore the presidents themselves, since a good deal of their time is spent planning their speeches and public appearances.

The other, more theoretical, conception of the rhetorical presidency refers to a doctrine or understanding of presidential leadership that has greatly influenced, though by no means fully determined, the development of the modern presidency. This doctrine, articulated originally by Woodrow Wilson, has helped shape how people conceive of the presidency and how presidents conceive of their role—or how they are compelled by public expectations to conceive of it. Its central idea is that of a president engaged intimately in the process of forming public opinion and speaking out on the issues that confront the nation. It refers to a president who not only attempts to promote his own agenda but who is expected to minister in some way to the moods of the public (or the moods of the public as identified by the media). Vague as this last notion may seem most on the East coast should have at least an intuitive grasp of what it means, for otherwise it would be impossible to understand the tireless exhortations of *New York Times* editorial page imploring presidents to exercise positive leadership.[2]

Although a great deal more than rhetoric in a literal sense is involved in this conception of presidential leadership, the term "the rhetorical presidency" is probably as good a choice to describe it as any other. Rhetoric, after all, refers to the art of public persuasion, and public persuasion is clearly at the center of this doctrine of leadership. Moreover, the term "rhetoric" has a slightly suspect connotation today, implying that what is rhetorical is not completely real, but somehow fictitious. This connotation identifies a characteristic that many feel to be part of the problem of the modern presidency and that on reflection may be an inevitable consequence of a theory of leadership that places so much emphasis upon persuasion through public speech.

There is, clearly, a connection between the two conceptions of the rhetorical presidency just outlined. Presidents have always spoken and engaged in rhetorical strategies, but the emergence of the doctrine of the rhetorical presidency—together, obviously, with changes in the media—have influenced when, in what ways, and how often presidents make use of rhetoric. If we did not have the doctrine of the rhetorical presidency, we might even today have a lesser institutional capacity for the performance of the rhetorical function.

During recent presidencies, for example, there have been many instances when it has come to be widely expected, given the prevailing conception of leadership trumpeted in certain quarters, that the president must somehow deal with an issue for which no concrete political action was planned or perhaps even possible. The easiest response in such circumstances has often been some kind of presidential media or speech, which has contributed to the growth in the presidential office of a sophisticated rhetorical capability. In fact, in the climate currently generated by the expectations of the rhetorical presidency, it is now not uncommon for the decision to "give a speech" to precede any decision about what should be said. The commitment to give a speech becomes father to the speech's ideas.

The line of influence also, however, runs in the other direction. Those who are part of the president's rhetorical institutional apparatus may act as a kind of internal pressure group in behalf of the doctrine of the rhetorical presidency. Presidential speech writers, pollsters, and media consultants may press the president to adopt more aggressive rhetorical strategies because this reflects their own understanding of what is important in politics and because it is likely to enhance their influence within the administration.

The role of these advisors as a pressure group must be understood in part in light of the current presidential selection process. That process—surely one of the most intensive (and perverse) rhetorical arrangements ever devised—requires candidates to spend the bulk of their time and energy for up to two years in the activity of public persuasion, often without any responsibility for making real decisions. The advisors most important to the candidate, and those who win reputations for being leading "conceptualizers," naturally include the masters of the rhetorical function. Once their candidate is elected, however, his responsibilities include governing as well as talking, and these advisors are in danger of losing much of their influence. To avoid this fate, they have a vested interest in impressing upon the president that the activity of governing is not after all very different from that of campaigning. A president, they will contend, must continue to heed the polls, the shifts in public mood, and the changing images the public holds of his character. Since so many others, particularly modern journalists, share this view of the importance of "opinion poll" considerations, and since there is some truth in this assessment (but not nearly as much as is commonly supposed), recent rhetorical advisors have sometimes managed to hold on and become close advisors to sitting presidents.

The Doctrine of the Rhetorical Presidency

As spelled out by Woodrow Wilson and his successors, the doctrine of the rhetorical presidency contains three basic elements:

1. The president should become the policy-making leader of the nation, preferably by a change in the Constitution or the party system that would bypass the roadblocks of separation of powers.
2. The president's position as chief policy maker is legitimated by his popular election and his role as a public opinion leader, constantly in dialogue with the nation through speeches.
3. The character of leadership is educative and uplifting—"moral leadership"—and transcends interest group calculations and mere partisanship.

This doctrine, which has waxed and waned in its immediate influence since Wilson, has been carried forward by some of the major figures in American political science, such as E.E. Schattschneider and James MacGregor Burns, and by political advisors like Lloyd Cutler, who served as President Carter's chief counsel. Even though only a relatively small number have ever subscribed to the radical idea of changing the Constitution advocated by these thinkers, many have accepted their diagnosis of the general problems with the presidency and the view of the kind of leadership necessary to resolve these problems.

A profound irony attaches to this doctrine. It has been promoted on behalf of the idea of a much stronger presidency and against the Founders'—and the Constitution's—conception of the office. Yet it has largely misunderstood that original conception, and by criticizing and undermining the Constitution and the Founders, it has tended to weaken, not strengthen, the presidency. Even more ironically, the doctrine of the rhetorical presidency has helped to lay the groundwork for the strong attacks on the executive power that have taken place over the past decade.

The doctorine of the rhetorical presidency, like the Founders' doctrine, consists of a view of both *how* the president should conduct the affairs of his office and of what the executive power includes. On both these points, the two doctrines are in conflict, though it is in respect to the powers of the office that the advocates of the rhetorical presidency have most seriously misinterpreted the Founders' views.

The Powers of the Presidency

Partly because proponents of the rhetorical model have been so influential in interpreting the Constitution, many Americans now fail to understand what the Founders had in mind for the presidency. In particular, many seem to have lost any sense of the difference between the president's primary, executive, power and his secondary, policy-making, role. This distinction was clear to many of the Founders and has remained clear to many foreign observers.

For many years—at least up until the Vietnam War and Watergate—proponents of the rhetorical presidency told the American people that the presidency was too weak and that the nation should consider adopting a parliamentary model. How ironic it is, therefore, that the one democratic nation that changed its constitution in modern times, France, looked to the American idea of the presidency to save itself from a crisis in executive authority experienced under a parliamentary system. In the transformation from the Fourth to the Fifth Republic in 1958, the French founders sought to escape the sort of crisis that occurred during the first few months of 1958, when parliament was unable to choose a prime minister and the nation was without a power that could act with the force of the community to save the state from disintegration. What France had lost in 1958 was the heartbeat of any government: its executive power.

In turning to the American Constitution for instruction, the French founders evidently saw what so many Americans have missed; that however weak an American President might be as a policy maker, and however divided the nation might be on policy questions, the Constitution provides (as best a constitution can) for the sanctity and continuance of the state by ensuring the existence of the executive power in the primary sense. Our constitution purchased the sanctity of this power and of a mechanism for its control at the cost of a unitary and energetic policy-making authority, although it should by no means follow that a unitary and energetic policy-making authority necessarily produces better, more acceptable, or even more democratic policies.

The executive power as understood by Montesquieu, John Locke, and many of America's Founders in 1787 entailed the responsibility of the executive to enforce the law with discretion and to act in situations of necessity for the good of the community, whether beyond existing law or, if need be, contrary to existing law. In addition, the executive power was understood by these same sources to include the greater part of the "federative" or foreign-policy-making power, since the arena of foreign policy involved decisions requiring broad discretion and sometimes speedy and decisive action. Regarding the conduct of foreign affairs, however, the Founders made a distinction between the executive power and the powers given to the president, probably in order to guard against one of the chief sources of executive abuse in the past—war as the sport of kings. The Constitution provides that specific aspects of the federative power (treaties and declarations of war) be shared with one or both houses of Congress; but, at least until quite recently, it was widely thought that aspects of the federative power not otherwise specifically provided for in the Constitution belonged to the president being part of the executive power or being executive in nature.

The effort of the Founders to establish a strong executive is a well-known feature of the story of the founding. The conflict over the Constitution involved a struggle between those who held to a Whig (or prolegislative) interpretation, of the doctrine of separation of powers and those who held a "federalist" (or proexecutive) interpretation. According to the former, the nature of government was such that the tasks of governing could be defined by law and thus managed chiefly by the legislature, with the executive playing a ministerial role of carrying out the legislature's commands. According to the federalist view, however, law could not handle all situations and therefore the nation required an independent executive endowed with its own grant of discretionary power.

The executive power in the sense just indicated is exemplified by such actions as President Reagan's decision to fire the air traffic controllers in 1981 (an action taken in his capacity as chief executive officer carrying out, with discretion, the enforcement of the law); President Carter's decision to undertake the rescue of the hostages held in Iran or President Reagan's decision to invade Grenada (actions undertaken by the commander in chief to protect American lives); and, of course, any action a future president might have to take to respond quickly to an immediate attack by strategic weapons. In such instances, the president acts on the basis of power that inheres in the office and in the function of being the nation's chief executive. The president may consult and take counsel with others, but the power rests, in the final analysis, with the president.

The executive dimension of the presidential power must be distinguished from presidential power in the policy making process. The policy making process, entails the functions of planning, mobilizing, proposing, legislating, and implementing laws. In this process, the Constitution provides that the power be shared and divided between the president and Congress (omitting here any consideration of the role of the court system). The greater part of the formal power of legislating is given to Congress, but the president has an important role deriving from his veto power. Implementing law is chiefly an executive function, although the power delegated to the legislative branch obviously circumscribes this function rather narrowly.

In the case of three of the important functions that make up the policy-making process—planning, mobilizing, and proposing—the Constitution does not explicitly define or assign the whole of the function to one or the other institution. Of course, by inviting the president to submit information on the state of the union and to make recommendations to Congress, the Founders clearly opened the door to the President as initiator and mobilizer in the policy-making process. But in no sense can it be said that these provisions institution-alize the president as the chief policy-maker, for as far as the formal division of powers is concerned, Congress can, and throughout much of the nineteenth century did in fact, play the major role in this area. The character of the policy-making structure, within the general boundaries of separation of powers was something that the Founders left to subsequent generations to resolve. They did so, it may be argued, because they did not think that a Constitution could or should attempt to institutionalize this process and because they may have believed that there was no one best arrangement, but that what was best might vary according to the needs and circumstances of each era and even perhaps according to the capacities of those holding office at any given time. In other words, for the Founders, the precise character of the policy-making process in all its dimensions was not a constitutional matter. A number of possible arrangements for this process are equally constitutional (although not thereby equally recommendable).

Interestingly, the Constitution's distinction between the two general dimensions of presidential power—the executive role and a role in policy making—seems to entail a distinction regarding the president's rhetorical responsibilities. When the president acts in his executive role, he is not *obliged* to speak. When he acts in his policy-making role, he is asked by the Constitu-tion to do so. This difference reflects a reality about presidential activity that continues to this day. Sometimes the boldest executive actions are followed by laconic announcements of the decisions taken, often by an official spokes-person, not the president himself; and when the president does speak, he often assumes the pose of informing the public of what he has already done and explaining his rationale for action. Since he acts in such matters at his own discretion, he need not persuade in the usual sense, unless it is to lay the basis for further action. In any case, his actions often speak louder than his words.

When, on the other hand, the president is involved in policy making, he is taking part in a process that was designed to be conducted by deliberation. It is a realm in which discussion was seen as integral to decision making, and the president as part of that process cannot command but is reasonably obliged to persuade. As Hamilton argued, "energy, activity and secrecy" are important characteristics of the executive acting in his *executive* capacity. In policy mak-ing, however, "promptitude of decision is oftener an evil than a benefit ... and differences of opinion ... often promote deliberation and circumspection."[3]

The doctrine of the rhetorical presidency was conceived by Woodrow Wilson at a moment when the president's role in the policy-making process had fallen to an historical low point. It was presented initially as a response to the Founders, but given the Founders' flexibility regarding the role of the presi-dent in policy making, the advocates of the rhetorical presidency might more reasonably have directed their fire against the particular view of the presidency that had grown up in the nineteenth century than against the office as defined in the Constitution. Much, though certainly not all, of what the advocates of the rhetorical presidency wanted was consistent with the Constitution, even if the Constitution did not require what they wanted. In any event, the doctrine of the rhetorical presidency has been sustained throughout much of this century, even after the president's policy-making powers had greatly increased, by those who believed that a greater concentration of policy-making authority in the presidency would help to foster the growth of the welfare state.

For many years now, the model of the rhetorical presidency was held up by many as an ideal and a fitting substitute for the presidency as it exists under the Constitution. This teaching has had important consequences for our understanding of presidential power. In the first place, while the doctrine of the rhetorical presidency proclaims its support for a strong executive, it downplays or ignores the executive aspect of the president's powers and speaks only of his policy-making role. The problem of governance is reduced to policy making, and the tougher side of executive power is forgotten. It is hardly a coincidence, then, that some former proponents of this view turned on the presidency after the Vietnam War and, having found a new faith as born-again Whigs, led the crusade to reduce the president's crucial discretionary powers in foreign affairs. The problem, then, with the rhetorical presidency is that it risks in the end turning the presidency into an institution that is all talk and no action.

Second, it is a regrettable development of constitutional history in this century that the "strong" presidency has largely been viewed by scholars as standing on a dubious constitutional foundation. This view is incorrect both in respect to the "executive power" (which the president possesses) and to an important role in the policy-making process. The Constitution, while it does not give the president the power to legislate, in no way precludes a president's playing the role as initiator of policy (as Wilson himself was to prove). For many years, and with no reason except historical accident, the "strong" president has been regarded as a nonconstitutional development, with the result that many of its proponents have forsaken the constitutional understanding of executive power and based the president's power on the quicksand of "rhetorical" model.

The Exercise of Presidential Power

The doctrine of the rhetorical presidency was addressed not only to what powers the president should have, but to how the president should go about effectively exercising such powers as he possessed. Here one can point again to a difference between the model of the rhetorical presidency and that envisioned by the Founders, although the difference in this instance is based on expected models or norms of behavior rather than on any firm constitutional grants of power.

Constitutional government for the Founders meant authority that was ultimately accountable to the public, but that was mediated by the formal grants of power given to each branch. The Founders had a slightly suspicious view of oratory and mass popular rhetoric, as distinct from the deliberative interbranch communications suggested in the Constitution. The term "leadership," which they associated with demagogic orators, is used in the *Federalist Papers* as a term of opprobrium. The president might represent the nation, but he was not to be a popular leader in the modern sense of the term. "Leadership" suggested to them a breaking down of institutional forms and a reliance on an informal relationship in which the source of authority of the president derived chiefly from the special contact between a leader and public opinion.

Woodrow Wilson took note of what had already become a recognized fact when he argued that power in modern democratic regimes could no longer rest on so formal a foundation. "Policy," he wrote, "means massed opinion, and the forming of the masses is the whole art and mastery of politics."[4] In Wilson's view, the greatest power in modern democratic regimes lay potentially with the popular leader who could sway or, to use his word, "interpret" the wishes of the people. After some indecision Wilson finally concluded that the presidency was the institution best suited to assume this role: "There is but one national voice in the country and that is the voice of the President."[5] And it is the "voice" that is most important for governing: "it is natural that orators should be the leaders of a self-governing people."[6]

This understanding of how power should be exercised, although it may exaggerate the importance of oratorical skill, does nonetheless acknowledge the centrality of public opinion in the formation of basic public policy. Here, clearly, Wilson had identified an aspect of politics that marked an evolution from what the Founders expected or desired. In any event, it was clear that, if the president was to play the role of chief policy initiator in the twentieth century, he could not remain silent or communicate only with Congress. He would have to go to the people, present his positions, and mobilize public support for his programs.

In this sense, the rhetorical presidency is, if not altogether desirable, then at any rate unavoidable. In modern democratic politics, public opinion counts for more in the short term, and almost anybody or any group seeking to exercise considerable amounts of power—from ambitious senators holding hearings, to pressure groups conducting grass roots lobbying, to sophisticated foreign governments running disinformation campaigns—may find it necessary to engage in efforts to sway public opinion.[7] Surely those who have occupied the presidency have not wanted to deny their office access to this source of power, even if it is only to protect its margin of influence relative to others. The issue today with regard to the rhetorical aspect of the presidency is thus not to attempt to restrict its use in order to conform to practices of another era, but to moderate its excesses and avoid strategies that are self-defeating for the president or dangerous to the nation.

Rhetoric and Politics

In a curious way, the relation between rhetoric and political power has just recently come full circle from the time when rhetoric was first discovered as a subject of study in Greece in the fifth and fourth centuries B.C. Rhetoric became an object of inquiry, first by the sophists and then by Plato and Aristotle, largely because of its new importance as a source of power in politics. As the traditional sources of authority in society faded—sources based on kinship, religion, and the warrior ethos—a new understanding of authority emerged based on the idea of rational political decision making carried out by citizens in public assemblies. Public speech naturally acquired more importance under such circumstances, obtaining its greatest influence in democratic regimes, where the power to persuade large numbers through public speech became not just an ancillary element of power, but its chief source. The demagogues of Athens—men such as Cleon—emerged as leading figures in politics almost solely because of their capacity to sway mass audiences in public assemblies. Even the celebrated Pericles, although he initially won reknown as a military leader, achieved his greatest power from being Athens' "great communicator."

The sophists, somewhat like modern campaign consultants, were the first to offer, for a fee, instruction in the new political technology of effective rhetoric. They sold their services as teachers of rhetoric throughout Greece, promising that knowledge of the art of rhetoric could help its possessors win political power. (In Plato's *Apology* we learn that one sophist, Evenus of Paros, received a fee of 500 drachmai for one job, which, even allowing for the strong dollar, makes his rate highly competitive with the best campaign consulting firms in Washington, D.C., or New York.)

Naturally, with their object being merely to teach persuasion, the sophists were unconcerned with the rational content of argument, except as it might prove effective in winning people over, and tended to give a great deal of weight in their teaching to certain emotional appeals and to rhetorical tricks. Given both the political importance of this art and the fact that it was being taught to the would-be tyrant no less than to the statesman, political philosophers could not afford to ignore it. They sought to co-opt or reform the study of rhetoric by connecting the art of public persuasion to a concern for rational argument and the public good, although they clearly acknowledged limits to rational exposition and recognized the need to employ, if need be, some of the "lower" appeals. The most developed product of this inquiry was Aristotle's *Rhetoric*, which even today stands as arguably the most informative work in the field of public communications.

Shortly after rhetoric was discovered, however, it began to lose its political importance. This change resulted from a shift in the dominant form of regime from the city state to larger units and eventually to the Roman Empire. In the Empire and then later, in the feudal period and in the monarchic regimes of later European history, political rhetoric in the sense defined lost its relevance at levels of government above the local assembly. With governments covering large territories and having no commitment to popular rule, popular rhetoric had little influence. (The Renaissance Italian city states were a notable exception, and there popular rhetoric again became a cultivated discipline, adding to the techniques of mass popular rhetoric a new set of emotional appeals and new categories of discourse and reasoning deriving from the Christian influence.[8] As a result of its unimportance in the political sphere, the focus in the study of rhetoric shifted from popular political persuasion to logical argumentation and belles lettres.

The advent of the printing press and then, in the eighteenth century, of constitutional government once again gave greater weight to the importance of public discussion, if not to mass political rhetoric. Some of the beneficiaries were politicians, but those initially gaining the greatest advantage were publicists, essayists, and journalists, who communicated to mass audiences through the medium of the printed word. In Great Britain, the power of Parliament once again made political discussion and deliberation central to the governing process, although the style of rhetoric, exemplified in the speeches of Burke and Macaulay, was more truly deliberative than popular. Speeches were addressed at least in the first instance to the relatively small audience of Parliament and only secondarily to the nation. In the United States, where mass suffrage was first introduced, public discussion conducted through political tracts, meetings, and newspapers assumed even greater importance. Speeches and party platforms were circulated and their contents discussed, while citizens were mobilized by party symbols and campaign activities.

Notwithstanding all this activity, the representative tone of the Constitution, along with the undeveloped state of the communications system, tended initially to discourage frequent direct appeals from the president to the public. Presidents and even presidential candidates during the nineteenth century rarely gave speeches or interviews. Direct communication was confined to three basic channels.

1. *The Inaugural address.* Delivered orally and intended for a broad public audience, the inaugural address has tended to connect themes of constitutional principle with general statements of the guiding principles of the president's political program.

2. *Constitutionally recognized communications.* The State of the Union message, special presidential recommendations, and veto messages were intended in the first instances as messages to Congress, although they were also clearly

used in some instances as appeals over the head of Congress to the nation at large. The State of the Union address, which Jefferson changed from a speech before Congress to a written report, became by the middle of the nineteenth century a lengthy document of little public interest and almost no mass rhetorical import. At a time when it was difficult to collect official information, the State of the Union message served largely as a report to inform members of Congress of what government had been doing. Special messages were used not just to inform, but to put forth new initiatives, occasionally in a rhetorical style calculated to stimulate public opinion. Finally, veto messages, when not merely technical, were also frequently directed at the public in the form of defense of the president's views against those of Congress.

3. *Presidentially initiated communications.* What is striking about such communications as Washington's Farewell Adress and Lincoln's Gettysburg Address from a modern perspective is their paucity. Very few such addresses or speeches were given by presidents, and most that were came with the president acting in an official capacity, for example, as commander in chief, which was the case when Lincoln delivered the Gettysburg Address.

In the twentieth century, the rhetorical dimension of the presidency has changed dramatically. Of the three established channels of communication inherited from the previous century, only the first—the inaugural address—has maintained its basic nineteenth-century form, although it sometimes now serves a more programmatic or policy-oriented function than before. In respect to communications in the second channel, Woodrow Wilson changed the State of the Union message into a speech addressed chiefly to the public. This was accomplished, ironically, by Wilson's return to the pre-Jeffersonian practice of delivering the message orally before Congress, which served to heighten its interest to the nation at large. As with the modern televised State of the Union address, Congress was more nearly the backdrop than the primary audience. Special messages and veto messages are today usually presented in written form, as they were in the nineteenth century, rather than delivered orally. Unlike the mass rhetorical use they were sometimes given in the nineteenth century, however, they serve today in most cases as communications designed for Congress or for special audiences. In most instances when presidents deliver a special message in person before Congress, the purpose is to gain an even larger public audience on television by calling attention to the solemnity of the occasion.

It is largely, however, through the third channel—presidentially initiated speeches and news conferences—that presidents now communicate with the nation and Congress.[9] The major addresses today are television speeches that presidents decide to give at their own discretion, addressing a topic of their choice or responding to some event or crisis. The president may use such speeches to explain actions he has taken, to mobilize support for his programs, or merely to show in some way that he is "in charge" and at the helm.

In comparison with the nineteenth century, the channels of communication between the president and the public have become less formal, and the less formal channels of communication have become more important. These changes reflect the view, central to the doctrine of the rhetorical presidency, that the president should now serve as the chief initiator of policy, a task he must accomplish as much by appealing to public opinion as by attempting to deal directly with Congress. As Woodrow Wilson wrote, "(The president) has no means of compelling Congress except through public opinion."[10]

The new rhetorical role of the president, however, also reflects a new rhetorical situation made possible by the advent of the electronic media. For the first time in history, it is possible for leaders in large nations to communicate directly with the public. It is in this sense that we have come full circle to the place of rhetoric in Greece in the fifth century B.C. A political leader is now in a position to use rhetoric and to mobilize public opinion to help achieve his or her objectives. Popular rhetoric has once again become an important tool of governing and an important resource of power.

To be sure, there are profound differences from the situation when citizens addressed the assembly in Athens. In the first place, the president speaks not as an ordinary citizen, but as the elected chief executive. His official position makes him the center of attention. If one wants to find a closer analogy to the Greek assemblies where rhetoric by itself is the source of influence, it would be the modern presidential campaign. George McGovern, for example, joined the Democratic presidential race in 1984 because he said he wanted to participate in the one great national "forum."

Moreover, the rhetorical situation is not that of speakers addressing their audience in assemblies, but rather that of rhetorical strategies being pursued in and through the mass media. The interposition of the media as the medium of communication has had profound implications. Only part of the president's total capacity to communicate is *direct*. This part occurs when a president gives a televised address or a televised news conference. Otherwise, the "picture" of a president and what he is doing comes to the public as it is filtered and interpreted by the media. Much of the rhetorical strategy of any modern president consists of efforts to have the president's actions and images presented in the way the president and his strategists would like.

Finally, the audience addressed by the president is the public, but the "questions" the public presumably is asking of the president are to some extent formulated by the press, which both influences public views by what it determines to be on the agenda and claims a subtle right to speak to the president as the representative of the public.

The Media

The role that the media now play in shaping the rhetorical situation of modern presidents is illustrated by events during two recent periods—June and July of

1979 and January of 1983. In the first period, President Carter, finding his popularity at a new low, dramatically canceled a scheduled televised speech on energy policy and gathered his advisors together for a domestic summit at Camp David. The cancelation of the speech was preceded and followed by an extraordinary barrage of journalistic stories in which one report followed another writing about the crisis gripping the presidency. By no means was this theme a mere invention of the journalists, for many of the president's own advisors were speaking in precisely the same terms. Gradually, as story fed upon story, many of the rhetorical advisors to the president—and indeed the president himself—came to the conclusion that the nation was experiencing a crisis of spirit or "malaise" that touched the very soul of our national existence. The president, it was thought, had fallen into the trap of being head of the government rather than leader of the people. It was now to be his duty to wake up the American people by an oratorical campaign. As a *Washington Post* headline declared, "Carter Seeking Oratory to Move an Entire Nation."[11] Yet after the emergence of the Iranian hostage problem, everyone forgot about national malaise. The entire crisis, built in the newspapers and the minds of those who read and feed them, had vanished.

The second period, in January 1983, saw Ronald Reagan reaching a low point in his poll ratings as the economy failed to respond to supply-side nostrums. Seeing a story here, the New York Times and the Washington Post dropped all semblance of restraint and entered an earnest competition to entertain their readers with "failed presidency" articles. Throughout the first part of January, the administration was variously said to be "troubled," "in disarray" or "unraveling," while the president himself was described as helplessly "detached."

Editorial writers and columnists sought different words to express the same theme. In a column titled "The Phasing Out of Reaganism," David Broder concluded that effective power in Washington has already slipped away from the president, and that top Republican officials were "working together to fill the vacuum of leadership that Reagan's phase-out has left."[12] Not to be undone, the *New York Times*, in an editorial titled "The Failing Presidency," chose to lead with a powerful olfactory metaphor: "The stench of failure hangs over Ronald Reagan's White House."[13] The news and commentary in this case, which proved at the least to be premature, leads one to wonder how mature observers of the presidency can become so caught up in such interpretation. Once the economy began to improve, this crisis too passed into oblivion without even a postmortem article titled "The Failed Presidency Watchers."

Again, it seems, journalists were not altogether responsible for creating this story. If accounts in the *New York Times* can be believed, talk of the troubled presidency in January was prompted as much by (unnamed) presidential aides as by those in the media. We are presented with the picture of a White House staff tied to the roller-coaster mentality of president watchers, urging policies to shore up the president's popularity from its momentary ebbs and flows. To the extent that this picture is accurate, it calls for extensive revision of our under-standing of a White House staff's role. Ever since George Reedy's *Twilight of the Presidency,* it has been assumed that one of the central flaws of the White House staff is that it isolates the president from the trends of opinion. Now, however, it seems that the opposite is also true. The staff may be all too closely in tune with Washington's ephemeral realities, and may counsel the president to raise the sails when he ought to be dropping ballast.

These two periods, though undoubtedly extreme, illustrate how the media, acting, so to speak, as a surrogate audience, create rhetorical demands on the president. Some might see in the media's activity an ideological vendetta, but the fact that it has been directed against presidents from both parties belies this claim. Others might see in this activity a sheer and willful perversity, but— tempting as such a conclusion may be—it does not fit the facts either, for the American media can sometimes give way to reporting that bespeaks an almost childlike naivete. Indeed, unlike France, where the news is often molded to ideology, American news is formed according to the criteria of news. The "news" in America is not in the service of something else, but precisely in service of itself—of what is newsworthy. If we are more conscious of the impact and influence of news today, it is only because other institutions, including to some extent the presidency, have allowed the criteria and "values" of news to shape their agendas.

To understand "news," it must be seen as a particular way of processing information. There are other ways of processing information, for example social science, that possesses different qualities and characteristics than news. Allow a political scientist and a journalist to view the same event and they are likely to choose different aspects of it to emphasize. To comprehend news, accordingly, one must seek out those of its characteristics that give rise to its distinctive view of reality. There are, I believe, three such features.

The first characteristic of news is suggested by the root of the word itself: news is what is new. From the mass of reality that impinges on us, the news tends to pick out the deviation of any event from expectations. Thus it is less important from a news perspective to show the whole picture than to emphasize a sharp, if minute, change within the picture.

The second characteristic of news is its frequently fictitious quality. More news is often demanded than actually exists, with the consequence that much of what passes for news may only be of a marginally "hard" quality. Daniel Boorstin has called such fictitious occurrences "pseudo-events." When the first American newspaper appeared in September 25, 1690, Boorstin tells us, the editor stated that the task of the journalist was to give "an account of such considerable things as have arrived unto our notice." The paper, its editor promised, would furnish the news regularly *once a month*—although it might appear more often "if any glut of occurrences happen."[14]

The notion was that a certain stock of "real" events are reported as news. Today, by contrast, we find news omnipresent and expect something always to be happening. The reader of an unexciting newspaper today is more apt to remark "What a dull newspaper" than to say "How dull is the world today." News under modern conditions can therefore move further and further from significant "real" events. It can generate itself, as in the case of the "failed presidency" or the "crisis of malaise." Usually of course reporting is of *real* events, in which case the way matters actually turn out will in the end govern the character of the news. Often, however, the media creates a fictitious reality; it builds on it; the story is "in" the news; it is the talk of the town; and then it may suddenly disappear.

The final characteristic of news as a method of processing information is interpretation of events within the framework of certain preestablished patterns or stories. In making this claim, one need not have in mind controversial structuralist theories that identify a small number of archtypes of human cognition; instead, one can speak more loosely of stories that evolved within our culture and that are used in an effort to "make sense" of what is going on. In the coverage of presidential campaigns, for example, observers of the media have identified several such "stock" interpretations, among which number the David versus Goliath (outsider slaying front runner) plot. Similarly, it would appear that there are a set of stories about the presidency to which journalists and the public have now grown accustomed. These form part of the rhetorical environment in which presidents now operate. Regrettably for presidents, these interpretative patterns give leave to the journalists to put the facts in their own framework, which is usually presented as an "objective" synthesis of the facts at hand, but which more often than not feeds off the "paradigm" of the president manipulating the public (a legacy of Watergate) or the "paradigm" of a coming crisis. Furthermore, the last thing that any journalist in America today wishes to be accused of is naiveté or being "taken in" by the president, with the result that reporters and commentators ordinarily cover themselves by adopting a cynical reductive posture in regard to presidential motives.

Perhaps the most striking story, already alluded to in the events of the Reagan and Carter presidencies discussed here, is the frightful spectacle of leaderless government. In this we are presented with the awful spectacle of a void, in which the president is depicted as having lost his grip on the office and the nation. Demands then emerge for the President to show himself and prove that his presidency is still "there." All this, of course, may sound like fourth-rate psychology; yet, odd as it may appear, can a better explanation be offered to explain the "news" in the periods earlier described?

From the seemingly critical remarks made about news coverage, it might seem that I have yielded to the fashionable pastime of media-baiting: blaming all the ills of our society of journalists. Yet this is not my point. While news coverage, like everything else, can be improved, the media do present what they take to be the news; and while some of the characteristics of news that I have sketched may seem extreme when presented in stark isolation, they do in fact constitute much of what is—and what we expect to be: the news.

The fundamental issue for those concerned with American political institutions is not to attempt to reform the character of the news, which in any case is the function of media critics and not those concerned with institutional maintenance and reform, but rather to determine the extent to which the particular methods the news media employ are permitted to set the agenda of American institutions. Even the most superficial analysis of the original purpose of our political system reveals that political institutions were designed to process information in ways very different from those characteristic of the modern news media. What the news media value, political institutions were intended to devalue, and what political institutions were intended to value, the news media devalue. Deliberative assemblies, long terms of office, and the protection of discretion were institutional properties designed to help process information according to political standards that value stability, a candid assessment of long-term trends, and a focus on reality and complexity.

One of the central problems of our system today stems from the "mediazation" of our institutional processes. More and more, institutions have been changed to allow the values of news to set their agenda and influence their decision-making processes. This has occurred most conspicuously in the presidential nominating process, where the judgment of political leaders has given way to a system heavily influenced by the making and reporting of news: and, to the extent we follow the model of the rhetorical presidency, we are in danger of witnessing the same development in the presidency itself.

Limits and Possibilities

"Public opinion," Alexis de Tocqueville wrote, "becomes more and more mistress of the world."[15] This observation, which lies at the center of Woodrow Wilson's call for a rhetorical presidency, focuses attention on the legitimate need for a powerful rhetorical instrument in our system that the Founders ever envisaged. Yet, like a good mistress, public opinion, while it needs to be wooed, courted, and at times to be enticed, at times flattered, and at times indulged, must at times be kept at a distance. Finding the right distance remains one of the central challenges of the modern presidency.

Rhetoric is an instrument of statesmanship, and the rhetorical strategy of any particular president should be designed to fit that president's own goals and purposes. General rules for rhetoric thus can tell us relatively little and can serve only as broad guidelines. It is with this limitation in mind that I offer the following four points.

First, presidents should attempt to set expectations at a realistic level and in line with what they can reasonably accomplish. Presidential performances, we know, are often judged today according to unrealistic standards, with people holding presidents accountable for many problems that they lack the authority to solve or that are insoluble. Such expections a president may be unable to moderate, even if he should preach the need for greater realism. But however great this dilemma may be, it can be compounded when presidents themselves indulge in setting unrealistic standards for themselves. This not only adds to the general tendency to judge matters unrealistically, but it is self-defeating, as a president's words will always be used against his own performance.

One must concede, however, that much of the unrealistic rhetoric that emanates from presidents today may be structural rather than deliberate. The modern presidential campaign, especially during the nominating phase, is so arranged that making appeals that, to speak politely, border on demagogy or pandering is almost necessary to stay in the running. In addition, the doctrine of separation of powers as it is currently interpreted, especially in foreign affairs, virtually forces a president to make unrealistic claims in order to receive permission from Congress to pursue policies that are based on nasty prudential grounds. Certification of progress on human rights in a country like El Salvador represents a case in point.

Second, presidents should avoid responding to pseudo events by means of oratory. In the course of any presidency, there will inevitably be "down" periods when some may charge that the presidency has "failed." There will also be periods when a president's opinion poll ratings fall and his image deteriorates. (For example, Ronald Reagan, who in 1984 enjoyed a great deal of popularity, was the least popular president at midterm of any president since Harry Truman—a "fact" that merited numerous front page news stories at the time.) It is very seldom indeed that any rhetorical strategy can solve these difficulties, and more often than not they will only compound them. Only actions and performance can "turn things around," and the best the president can do is either wait for (or help create) the kind of opportunity or event which will allow him (or her) to regain the initiatives and silence his critics. Such events do arrive. Margaret Thatcher had the "opportunity" of the Falklands War and Jimmy Carter had (or took) the fateful decision on the Iranian rescue mission, which had it turned out differently, might have erased much of the reputation he had as a weak and ineffectual leader. The swiftness with which perceptions can change in response to deed rather than words should lead a president to treat with great caution the panicky advice of rhetorical strategists to say something to reverse his fortunes.

Third, although the modern president is the nation's chief policy initiator, it does not follow that he must assume the initiative on all matters of public policy. What presidents emphasize in their policy-making capacity (and in their rhetoric) should be matters that they choose to emphasize or they cannot avoid. By a bit of modesty presidents can make use of their ambiguous constitutional role in the policy-making process and turn it to their advantage by delegating responsibility to cabinet officers and to Congress.

Finally, presidents do have a proper role to play as moral leaders. The danger, however, is when that role becomes a cliché, an empty formula, and when the demand for moral leadership substitutes for attention to the substance of the policies that the president should follow. It should be borne in mind that Americans live in a regime that accords a great deal of weight to the pursuit of interest, a fact which in turn makes it necessary for leaders to be involved in the "lower" task of accommodation among various interests. Presidents, accordingly, must be wary of preaching a moralism that is at odds with the predominant "genius" of American politics. "A nation," Calvin Coolidge once said, "cannot dwell constantly on the mountaintop." At the same time, precisely because of this practical and self-interested component to the regime, presidents have an important role to play in covering the struggle of self-interest with a veneer of poetry and in calling at certain moments for sacrifice for the common good.

Very often Americans find it difficult to discover the meaning of their principles from domestic politics alone. It is for this reason that presidents can often teach the higher lessons of American principles by holding up the picture of our society against that of our ideological foes.

Notes

1. *The Washington Post,* May 5, 1977, p. 7.

2. For a full development of this doctrine, see James Ceaser, Glen Thurow, Jeffrey Tulis, and Joseph Bessette, "The Rise of the Rhetorical Presidency," in *Presidential Studies Quarterly 11* no. 2 (Spring 1981):233–251.

3. *The Federalist Papers,* Clinton Rossiter, ed. (New York: Mentor, 1961), pp. 426–427.

4. Woodrow Wilson, "Leaderless Government," in Ray Stannard Baker, ed., *College and State,* 2 vols. (New York: Harper Brothers, 1925), vol. 1, p. 339.

5. Woodrow Wilson, *Constitutional Government* (New York: Columbia University Press, 1908), p. 73.

6. Woodrow Wilson, *Congressional Government* (Boston: Houghton Mifflin, 1885), p. 209. For an in-depth treatment of Wilson's view of rhetoric, see Jeffrey Tulis, "The Two Constitutional Presidencies," in Michael Nelson, ed., *The Presidency and the Political System* (Washington, D.C.: CQ Press, 1984), pp. 59–86.

7. I am obviously omitting here those who seek power through a reliance on litigation or through influence with the bureaucracy, both methods of achieving power that have also increased in recent years.

8. One of the most astute observers (and collectors) of the rhetorical tradition of the Italian city state was Machiavelli.

9. See Samuel Kernell, "The Presidency and the People: The Modern Paradox," in Michael Nelson, ed., *The Presidency and the Political System* (Washington, D.C.: CQ Press 1984), pp. 233–263.

10. Wilson, *Constitutional Government,* p. 71.

11. *Washington Post,* July 16, 1979, p. 1.

12. *Washington Post,* January 12, 1983, p. A19.

13. *New York Times,* January 9, 1983, p. E22.

14. Daniel Boorstin, *The Image* (New York: Atheneum, 1978), p. 7.

15. Alexis de Tocqueville, *Democracy in America, Volumes One and Two* J.P. Mayer, ed. (New York: Anchor, 1968), p. 435.

4

The Presidency in the Era of Mass Communications

George E. Reedy

In terms of public discussion, much of the analysis of presidential rhetoric is based upon the assumption that its objectives are persuasion and education. Obviously, both elements are involved, even though the word "education" must be defined very broadly for the assumption to have validity. Experience shows, however, that there are far more important elements which must be taken into consideration. They rest upon the roles which a president is called to play—some of which make contradictory demands upon him. Two of them can be very confusing. They are the necessity of providing the nation with political leadership and the necessity of serving as the primary symbol of national unity.

There are occasional moments when the two roles dovetail, such as the initial honeymoon; a declaration of a popular war; or the initial reaction to national disaster. But such ecstatic experiences are rare and have no lasting impact. The day-to-day operation of the presidency requires a continuing effort to balance the moves that must be made to carry out political objectives against the symbols that must be manipulated to maintain the cohesion of the United States. This never-ending effort to reconcile the irreconcilable may well be one of the most exhausting burdens of the office. It certainly is a prime factor in determining the style of presidential rhetoric.

Politics is a form of warfare, the reverse of the famous dictum by the German general Clausewitz. At any and every level it pits people against each other and, in a democracy, its principal (though not its only) weapons are rhetorical. Unfortunately, the principal instruments for sustaining unity (although again, not the only instruments) are rhetorical. In a parliamentary system, where the prime minister can concentrate on political leadership and leave questions of unity in the lap of a monarch, this situation presents no difficulties. But in the United States, there are many nights when a president goes to bed searching for a graceful method of eating the divisive words he spoke during the day. Our system of government requires eternal shuttle travel between two extremes. That consideration affords the context for this chapter.

In the United States, one of the most important elements of the context is the distinction between the forms of political warfare that precede and follow an election. It is a distinction that is unique to our country and flows from the character of our election process. We do not, when we go to the polls, decide *how* our country is going to be run but only *who* is going to do the running. The *how* is a question reserved for our postelection politics, which is basically a continuing struggle among the president, the Congress, the courts, the states, the cities and the pressure groups of our society—a struggle in which the people have a very direct voice. It can be said that in our nation, active politicking never stops or even slows down; it merely changes its form.

This feature of the American political scene can be very confusing to observers from other countries. Most foreign democracies rest upon a parliamentary form of government in which an election can be interpreted with validity as a voter mandate on how the nation will be run. When a British voter, for example, votes for the Conservative party, he or she can do so after reading a party platform which states, with a high degree of reliability, what will happen if the Conservative party gets enough votes. There are, and can be, no similar set of assurances in an American election.

This is not because our political leaders are duplicitous but because we really have separated the powers of government in our system. Presidents discover—sometimes with a shock—after they enter the White House that their only real "power" is an authoritative position from which they can negotiate with other constitutional branches. They are not without important weapons to use in that struggle, and the most important of those weapons involves rhetoric. Ultimately, whether they go down in history as a "strong" or a "weak" president depends upon how effectively they use the weapons. The command authority inherent in the office has little to do with ultimate judgments upon their performance.

Presidential rhetorical style, aside from individual idiosyncrasies, has been directly affected by the considerations outlined above. There has been a distinct difference between the types of rhetoric employed during and after the election process because the words are employed to achieve different goals. In the "before" state, words are used to achieve power; in the "after" stage to manipulate it.

In practice, what this has meant is a style of pre-election rhetoric which tends to sidetrack issues and concentrate instead on questions of philosophy and personality. There have, of course, been candidates who discuss, with some specificity, issues. But there is very little evidence that such discussions have much to do with voter decisions. When people are questioned on what they remember that was striking from past election campaigns, they usually recall a slogan (Keep Cool with Cal); an epithet (that do-nothing, good-for-nothing Eightieth Congress); a symbolic event (Nixon's appearance in the 1960 television debates); or an overly simplistic issue summation (Are you any better off today than you were four years ago?). The allegedly low level of political debate in the United States has been deplored for many years by observers who believe speeches should be "educational" and offer the voters ideological choices.

Actually, it can be argued that ideological debate in an American election campaign is quite inappropriate. In the first place, the candidates really do not know what they are going to do if they are successful. Issues have quite a different appearance *inside* the White House than they do *outside* the White House. Frequently, the "issue rhetoric" on the campaign trail can be quite embarrassing, as Franklin Delano Roosevelt discovered in 1933 when he was pressed for fulfillment of his 1932 campaign promise to cut the federal budget. In the second place, however, the people with whom the president must negotiate on *how* to run the nation have been placed in power by voters operating on a different set of premises than those who selected the chief executive. In 1948 Harry S Truman, for example, presented the electorate with a "laundry list" of proposals and was elected to the presidency. He then presented the same list to Congress and was turned down with little more than a face-saving response. There were no indications that the electorate, as a whole, disapproved of the rejection.

As a consequence, the more appropriate presidential campaign rhetoric would appear to be directed toward questions of personality (defined as qualities of prudence, steadfastness, and reliability) and philosophy (defined as attitudes favoring or denigrating patriotism, businessmen, workers, farmers, and minorities). Of course, "must" issues in the sense of current events which demand a presidential response are always discussed. But the discussion rarely goes very deep. Having been both an observer of and a participant in the process, I find it obvious that issues play the same role in a campaign that a football plays in a football game: the football does not cause the game, but the game cannot be played without a football.

One final point should be noted. It is that our elections are held at stated intervals rather than at times when political circumstances demand a voter reevaluation of governing authority. Under such conditions, it is inevitable that issue discussion will have something of a contrived air except in unusual circumstances such as those of 1860 or 1932.

The circumstances that govern presidential rhetoric shift immediately after the results have been announced. A number of important considerations at this stage enter into play. The first is the necessity of healing wounds that may have been inflicted during the campaign. Whatever the candidate may have felt when striving for the office becomes unimportant. His task now is to manage the affairs of the country, and here he stands in a special relationship to the American people. The election left Congress with outlets for partisan feelings. But there are no such institutionalized outlets in the executive branch. The president finds that there are pressures bearing upon him to represent not only the people who voted for him but the people who voted against him. He must now deal with a different set of realities and is not going to be successful unless he can secure consensus votes out of a Congress which has a strong tendency to be sensitive about the feelings of its own minorities.

The president, naturally, is in a unique position to resist pressures immediately following an election. But in terms of rhetoric, what is usually appropriate at this stage is the "bind up the wounds" approach—and that is the customary pattern. In the opportunity I had for close observation, the president had something of a feeling of a "father" relationship to the nation, and this seems to have been the case with most new presidents. The consciousness that they face four years of *being* the United States appears to have had a sobering effect. The loftiest presidential rhetoric usually takes place during the honeymoon period.

There are other circumstances which tend to produce lofty forms of rhetoric during the first few months to a presidential term. One is the concentration of the press, in the friendliest of tones, upon the "first family." This is usually quite favorable as the journalists are merely reflecting the public desire for symbols of identification. The second is the reluctance of Congress to lock horns with a chief executive whose real hold over constituents has yet to be measured and whose reaction to opposition is still uncertain. There is a tendency to let the new occupant of the White House "prove himself" (soon probably "herself") and the legislative attitute is to be as reasonable as possible.

This is the famous honeymoon period, which may resemble its counterpart in marriage by creating illusions as to what is to follow. It does not and cannot last. The press finally exhausts personality questions and the Congress settles down to its normal partisan battles. At this point, presidents find themselves torn in two different directions—the use of rhetoric to gain political ends versus the use of rhetoric to sustain the unifying function of the office. Very few presidents since George Washington can be given high marks on both scores, although in modern times Dwight D. Eisenhower came reasonably close. What results is running warfare between the White House and Capitol Hill—usually resulting in compromises that are not totally satisfying to either side but with which both sides can live.

During this period, the unifying rhetoric is confined almost entirely to ceremonial affairs—the "Rose Garden rubbish" so annoying to many White House assistants. Much of this, of course, can be turned over to a vice president. But the wiser chief executives usually decline to do so. The speeches may be inane and the occasions trivial, but both serve a purpose. They contribute to the mystique which is one of the main strengths of the presidency in dealing with the Congress. He needs all he can get. Congress has some formidable weapons with which to frustrate a president when the legislators wish to use them.

The principal instrument of the president in the partisan warfare with the legislative branch is the power of the initiative. This may well be decisive. The ability to set up the issues—virtually to determine the legislative agenda—gives the chief executive an edge. Here rhetoric is of considerable importance as skillful statement of a question is often tantamount to a victory. It takes a real curmudgeon to say "no" to the leader of the whole nation who wants to feed the hungry, clothe the ragged, and house the homeless. Franklin Delano Roosevelt was the master of the initiative and almost every one of his successors has tried to follow his lead.

The operative word in this equation, however, is "skillful," and few of his successors demonstrated the same skill. Harry S Truman, for example, was probably unsuccessful with the legislative branch because he sent it too many initiatives. There were so many that it was simple to play them off against each other in the labyrinthine committee structure of Congress. They were sunk without a trace.

In the battle with Congress, the president has a number of weapons. He can release funds for very public projects in key districts; he can confer distinction upon some legislators and withhold it from others; he can manipulate key appointments; he can offer political support to those who will go along with him. But the efficacy of these instruments has declined with the decline in the cohesion of political parties. To an increasing extent, chief executives find themselves resorting to direct appeals to legislative constituents. In the last analysis, no pressure upon a senator or a representative is as potent as the pressure of his or her voters. It is here that rhetoric assumes the highest importance and it is also here that modern technology has given the White House a tremendous advantage in access to radio and television.

The full dimensions of that advantage have yet to be measured. They arise out of the fact that the president can literally *command* the air waves. He can come into the homes of the overwhelming majority of U.S. citizens every night of the week and—depending upon his rhetorical skill—speak to them as the leader of the nation. There is no way in which this performance can be matched. Individual legislators have only limited access to the electronic media, and there is no method by which they can speak from a platform as impressive as the Oval Room of the White House. As for the Congress, there is no way it can speak as a single body except through its votes. Legislative responses to executive statements are usually feeble, nor do the officials of the two political parties have the standing to make a response on their part feasible or effective.

There are, of course, entries on the debit side of the ledger. Television in particular can magnify an *inept* presidential performance as well as it can project a skillful performance. There is always the danger of overexposure—of making the president such a familiar figure that he becomes associated with toothpaste and laundry soap commercials. And it is very obvious that every presidential appearance displaces a regularly scheduled program and can, under the right circumstances, generate hostility. Nevertheless, there can be little doubt that modern technology has placed an important weapon in the hands of the president and the weapon can be decisive *when he knows how to use it.*

Franklin Delano Roosevelt was the first president to use the electronic media, through his famous "fireside chats." He was in a good position to do so as he had experimented with radio during the period that he was governor of New York and had already determined what it would do and what it would not do. He recognized rhetoric as an adjunct to the political process rather than a substitute for it and was always careful to put together words and organizational considerations. It was a potent combination.

The stage of appealing to the public is probably that phase of the presidency which resembles most closely the "educational" model. Obviously, the chief executive on such occasions is attempting to bring the public to a realization of his approach to an issue. But the history of such appeals would suggest that the process is more akin to rallying the troops than to enlightening eager students. Certainly, one would be hard pressed to identify an example in which presidential rhetoric altered political currents by presenting the electorate with an overwhelming combination of facts and logical analysis.

Woodrow Wilson's barnstorming in favor of joining the League of Nations was cut short by deteriorating health. But contemporary accounts indicate that the effort, as far as it went, was not successful. Franklin Delano Roosevelt received a negative response to his "quarantine the aggressors" speech, and it took an outright attack upon Pearl Harbor to galvanize the nation into action. Mr. Roosevelt also discovered that his oratory was unable to sell voters on his campaign to purge the Democratic party of conservatives or to alter the liberal-versus-conservative balance on the Supreme Court.

The role of the presidency is performed on such a high stage and before such a large audience that there may be no means of breaking down a president's rhetoric into its essential elements and sorting out those which are effective from those which are ineffective. But as an observer and a participant, it has seemed to me that these are the objectives that can be achieved by skillful mastery of the channels of communication:

1. To arouse the public to what the president perceives as a need for action
2. To set up standards around which presidential protagonists can rally
3. To provide the "faithful" with quick arguments and quick rebuttals to opposing arguments in the verbal battles that are waged in the streets
4. To assert the legitimacy of the president's position as "national policy" in contrast to the "special interest" policy of his opponents

In order to be effective, the president must realize that the "educational process" on any issue has taken place long before it is time for his speech. It has come through the continuing dialogue that is constantly underway in the United States through organizations not normally defined as political. These include newspapers, magazines, radio and television talk shows, public forums, churches, and, what may be the most important of all, lobbying and pressure groups. All of these must be taken into account and the rhetoric shaped to achieve the maximum possible in terms of what Americans have come to believe before the speech was made.

In summary, the importance of rhetoric in the operation of the presidency has increased in proportion to the decline in party cohesion in the United States. In the modern world, the ability of the chief executive to command the nation's channels of communication must make up for the loss of Democratic and Republican machinery for garnering votes and distributing patronage in a politically effective manner.

The increased reliance upon rhetoric in the political process has also coincided with new technologies which give the occupant of the White House a decided edge in reaching the electorate. The president is capable of entering people's homes every night with a message presented precisely as he wants to deliver it, whereas his opponents must filter their rebuttals through the mass media. In the few instances where opposition voices can secure time for a complete statement, it must be made from a platform much less impressive than the Oval Office.

Finally, under these circumstances presidential rhetoric can be seen as the use of weapons in political warfare. It is possible to regard his speeches as "educational" and "persuasive," but only by giving those words very broad definitions. Fundamentally, a president must, to be successful, shape what he says both strategically and tactically in accord with the particular function of the presidency at any given time.

5
Comments on Part II

James M. Fallows

There are two parts of Professor Ceaser's argument about which I have either a different or a supplementary point of view. In the crucial part of his chapter he suggests a crystal clear distinction between two roles the president plays; the executive role and what he calls the policy-making role. By labeling the policy-making role part of the rhetorical presidency, he is able to cast it in a fairly chilly light as the part that leads to inflamed expectations; to a government that is all talk and no action, and to a corruption of the Founders' original intentions. Essentially, it's a view of two presidential roles, one of which is Gary Cooper doing the job laconically, not messing around; the other is Woody Allen, Rodney Dangerfield, or some other blathering person of that sort.

The problem with the rhetorical presidency is that it risks in the end turning the presidency into an institution that is all talk and no action. By contrast, when a president acts in the executive role, he is not obliged to speak. Now this is a vision of the role of the presidency which is, in my mind, more judicial than executive. It is essentially the job of a Supreme Court justice. It is also, by coincidence, the interpretation of the presidency that I think Jimmy Carter, my one-time employer, found most compatible. He would have been happy with a job in which he just resolved issues and then did not have to explain them—as opposed to a different role which I am going to suggest.

My own interpretation is that the distinction between these two roles, while perhaps clear in theory, is unclear to the point of insignificance in practice. My point is not to argue whether the merging of these roles came with Franklin Roosevelt or Woodrow Wilson or with Andrew Jackson or with Thomas Jefferson, nor whether or not it confirms the Founders' intentions. I am not arguing that at all. I am arguing only that, as a practical reality for the modern presidency, these two roles have been merged and this merger casts a different light on this function of rhetoric: how the president goes about doing the business he has to do. If you take even the extreme of the range of powers that a president has, from those outlined in the Constitution to the vaguest ones that have come in the modern media age, you can find that there is still some check on them if he does not maintain some consensus for the actions he wants to undertake. What I have in mind here, if reports in the *Atlantic Monthly* can be believed, is the recent story by Seymour Hersh pointing out that during the final months of Richard Nixon's reign he lost his power to make military decisions. The secretary of defense, James Schlesinger, told the members in the military chain of command not to honor a request for a nuclear strike if it came from Richard Nixon. Why? Because Nixon had, in various ways, squandered the legitimacy of his office. So, even this power of the presidency, the most inherent one, was given away because he had not maintained the rolling consensus the president needs.

Under the more normal circumstances in which other presidents work, my contention is they must build consent day by day. Rarely do they have to establish it with the joint chiefs of staff or the secretary of defense. Frequently, they have to build it in Congress, and even among members of their own administration. When you have an organization of several million people which the federal government is, or several thousand people, which the office of the president is, you do not just tell it to do something and it happens. Its members must be persuaded as in any other organization. To quote Professor Ceaser on executive action, "since the president acts in such matters at his own discretion, he need not persuade in the usual sense unless it is to lay the basis for future action." My point is that it is an enormous "unless." That "unless" encompasses virtually everything a president must do. He must build the base for consensus and consent within his government, outside his government, in the Congress, and elsewhere.

In pursuit of that goal, the rhetorical functions of the presidency are indispensable because giving some clear picture of the direction in which government policy is to proceed is one of the important means for building the consensus that the president needs to get his job done. This is important at the abstract level. People can say, yes, I support President Reagan because he's doing this and that about the income tax or the Russians. Consensus is also important at a very gritty and tangible level.

One of the most serious problems in the Carter administration arose from its rhetorical deficiencies. Arguments down at the fifth level of the State Department, or between departments, could never be resolved by someone saying "Let's stop fighting about this. We know what the president is going to say." They could not be resolved that way because nobody knew what the president would say on each case as it came up. They did not know because there were no speeches giving the broad brush picture saying, This is where our policy lies. By contrast, you have the Reagan administration. In the modern presidency as it really is, the lines between the executive and the policy-making functions are hopelessly blurred and to be able to carry out any of his powers, a president must skillfully exercise this rhetorical part of his job.

My second point concerns the degree to which the media dominate this part of the president's job, and how it sets the agenda. I yield to no one in my hostility to the way the White House press corps does its job, and I have vented myself in print with much more sarcasm than Professor Ceaser did on this point. But, I do think that his indictment slightly misstates what the pathology is and overstates the influence that the press has on setting the government's agenda.

For the misstatement of the indictment, I return again to one of his central illustrations, the 1979 "crisis," in which President Carter went away to Camp David. It seems to me important to distinguish between two very different "crises" going on at that time. One of those indeed was exactly as Professor Ceaser described. This was the "manufactured crisis" about whether Carter had lost his grip. There was one day in which newspapers reported he had gone insane because he didn't show up for his speech at the right time. I agree with him entirely that this was a bogus event, a media pseudo-event, and it reveals some tendencies of the press which I will describe shortly. There was, however, another crisis that was of far graver import, one whose existence was essential for the bogus one to be generated. That was a generalized feeling of disgruntlement with major American institutions.

There were any number of opinion polls generated during those years showing people feeling malaise about business, government, military, and academic leadership. There were other straws in the wind which made people think American businesses could not compete with Japan's, American schools couldn't work, and so on. That is what I believe President Carter was trying to address when he gave his speech about the nation's mood. There was a genuine crisis of spirit that Carter was trying to talk about as well as the manufactured crisis. When those weeks at Camp David were over, these crises did not just disappear, as Professor Ceaser has suggested. The Carter "crisis of competence" disappeared only in the sense that he was forever after a beaten man in office and was driven out with a landslide vote.

The more serious feeling about American institutions I think is only now being unraveled. It was part, I believe, of the impetus for Ronald Reagan's election: people wanting to feel they could take pride in America's institutions as part of a generalized effort to pull themselves up.

What is it in the press that makes them look for these things? I have a different interpretation from that of Professor Ceaser. I think that reporters, like other people, are more afraid of making a mistake and being embarrassed than they are attracted by taking a risk that might prove to have some kind of unusual virtue attached to it. And so, the first instinct of a reporter is to write something that is safe and to deal on grounds where a reporter feels confident. The grounds where political reporters feel confident is the horse race aspect of politics—Who is up? Who is down? Who's ahead in the race?—how a president is doing as opposed to what he is doing. And that is why you see reporters following one another in packs with these "up and down" stories about a president. It is what they feel confident about and they are afraid of making mistakes by shifting away from that trend.

6
Comments on Part II

Irwin "Tubby" Harrison

The title "The Rhetorical Presidency" is an awful one, because it invests our topic with a level of abstraction and a depth which perhaps it doesn't really have. I am a political animal and I tend to think about the presidency, or any other office, in terms of winning and losing, popularity and unpopularity, and support and lack of support; I am also one of the fellows who gets a little bit less than the "500 drachmai," but nevertheless does get it. I'm often asked, apart from providing the numbers, to interpret them in terms of what can be done about them. What we're really talking about is a president's ability to, through his rhetoric, influence opinion and improve his popular standing; to enhance his re-electability, and to mobilize public opinion in support of or against a particular policy or program. In those terms, the media has enormously enhanced the president's ability to do certain things. But what we have really not addressed too much (although Mr. Reedy did to some degree) is the extent to which the media has also limited the president's ability to influence. By "limited" I mean limited the time in which a president can do it.

The president has a lot of influence during the immediate postelection period, the so-called honeymoon. After that, the public, through a variety of media, begins to know him; begins to see what he's like; begins to see what they like, trust, or dislike about him. And it becomes harder for him to do certain things. For example, in the Mayaguez situation Ford did something; his popularity went up immediately, but it went down almost immediately after. It was not a lasting thing. Incidentally, my view was that Carter's "malaise" was not a creation of the press or of the media, it was a creation of Carter. I view it in a much more cynical sense. Here was a guy who was in trouble, who was trying to get out of it, and who used those few days to attempt to improve his image with the public. Unfortunately, he didn't quite succeed.

But perhaps the best illustration of the limitations on a president's power to influence opinion is the Reagan presidency. Here is a guy who is regarded widely as a very skillful communicator, as having an ability to communicate and get across to the public. My opinion was that when the economy started to recover, his popularity would zoom, and, if you wanted to take the real test of that popularity by pitting him against John Glenn or Walter Mondale in trial heats before the 1984 Democratic party primaries, he would destroy them. But he did not destroy them according to the presidential polls that appeared in the press from time to time; nor did his popularity zoom. There were some lasting effects from the series of articles criticizing Reagan, which Professor Ceaser mentioned, in the *Washington Post* and the *New York Times*. Those articles were reflecting questions the American public was asking. The public was not asking: Is he powerless? Is he sitting there just looking at the wall? But they were worried about the economy, and President Reagan had not convinced them that it's all better, the recession is all over, and now we are all going back to a rosy picture—this despite all his ability to appear on television and his skillful use of all the media.

The main result of the media exposure of the president in recent years is, more and more, the idea of a one-term presidency. After a while the public just gets tired of a president. Part of the disenchantment also has to do with the immensity of the problems a president faces. Really, none of the presidents, not through any fault of their own but by virtue of the enormity of the problems, does much about them. I sense the beginning of widespread cynicism: What difference does it make who's there?—nothing happens anyway. We lose some of that cynicism in the excitement of the election campaign, which is a totally artificial situation when rhetoric does have a lot to do with things. But within a couple of years after the president comes into office, the limitations begin to appear and at that point he is beginning to run for re-election anyway, if he is wise.

Part III
The Institutionalized
Presidency

7

On the Separation of Brain and State: Implications for the Presidency

Thomas E. Cronin

One of the primary functions of the president of the United States is to serve as a teacher, as someone who will point the way, who can enlighten the nation about the possibilities and the priorities. To serve as a teacher or educator, the president has a constant challenge to be a learner. Much of the institutional presidency in modern times is organized around the tasks of gathering information and seeking to make sense out of large bodies of information.

Our other political institutions often have more defined ways of learning on a regular basis. Thus the Supreme Court learns from formal oral argument, from materials submitted to it from contending sides of a case as well as from lower courts, from judicial conference meetings that involve peer discussions, and from advice gained from law clerks and from new legal research.

Members of Congress learn from a variety of sources. Chief among these are learning from their colleagues (especially like-minded party and home state colleagues), learning from testimony and research presented at hearings, and learning from trips and countless communications from constituents back in their districts. Members of Congress also learn from the communications sent them from the White House and cabinet officials.

In recent years, a somewhat predictable learning process has evolved for presidents. The following are some of the major learning and advising routines that shape how presidents learn.

1. Senior staff memoranda and briefing sessions (including intelligence and economic estimates)
2. Cabinet advocacy and counsel
3. Congressional party leadership meetings
4. Advocacy from leading business and economic leaders
5. Discussions with (and communications from) other heads of state
6. Reports and counsel from presidential advisory commissions
7. Proposals and ideas from the Washington bureaucracy

8. Advocacy from interest groups, Political Action Committees, and political movements
9. Lessons learned from the mistakes and successes of former presidents
10. New books and inventions that come to the attention of the White House
11. Criticism from intellectuals and opposition political leaders
12. Public opinion survey data
13. Newspaper and media opinion and interpretation
14. Contact and conversations with friends and citizens at large

Presidents learn also from what is going on within the Congress, within the parties, and from messages sent by the various courts.

Note, however, that there is no prescribed learning process. Each president has to devise anew the learning process, and each also decides how much time and how much White House energy is devoted to learning. Still, the process has become reasonably institutionalized. That is, processes have become established in one administration and more or less passed on and adopted or adapted by succeeding administrations. The current cabinet councils are illustrative. Often there are congressionally mandated reports or requirements that help to enforce institutionalization. Political and press expectations sometimes also encourage the continuation of some of these practices. In this chapter I comment on and raise questions about certain aspects of the presidential learning process. I suggest the following:

1. Much of what the president learns is learned after winning election to the White House.
2. Most of what is important to learn often comes from outside the normal inner circle of the presidential advisory circles.
3. A strain exists between intellectuals and creative entrepreneurs and the political leadership in the nation. What may be called *the separation of brain and state* often exists and while it is inevitably in tension, presidents and their close advisers need to work to make sure that the separation is not total.
4. The use of presidential advisory commissions, the media to the contrary, makes considerable sense and perhaps should be used more frequently.

Unpreparedness of New Presidents

Most U.S. presidents in recent years have come from governorships or from Congress. In such positions, these future presidents have obviously learned about many of the more important problems facing the nation. But seldom have they developed extensive expertise about major policy issues—especially issues of international economics, arms control, and complex developments in distant regions of the world.

To campaign for the White House requires only a superficial knowledge of the controversies of the day. Candidates repeatedly are asked about the same issues, generally the issues currently in the headlines. Many of the issues discussed and debated in the campaign cease to be critical issues after the election. And some or even many of the major problems and crises that arise during a presidential term are new or unexpected issues.

John F. Kennedy, for example, did not discuss what he would do in Vietnam during his 1960 campaign. He mentioned Vietnam just once or twice in passing. The pressing issue in 1960 was what to do in Quemoy and Matsu, islands off of Formosa. That issue was widely debated, but it was not controversial once Kennedy came to the White House. Vietnam, on the other hand, became one of Kennedy's greatest tests.

Lyndon Johnson had even less preparation for foreign policy responsibilities—and this deficiency later became evident. Countless other new and demanding issues arose during his presidency, even after he was elected in his own right: matters such as crime policy. Neither Johnson nor anyone else on his White House staff knew much about the crime problem, the criminal justice system, or crime research. The crime issue was raised or generated by Barry Goldwater and others; Johnson and his advisers sought to ignore it. But that strategy failed, and they groped with considerable unease toward some form of political response to the crime issue. While responding to the issue they often ignored most of the problem.

Richard Nixon won the presidency in 1968 by promising that he had some kind of secret plan to win the Vietnam War. It took four years and numerous plans, as Nixon was to discover. Jimmy Carter claimed in 1976 he had ideas about reforming the federal bureaucracy and simplifying the budget process. He, like Ronald Reagan, said that he would balance the budget. Somehow the job is almost always more complex and the candidates seemingly come with much to learn.

The impression is often conveyed (an impression fostered by presidential public relations aides) that presidents and their staffs are more informed and better advised than they really are. Again and again, presidents and their staffs have to embark upon major learning undertakings after the election. The reasons are simple.

First, to win an election requires general responses to general issues. But policy making and decision making require much greater understanding of root problems and alternative policy responses and their consequences. Second, many of the major issues facing presidents are issues that were only superficially treated, if raised at all in the election (for example, the missile gap, Vietnam, crime, energy, Iran, Central America, and industrial policy).

Another reason the president and his staff must learn so much is that the pace of change has dramatically increased. Policy proposals that have been posed in a campaign or in the first year of a presidency often become obsolete, overtaken both by events and technologic changes. The problems become very different and often require a different approach. Such problems as social security, arms control, educational quality, and human rights change with changing circumstances.

Moreover, the aides and supporters a candidate needs to win the White House are often decidedly different from the advisers a president needs to govern and lead. Delegate hunters, political brokers, and campaign strategists are gradually replaced by policy advisers and experts—and the latter often take a while before they can understand a president's style and contribute productively to the president's new learning processes. It took a year or more before Carter became adjusted to his policy staffs in 1977–78.

Presidents are generalists. The best we probably can expect is that they are reasonably bright and curious, ask good questions, and can make sensible and quick decisions when they are pressed to do so. It is justifiably expected in addition that they have the ability to recruit gifted advisers and that they are reasonably quick studies. As analyses in recent years suggest, we should certainly look for presidents who will avoid "group-think" tendencies, who can develop some form of competing advisory systems (sometimes called multiple-advocacy processes), and avoid dogmatic and simpleminded approaches to the crucial task of learning about or rethinking national policy choices.

If knowledge is power, as the proverb has it, the constant challenge for those in the White House is to reach out to those who can supply more information, explanations, and understandings. Information is almost always incomplete. Uncertainty is ever present—so much so that knowing what you do not know is often the first step in the right direction. Asking the right question becomes critical. A problem well stated, as an old saying put it, is a problem half-solved. Knowing when and where to turn for advice is also an important skill.

Hence, despite the growth of White House staff, the executive office of the president, and staff organizations like the Office of Management and Budget, Council of Economic Advisors, Council on Environmental Quality; every four years the institutionalized White House needs to be reorganized as an institution for learning.

Broadly Dispersed Leadership

Policy leadership seldom originates at the White House. Ideas come from a variety of sources—from experiments in states or in other nations, from research breakthroughs, from think tanks, from enterprising members of Congress and their staffs who have been on the outlook for new ideas, from interest groups, and from political movements in the country.

Generally speaking, presidents and their top aides are brokers. They have fought to win election by appealing in broad terms to as many groups and sections of the nation as possible. They have viewed their campaign as a fight to win plurality and majority support—and not as occasion for adult education, or for stirring up divisiveness in the nation. Most of the time, too, they have skillfully phrased much of what they might do in ambiguous terms: "I shall go to Korea"; "Let's get the Nation moving again"; "I have a secret plan to win the war"; "I am not a lawyer, I am not from Washington, and I will not lie to you."

Breakthrough ideas seldom come from the White House. It is much like the invention of new ideas in the private sector. The large so-called expert organizations often get bypassed by smaller, newer, more risk-taking and entrepreneurial outfits. Thus the automobile was not invented by the transportation experts of that era, the railroads. The airplane was not invented by the automobile experts. Polaroid self-developing film was not invented by Kodak. Hand-held pocket calculators were not invented by IBM. Digital watches were not invented by the watchmakers. Apple Computers beat IBM for a couple of years in the home computer market. The list is long and the moral vivid.

Domestic policy change often takes place over a lengthy period, and sometimes it seems as though the White House is the last to learn about the pending change. This is in part because we have created a presidency that necessarily is a brokerage institution: it waits for other groups, individuals, and institutions to take the lead. The White House responds to ideas and suggestions for change, but usually not until such ideas or proposals have gathered substantial public support.

Some would say that presidents are followers more than they are leaders. This overstates the point. Presidents plainly have to exercise decisive leadership in emergency situations and often in secretive national security activities. Presidents often can assist those who are advocating change. They can nurture or facilitate a national debate and in doing so can often help expand the public support for an idea whose time has yet to come.

Still, most presidents most of the time are cautious. They fear being in advance of their times. They are tremendously concerned with appearing prudent, sensible, and effective. Thus they act upon ideas for which they can gain congressional passage, or public opinion support, or compliance.

Presidents Cleveland and McKinley, for example, were not leaders of the women's suffrage movement. Presidents from Hoover to Kennedy can hardly be called civil rights leaders. Nixon was hardly an environmentally concerned person and he most assuredly was not an antiwar leader. Nor were presidents in the 1970s advocates of tax cutting. Yet during all of these periods, policy leadership and policy incubation was going on in the nation—often in highly activist and vigorous ways.

Policy ideas often go through a series of stages or acts prior to their gaining acceptance by a president or a presidential candidate. I find helpful the idea of borrowing from the theater to suggest that policy change requires leadership in at least three distinct acts. This oversimplifies and suggests an all too tidy frame of reference, yet it is a step in the right direction. Just as there are three acts in most plays, I will illustrate policy leadership as moving along in three acts, and being nurtured or carried by three fairly distinctive kinds of leaders.

Act I	*Act II*	*Act III*
Agitators	Coalition builders	Office holders
Inventors	Consciousness raisers	Elected politicians
Crowd gatherers	Lobbyists	Policy makers
Policy prophets	Movements organizers	White House staff
Movement founders	Policy advocates	Party leaders

Act I leaders are classic crowd gatherers and agitators. They stir things up, raise new and often troublesome ideas and are often viewed as cranks, rebels, and revolutionaries. Patrick Henry, Samuel Adams, and Thomas Paine provided some of this Act I leadership as a prelude to the American Revolution. Nat Turner and John Brown provided dramatic nineteenth-century civil rights agitation. Howard Jarvis in recent years agitated for property tax relief. Saul Alinsky, Rachel Carson, Jonathan Schell, and Michael Harrington also illustrate the act I types. Few of them get elected. Many of them are kept at distance by politicians. Yet all of them catalyzed protests or generated ideas in ways that aroused large numbers of would-be citizen activists.

Act II leaders are the coalition builders. Their ranks include Susan Anthony, Martin Luther King, Jr., Jack Kemp, Jerry Falwell, Ralph Nader, Allard Lowenstein. The leaders of the temperance, progressive, populist, consumer rights, anti-Vietnam War, nuclear freeze, and new right (Richard Viguerie) coalitions are all act II leaders. Often unelected and even unelectable, they galvanize movements and coalitions in such a compelling way that politicians at least begin to heed their message and listen—even if only cooly at first. Their objective is to raise interest and enlarge their ranks. They wish to publicize new ideas (and sometimes to revive old ideas) and bring pressure on those who serve in the White House and other political establishment centers.

Act III leaders typically are elected officials. Some have highly publicized and sometimes even glamorous careers. But the act III types have to follow public opinion as much as mold it. Act III types are usually more constrained than the nonelected political leaders, and they often find themselves dependent on act I and act II leaders for fresh thinking and novel approaches to public problems. Act III leaders invariably become enmeshed in the challenge of reconciling competing claims about the public interest. They become preoccupied too with what is do-able and with the pragmatic options.

The most serious charge against many of the act III types is that they are simply horsetraders, bargainers, transactional brokers, and Johnny-come-lately's. They are often pictured as lacking strong convictions and moving in whatever direction the wind is blowing, as opportunists willing to sell out to the highest bidder in money or votes. The charge is usually overdrawn but a core of truth remains, act III types and the occupants of the White House not only are brokers but have to be the brokers in order to make the system work. The American political system has so much built-in conflict, so many representatives of competing or warring constituencies, and has so many checks and balances that higher level adjustment and compromising are essential.

Presidents are frequently criticized for not providing leadership for all scenes, for all acts, for all seasons. A more refined appreciation of how our political system is fashioned would lead to a recognition that most presidents most of the time have to operate in the act II-and-a-half to act III range. They are necessarily dependent on other types of leaders to generate the inventions and the movements that help the nation to renew and change itself. We would all be better judges of presidents if we recognized the considerable degree to which leadership in this nation is very dispersed and that much of the leadership we need—at least on very many occasions—is not leadership from the top, but movement, group, and entrepreneurial grass roots leadership from outside of Washington and outside of government.

Note that sometimes an individual may move from one act to another. Thus a Reverend Jesse Jackson, for example, performs act I functions when he is an outspoken advocate, act II functions when he is an organizer of Operation Push, and in 1984 he very nearly became an act III operative as he sought the Democratic party's nomination for the presidency. Ralph Nader operated in act I or Act I-and-a-half when he wrote *Unsafe at Any Speed*, the book that condemned General Motors and its shoddy automobiles and its neglect of automobile safety. But Nader was an act II type when he organized research and advocacy activities and recruited money and staff to lobby for his political agenda.

Leadership comes from all three acts. Presidents may be dependent, more than either they or we realize, on act I and II types for ideas and new initiatives—but so also the act I and II types must depend on presidents or other national act III leaders to bring about the compromise or brokered decisions that permit needed change or breakthroughs in legislation, court decisions, or executive actions. Act III leadership can be just as creative and innovative as leadership in act I or II. Similarly officials in act III can fail—because of caution or ineptitude and so on—just as act I and II types can fail in their undertakings. The lesson is that leadership rarely comes from a single person or a single institution. Leadership is dispersed, and leaders are extraordinarily dependent on other leaders to help shape, develop, enact, and implement the policy changes the nation needs.

Separation of Brain and State

There are countless definitions of an intellectual. These range from the uncharitable description of intellectuals as people who take more words than necessary to say more than they know, to the more general definition of the intellectual as a person devoted to matters of the mind, to study, reflection, and speculation. Arthur Schlesinger, Jr., suggests an intellectual is a person happy with ideas, likes them, thinks about them, talks about them, and worries about them. Most would agree intellectuals like to build ideas up, break them down, refine them, and, in the larger sense, connect ideas together to build theories about the meaning of life, the universe, truth, beauty, and justice.

An intellectual is also in part a philosopher, a lover of truth and knowledge. Someone interested in ideas for the love of wisdom. Someone who has an innate love and curiosity for knowledge and seeks ends beyond the immediate practical needs of society. Intellectuals question the truth of the moment and view things in the longer, higher, and wider sense of "truth" and "justice." In short, the intellectual dreams of what might be, of the "impractical ought."

This nation was shaped and founded in large part by a number of intellectual activists. Adams, Franklin, Hamilton, Jefferson, James Wilson, Madison, and scores of others helped construct and invent the ideas that empowered this new Republic. But, more often than not, the intellectual has played a detached role, often skeptical, critical, or even outraged by the misuses and abuses of power. This is not always the case. Many, like Aristotle, have been tutors to presidents and the powerful. In our time, we have had Roosevelt's Brains Trust and scores of John Kenneth Galbraiths, Edward Tellers, and individuals like Arthur Burns, Arthur Okun, Henry Kissinger, Daniel Patrick Moynihan, and advisers like Arthur Schlesinger, and Martin Feldstein.

What Theodore White once hailed in 1967 as the rise of the "action-intellectuals" also poses some problems. Can an intellectual become involved in the exercise of power without losing the perspective and perhaps even the credentials of a disinterested scholar? Walter Lippmann suggested this was risky business:

> It is only knowledge freely acquired that is disinterested. When, therefore, men whose profession it is to teach and investigate become the makers of policy, become members of an administration in power, become politicians and leaders of causes, they are committed. Nothing they can say can be relied upon as disinterested. Nothing they can teach can be trusted as scientific. It is impossible to mix the pursuit of knowledge, and those who have tried it turn out to be very bad politicians or they cease to be scholars.[2]

Some observers go even beyond Lippmann's point and say the essence of intellectual thinking is disagreement. Solzhenitsyn writes, "The task of the artist is to sense more keenly than others the harmony of the world, the beauty and the outrage of what man has done to it, and poignantly to let people know."

Intellectuals as critics commonly disparage the things associated with politics. Manipulation, compromise, pragmatism, wheeling and dealing, coercion and the endless bickering and squabbling that make up the practice of politics leave the intellectual indifferent or hostile. Henry David Thoreau wrote that what is called politics "is comparatively so superficial and inhuman that practically I have never fairly recognized it concerns me at all."[3] The novelist J.D. Salinger was quoted not long ago in a rare interview as saying "I don't care about politicians. I do not have anything in common with them. They try to limit our horizons. I try to expand our horizons." Linguist Noam Chomsky, of the Massachusetts Institute of Technology, is even more blunt: "Intellectuals are in a position to expose the lies of the government." Gore Vidal is just as blunt on politicians:

> All of the major politicians are interchangeable. They are all paid for more or less by the same people, and they do not even pretend now to be representative of the people at large.[4]

"Pet them, but do not give them any power," Eric Hoffer warned President Lyndon Johnson. Woodrow Wilson saw it this way:

> The men who act stand nearer to the mass of men than do the men who write. ... The men who write love proportion, the men who act must strike out practical lines of action and neglect proportion; here, unquestionably, we come upon the heart of the perennial misunderstanding.[5]

Wilson in the 1912 campaign went on to say, "What I fear is a government of experts. God forbid that in a democratic country we should resign the task and give the government over to the experts."

We are unlikely to realize Wilson's fear—most especially at the current time. Still there are serious questions. Presidents must recognize these tensions and what Wilson called the perennial and doubtless persisting misunderstandings. But presidents and their closest lieutenants should also make efforts to encourage the creative inventors in the land. This nation has remained great in part because it has been, on the whole, an open society—a society where ideas are encouraged and where the dissenter in politics as well as in the arts and sciences is free to innovate and develop fresh ideas and fresh approaches. The challenge is how to encourage intellectuals, inventors, and researchers (and artists and poets) to contribute positive and constructive as well as critical ideas, to suggest and point they way toward ideas that might make government work better.

Intellectuals doubtless will be gadflies, outsiders, and critics commonly immune to the seductions of power. Some have even suggested that their powerlessness is the precondition to their being creative and imaginative and to their ultimate wisdom. The true transcending intellectual is a questioner—always concerned with the higher goals, purposes, and values of both society and humankind. At their best, they are often a shadow or opposition government—in the best sense of those phrases. Shelley even went so far as saying the "poets are the unacknowledged legislators of the world." Solzhenitsyn adds, "The great writer is, so to speak, a second government; that's why no regime anywhere has ever loved its great writers, only its minor ones."[6]

Presidential Advisory Commissions

The conventional solution for information-starved presidents is to build up their White House staffs. This has been done extensively since the time of FDR. But there are limits to the number of useful staff a president can have. After a while the addition of new staff and more and more staff units and cabinet councils just multiplies a president's managerial problems without giving valuable service in return. Giving a president more staff often actually insulates a president from currents of thought he should be aware of—both within the government and from outside.[7]

It has long been fashionable in journalistic circles to poke fun at presidential commissions. But they are also one of the solutions to the need for more enriched presidential learning. Not all presidential commissions have worked out well, but, more often than not, these short-term advisory units have added to presidential and national learning. And they are a plausible way to overcome the potential separation of brain and state. If they have not worked as well as they should have, the answers why this has been so need to be examined. The effectiveness of outside advisory units rests upon a variety of factors—especially these:

The determination and definition of a worthy need for outside advisers

Recruitment of appropriately talented and concerned members

Intelligent staffing and relevant briefings

Informed analysis and high-level independent analysis of the resulting reports and recommendations

Presidential advisory commissions are essentially a twentieth-century creation.[8] There have been some 150 or more White House level advisory commissions over the past eighty years. They are ad hoc rather than permanent in nature. Research indicates that commissions are generally created by presidents who seriously want policy advice, and want to learn. Research indicates—and the Ronald Reagan use of these bodies confirms this as well—that most presidents most of the time act favorably on the reports they receive from commissions. The conventional wisdom is almost always the opposite: namely, that presidents appoint commissions and similar study groups in order to avoid issues, delay action, or to deflect public attention. Members of Congress are sometimes jealous of this practice because they view it as a legislative responsibility to gather ideas by holding hearings, conducting investigations, and by other methods devised by Congress to fulfill its constitutional mandate.

Occasionally, presidents have used commissions for those other purposes. In practice, a variety of motives or concerns prompt presidents to create these commissions.[9] A commission is created

1. When a president needs outside help to analyze a controversial question because his own top officials are not providing enough information
2. When a president genuinely desires a fresh outside perspective and fully intends to offer leadership on the topic when the commission is finished with its work
3. When the president may not need further information for himself but wants a bipartisan group of experts to help him build bipartisan support for a policy or program initiative
4. When a controversial issue has to be resolved and a president is less in need of new information than in need of new negotiations and presidential-congressional bargaining
5. When a president is responding to a major crisis or tragedy (the death of John F. Kennedy, Three Mile Island) and needs an investigation that will find answers and reassure the president and the public
6. When a president (as did Hoover, Eisenhower, Carter) wishes to forecast trends and anticipate new challenges and possible solutions

Despite the fact that presidential commissions are often the butt of jokes—and they will continue to be the object of satire—presidents will continue to appoint them. This resource for presidents carries risks, but it generally provides more opportunities than liabilities. Their use and abuse need evaluation and oversight by Congress, the press, and other outside institutions. A few generalizations may be helpful in this regard.

Defining the success or effectiveness of a presidential commission is not easy, for one has to take into account the variety of purposes for which they are used. Some are useful for their findings. Some are useful for the general education they provide, like Milton Eisenhower's Commission on Violence. Some, like the 1982–83 Social Security Commission, are useful for legislative initiatives. Others, like the 1983 Kissinger panel on Central America, help survey a thorny situation and may perhaps provide new information and fresh perspective for both president and Congress. An outright failure is rare for a presidential commission—as long as the definition of success is broadly defined.

We should rightly ask what this device may do to the existing channels for helping presidents to learn. Does reliance on advisory commissions diminish the vitality of the cabinet, the various units in the executive office of the president, or even the Congress? This is probably not the case, but this question needs further study. Sometimes members of Congress have served on these commissions. Moreover, Congress can always appoint its own commissions and has occasionally done this. A performance shootout (to borrow an IBM term) between presidential and congressionally appointed commissions might occasionally be a productive competition.

Commissions, when properly designed, can sometimes be a useful device for bridging some of the gap between those who are detached thinkers and researchers and those who have to make practical decisions in the world of government. They can also sometimes serve as a catalyst to raise questions or to pose issues for further research. A few years ago, James Sundquist of the Brookings Institution called for more attention to be paid to what he called research brokerage—the people or institutions who can translate research findings and information into the kinds of usable information that policy makers can readily absorb.[10] He suggested a model that links researchers, research administrators, information brokers, and policy makers that looks like this:

A		B		C		D
Researchers	⟷	Research administrators	⟷	Information (research) brokers	⟷	Policy makers

He noted too that the flow had to go in both directions. While policy information moves to the right, research funds and guidance about critical pending public or societal problems should flow in the reverse direction.

Presidential commissions—such as those on violence, Three Mile Island, the strategic forces such as the MX missile, or the Commission for the Study of Ethical Problems in Medicine and Biomedical and Behavioral Research—obviously pose vital policy problems, problems that cry out for more attention from the nation's researchers, inventors, citizens at large.

In sum, presidents go about learning in a variety of ways. No one way is adequate. Plainly, their styles and temperament affect how, and how much, they learn. But much of their learning takes place, it would appear, after they get to the White House. Much of their learning comes about because of messages sent from a distance, rather than coming in neat tidy packages from the West Wing or from across the alley in the Executive Office Buildings. An inevitable tension between brain and state often grows worse during presidential terms and presidents will not likely be able to solve that clash of styles and values. We need to conceive of the potential learning process at the White House in wider, broader terms. We need to conceptualize a presidency without walls. Presidents as both learners and educators, and ultimately as teachers, need in a larger sense to encourage the nation to learn along with them and to encourage the nation to help discover the ideas and approaches needed to solve problems.

Notes

I have drawn upon several books for some of the general ideas and references in this essay. See especially Thomas E. Cronin and Sanford Greenberg, eds., *The Presidential Advisory System* (New York: Harper & Row, 1969); Thomas E. Wolanin, *Presidential Advisory Commissions* (Madison: University of Wisconsin Press, 1975); Arthur M. Schlesinger, Jr., *The Crisis of Confidence* (Boston: Houghton Mifflin, 1969); James MacGregor Burns, *Leadership* (New York: Harper & Row, 1978); Lewis A. Coser, *Men and Ideas* (New York: Free Press, 1960); and Alexander L. George, *Presidential Decisionmaking in Foreign Policy* (Boulder, Colo.: Westview Press, 1980).

1. Schlesinger, *Crisis of Confidence,* pp. 57–58.
2. Walter Lippmann, "The Deepest Issues of Our Time" *Vital Speeches,* July 1, 1936.
3. On Thoreau, see Charles A. Madison, *Critics and Crusaders* (New York: Henry Holt, 1947), pp. 174–193.
4. Gore Vidal, quoted in "Gore Vidal: His Life Is an Opened Book," by Kay Mills, *Los Angeles Times,* July 15, 1984, part VIII, p. 10. Copyright, 1984, Los Angeles Times. Reprinted by permission.
5. Woodrow Wilson, quoted in James Reston, "On Kennedy's Disenchanted Intellectuals," *New York Times,* October 7, 1961. Copyright © 1961 by The New York Times Company. Reprinted by permission.
6. The Shelley quote and some related themes come from William M. Gibson, *Theodore Roosevelt among the Humorists: W.D. Howells, Mark Twain and Mr. Dooley* (Knoxville: Univ. of Tennessee Press, 1980).
7. See Thomas E. Cronin, *The State of the Presidency* (Boston: Little, Brown, 1980), ch. 7.
8. See Wolanin, *Presidential Advisory Commissions.*
9. I have drawn upon here from a personal letter sent to me March 14, 1983, by Bradley H. Patterson, Jr., a former White House aide and veteran government civil servant who has worked with several commissions.
10. James L. Sundquist, "Research Brokerage: The Weak Link," Brookings Institution Reprint Series #342, 1978, p. 127.

8

The Executive Office of the President

Hugh Heclo

T he executive office of the president is a very peculiar subject. It is not really "executive," for the executive office of the president itself executes or runs almost nothing. It is not really an "office," but a holding company for many offices. And any president is likely to know next to nothing about "his" office's operations. No one has ever tried seriously to manage the executive office of the president as a whole. No one, apart from a few congressmen on obscure appropriation subcommittees and a handful of White House clerks, pays any sustained attention to the executive office.[1]

And yet the executive office of the president is more than an exercise in creative labeling. Its development and its status as almost a nonsubject in American government tell us some important things about the presidency. Because our attention is normally riveted to the particular doings of the individuals who occupy the presidential office, it is doubly important to try to think institutionally about the larger organizational milieu surrounding presidents.

What it means to think institutionally about the presidency can be best conveyed by an anecdote about the former executive clerk of the White House, Rudolph Foster. By 1944 Foster had worked in the White House for over forty years, that is to say, since the McKinley administration. Throughout Republican and Democratic years, Foster had supervised the handling of presidents' routine business (state papers, mail, files, messengers, and the like), and FDR had made special provisions to keep him on past the legal civil service retirement age. In October 1944, as a weary FDR left the White House for one of his last campaign trips, the old chief clerk approached, warmly shook the president's hand and wished him good luck. Watching Foster wave to him from outside the executive offices, FDR turned to his companion in the car and said with emotion in his voice, "That is practically the first time in all these years that Rudolph has ever stepped out of character and spoken to me as if I were a human being instead of just another president."[2]

To treat the president as just another president is to have adopted a larger view of time and place and office. It is something of that perspective that I would like to capture by focusing on the executive office of the president—the organizational life of this nonoffice rather than its power or personalities. In this chapter I try to recreate some of the ancient history and original intentions surrounding the executive office of the president and then look at the results of these intentions and the trends that overtook them. The most important developments for the executive office of the president were often things that did not happen, unsuccessful efforts to create a more orderly set of relationships at the executive center. The final section of the chapter spells out what I regard as the more interesting implications of this survey. If I am correct, the executive office of the president is going to merit much more serious attention in the future than it has received in the past.

Intentions

Prior to 1939, the "executive offices" (the plural was usually used) was a term conventionally applied to those facilities through which presidents conducted the business affairs of their office—correspondence, signing of state documents, recordkeeping, and so on. The clerklike function of these offices was typically contrasted with the many social functions of the presidency. In fact it was only late in the nineteenth century that a staff organization distinctly for business as opposed to social duties began to emerge in the White House. Congress had first appropriated funds for presidential staff in 1857, namely a private secretary, a steward, and a part-time messenger. There is no neat dividing line, but certainly by the end of the McKinley administration White House business was much less subject to the personal whims of unemployed presidential relatives, rascals, and other characters who followed earlier presidents into the executive mansion. Ideas of business efficiency were penetrating the presidency from the private sector just as the workload was increasing and being spurred on by a more sensational national print media. From the Cleveland to the McKinley years to the Theodore Roosevelt years, an important White House bureaucrat for the first time stayed on across administrations to supervise the rapidly growing clerical staffs.[3] In 1902 Roosevelt demolished the greenhouses at the west end of the executive mansion and built a temporary executive office bulding. In 1909 the west wing executive office building was doubled in size and the Oval Office built for President Taft.[4] In the next several years, attempts to create a more professional, high-level career staff in the White House modeled along private management models ran aground amid the Taft administration's political difficulties and the heavy-handed manipulations of the president's private secretary, businessman Charles Norton. Still, an important transformation in the direction of a more bureaucratic presidency had occurred. As Ira Smith, the veteran White House mail clerk later recalled:

> The small, intimate group that had previously gathered devotedly around the President and had considered itself on familiar terms with him was never

completely restored. This was not entirely a result of Norton's operations, although they delineated the change. The fact was that the office of the Presidency was becoming too big and too busy to permit the continuance of the old set-up. Somewhere in Taft's administration the one-big-family atmosphere faded out, and when Woodrow Wilson became President, the times had changed and we were in for a busy office that had little chance for byplay, gossip, or an occasional game of craps in the basement.[5]

One may doubt that gossip ever went out of fashion without quarreling with the view that something important had changed. The arrival of Franklin Roosevelt brought another major expansion in the White House staff and a much more complicated organization that in some respects is still familiar. To the outside world the presidency was, if anything, more intensely personal than ever. The personae of FDR, his family, and intimates dominated attention. But the organizational underside of this attention was more people working for the president to answer letters, handle the press, arrange White House tours, schedule public appearances, respond to congressional requests, cultivate interest groups, maintain contact with the executive agencies, work on hot policy problems, and do all the other chores associated with what we now think of as the modern presidency.[6] As the initial emergency measures of the New Deal were taking effect, Roosevelt's attention increasingly turned to ways of bringing more order to the melange of executive aides, offices, and councils that he had created. From that effort finally emerged the first formal organization of the executive office of the president in 1939.

I doubt that there will ever be enough historical documentation to allow one to speak conclusively about FDR's "true" motives. Probably he himself did not always know what they were. Still, it seems that there is now enough historical information to indicate that FDR, if he did not have a simple coherent plan for the executive office of the president, was doing much more than merely extemporizing. Roosevelt had after all been schooled in Progressive ideas about good government, and as assistant secretary of the navy in 1919 had testified to Congress in a brilliant exposition of the case for an executive budget centered in the presidency. FDR admired savvy administrators like Louis Brownlow and himself had been a reforming governor of New York's outmoded administrative apparatus. In the spring of 1934 the New Deal was one year old and the White House was seeking approval from the Washington Fine Arts Commission to remodel the executive offices of the west wing. FDR noted to the assistant who was handling the matter that he regarded this as a temporary solution and looked forward to the day when the old State Department building would be put to use "for the president's offices and bureaus."[7]

The road to the 1939 executive order creating the executive office of the president in the State Department Building (renamed the Executive Office Building) was a twisting one.[8] To produce his reorganization plan, Roosevelt appointed and consulted closely with a three-member Committee on Administrative Management chaired by Louis Brownlow. Often forgotten now is the fact that the Brownlow Committee was originally intended by the president to be an outgrowth of the administration's planning activities; more effective regional planning of public works and the growing list of other federal services required more effective and centralized executive reorganization. The focus of such ultimate coordination was to be in the presidency itself.

Had President Roosevelt and Brownlow Committee gotten their way in 1937, the contours of American national government would have been transformed. A central planning board under the president would have overseen a series of regional planning centers spread around the country distributing federal services. All independent regulatory commissions would have been merged into existing cabinet departments and led by the president. A central personnel agency under the president would have replaced the Civil Service Commission in managing the permanent federal work force. In the event, FDR's 1937 proposals became caught up in a firestorm of controversy surrounding his attempt to "pack" the Supreme Court and cries of dictatorship. In 1939 the president brought forward a much scaled down version through a reorganization plan that would take effect unless vetoed by Congress. Eager to avoid more political controversy, the president took what he could get of the original Brownlow proposals and tried to implement the 1939 reorganization so as to get more of what he wanted. The executive order creating the executive office of the president was issued on September 8, 1939, but received scant attention, for on the same day, Roosevelt issued his Limited National Emergency Proclamation after the outbreak of war in Europe.

The new executive office of the president was composed of six major subdivisions:

1. A White House Office with six administrative assistants for the president in addition to FDR's existing personal aides and the clerical offices under Rudolph Foster
2. The Bureau of the Budget relocated from the Treasury Department
3. A National Resources Planning Board, bringing to the presidency a planning staff formerly under a cabinet council but without regional offices as originally hoped for
4. A Liaison Office for Personnel Management following the unsuccessful bid to place the Civil Service Commission in the executive office of the president
5. An Office of Government Reports combining earlier scattered functions of public information
6. An Office of Emergency Management to serve as a home for temporary units concerned with the anticipated problems of national defense

The story of what actually happened in this new executive office structure is buried in long-forgotten files and fading memories of the few surviving participants. To some extent the 1939 reorganization simply formalized existing arrangements. But to say that it did no more than that would, I think, be to seriously misunderstand the underlying intentions that emerged as problems of central staffing were discussed privately among FDR, the Brownlow group, and other insiders during the period 1936–1939. Three points merit attention.

First, the executive office of the president was not seen as simply a collection of convenient staff functions; it was to be a compact organization with a unifying logic of its own. Taken as a whole, the executive office of the president would embody those nondelegable central functions without which a top executive could not do his job. These services to the president—administrative assistance, budgeting, planning, personnel policy—were a kind a model of administrative management that would, it was hoped, eventually be mirrored in the provision of similar services for department heads everywhere in government.

Second, the executive office of the president was primarily to furnish a central capability for executive branch coordination, not a staff for policy making or operational competition with the departments and agencies. It was recognized, of course, that any central clearance of agency actions or national resource planning would affect policies. But executive office staff would not be in the business of formulating policies from the ground up nor themselves operate programs. They would be conveners, facilitators, expeditors, and intelligence gatherers for presidents. The executive office of the president was essentially viewed as a manager of processes cutting across programs.

With FDR's approval, for example, the Brownlow committee considered and rejected the idea of creating a cabinet secretariat as a central coordinating device, seeing this as an undue restriction of the president's tactical freedom in dealing with his department heads. Yet the alternative was not for the president to organize his staff on just any basis. Instead the president was to have a half-dozen administrative assistants with subject matter assignments (economics, foreign affairs) and serving as the president's eyes and ears around government; one of these assistants ("the fellow who never goes out" as FDR liked to call him) would serve as an in-house coordinator of the others.[9] These administrative aides, supplemented by temporary assistants hired to work on special problems as they arose, would consult with department heads either singly or in groups depending on the amount of policy overlap involved. Backstopping these aides would be the larger staffs of the institutional units in charge of the four key management processes—planning, budgeting, personnel, and reporting.

Finally, the executive office of the president was foreseen as having a strong component of government careerists. It was expected to include government professionals, especially generalists, who would be capable of performing at the highest levels in both functional units of the executive office of the president and on rotating assignments in the White House Office. For example, from 1937 onward FDR indicated privately that his in-house coordinator "who never goes out" was to be William H. McReynolds, a widely respected civil servant of twenty-five years standing. Likewise, the president repeatedly pressed acting Budget Director Daniel Bell, another long-time federal careerist in the Treasury Department, to become official budget director in anticipation of moving the budget agency into the executive office of the president. Bell's firm refusal eventually led to selection of another professional public administrator, Harold Smith, Michigan's budget director in a Republican administration, for the job. Likewise, in November 1936, again with FDR's apparent support, the Brownlow Committee looked forward to arrangments by which departmental officials would be given tours of duty in the White House Office.

In summary, the intentions behind the organization of the executive office of the presidency ran in the direction of providing a fairly coherent central capability to bring greater unity of purpose and consistency of action to the executive branch. It would be easy to overinterpret all this as a grand design to curb FDR's messy administrative habits through scientific management. It was not. The ideas behind the organization of the executive offfice of the president constituted an architect's sketch rather than an administrative draftsman's blueprint.

This sketch aimed at providing continuous administrative support to an office that everyone recognized to be highly dependent on particular political personalities. The EOP capability would be institutional—in the sense of having a distinct set of logically related functions and focused continuity—but it would not have the layered, specialized trappings of a large bureaucracy. Staff would be arranged in an orderly way to operate under the imprimatur of the presidency, but they would not be so rigidly structured as to destroy the president's flexibility as a political leader. The ultimate intention was not to organize FDR but to provide the necessary and sufficient tools with which each president could organize himself.

Results

The intentions behind the organization of the executive office of the president failed to be realized, and quickly so. FDR's immediate need to deal with the emergencies produced first by the European war and then Pearl Harbor soon overpowered any intentions for a more orderly operation of the executive office of the president during 1939–1942. Adding to this were particular problems of personality and circumstance that are far too intricate to describe here. In general, the only part of the original design to survive was the Bureau of the Budget, an important exception but one whose subsequent strength has tended to obscure how much of the larger picture was lost. For example, FDR's administrative assistants became absorbed in ad hoc assignments and only rarely performed the coordinative work that had been intended. McReynolds, rather than playing any in-house role among them, became head of the Liaison Office for Personnel Management, an office that eventually fell into disuse. In 1943 congressional opponents destroyed a National Resources Planning Board that was internally divided as to the nature of its mission, either as a presidential staff developing coherent national plans for physical and human resources or as a more traditional agency shaping its work to the distributive politics of Congress. The Office of Emergency Management did for several years serve as a holding company for temporary offices associated with defense and then war. But as was not intended, OEM became the spawning ground for new and largely improvised central units that progressively shifted from liaison and coordination to operations-oriented hierarchies. Its main offspring was an Office of War Mobilization and Reconstruction that by 1944 had its own statutory base, a head with president-like powers of command over the departments and a two-year fixed term of office.

Attempts at Reorganization

As it became apparent that original hopes for the executive office of the president were not being achieved, a number of efforts were made to reformulate arrangmenets at the center. These attempts have continued down to the present day. They are generally characterized by an urge to provide for more systematic procedures above the level of departments but short of telling the president how to run his own immediate affairs.

The first generation of such attempts occurred among a small set of persons who were familiar with FDR's methods, remarkably rich in practical experience at the center of government, and deeply reflective about the presidency. By and large their discreet efforts have been lost in the mists of history, and here we can recount only a few highlights.

At FDR's request, for example, Brownlow returned in 1943 with a draft proposal on the postwar organization of the president's office. He recommended a system of interdepartmental committees directly under the president and moderated by a neutral representative of the president, with one staff secretary drawn from OEM for each committee. These cabinet committees would coordinate the development of policies for the president's approval or rejection. A strengthened Bureau of the Budget would see to it that approved policies were carried out and would develop new means of reporting on departmental operations.[10] As we shall see, this has been roughly the system hit upon by the Reagan administration.

During the mid-1940s a number of efforts were made to create some form of staff secretariat under the president, paying special attention to the need to coordinate not only defense and diplomatic policy streams but also presidents' often freewheeling role in foreign affairs. Most noteworthy was General (and later Secretary of State) George C. Marshall's quiet lobbying for a permanent White House secretariat modeled on British lines. Had Marshall's plan succeeded, Ambassador Averell Harriman would have returned from Russia in 1945 to be cabinet secretary. As it was, Roosevelt's death and the initial uncertainties of the Truman administration raised many sensitive issues of presidential staffing. Remnants of Marshall's ideas continued in the efforts of James Forrestal and Robert Lovett to create a permanent executive council for national security affairs. The National Security Council that eventually ended up in the executive office of the president was at first resisted by President Truman as a threat that would collectivize presidential leadership; gradually the NSC became accepted as an expression of the president's individual leadership.

The Bureau of the Budget produced its own cadre of serious thinkers about the executive office of the president. In addition to Harold Smith himself there were people in and at the fringes of the budget agency who took a lively intellectual interest in the problems of central executive staffing, persons such as Arnold Miles, V.O. Key, Don K. Price, Wayne Coy, and others. No single, authoritative proposal was ever produced from this quarter. In the name of preserving presidential prerogatives and flexibility, they were constantly at pains to argue against statutory arrangements and other forms of congressional entree into presidential staffing. At the same time they were dissatisfied with the haphazard, sporadic attempts to provide coherent leadership from the presidency. The results were inconclusive. There was some thought that the Bureau's mandate should be broadened to explicitly include the interdepartmental management of domestic policy development and execution. Or perhaps there should be a cabinet officer without portfolio and a small central staff, a kind of formalized Harry Hopkins. For a time Harold Smith hoped that the Bureau's fiscal analysis division would undertake the tasks that Congress in 1946 assigned to a statutory Council of Economic Advisers in the executive office of the president. Like the National Security Council, the CEA was created by the so-called do-nothing Eightieth Congress controlled by the Republicans, and like the NSC the CEA gradually clarified its ambiguous standing by becoming oriented solely toward advising the president of the day (rather than Congress or a collection of executive officials).

Thus by the end of the 1940s the executive office of the president contained the three core components that would survive to the present day—the Bureau of the Budget, National Security Council, and Council of Economic Advisers. What it did not have was the kind of internal logic, coherence, and continuity that reformers had hoped for in a system of central staffing.

The next major attempt at rethinking the executive office of the president occurred in Eisenhower's second term under the auspices of the President's Advisory Committee on Government Organization (composed of Milton Eisenhower, Arthur Fleming, and Nelson Rockefeller, and later Don K. Price).[11] Eisenhower had already established and made use of a cabinet secretariat to manage his regular cabinet meetings and an Operations Coordinating Board to oversee implementation of National Security Council policies. During his second term Eisenhower and his Advisory Committee mulled over a variety of major reorganizations without ever producing a final proposal. The only public airing of these ideas was in Nelson Rockefeller's congressional testimony (proposing a single central "Office of Executive Management" headed by a powerful executive assistant to the president and a first secretary serving as a kind of prime minister in national security and foreign affairs) and Milton Eisenhower's subsequent advocacy of two presidentially appointed vice presidents for foreign and domestic affairs. The president himself was apparently intrigued by these ideas but saw no political opportunity to push them. In the end, the incoming Kennedy administration simply discarded the cabinet secretariat, Operations Coordinating Board, the Advisory Committee, and the ideas for reform of the executive office of the president. The Eisenhower apparatus was seen as too cumbersome and bureaucratic for a young president promising vigorous action.

The next generation of efforts to reformulate the executive office of the president occurred in the Johnson and Nixon administrations and were led not by public administrators but by businessmen. The Task Force on Government Organization, chaired by Chicago industrialist Ben Heineman, was appointed by Lyndon Johnson in late 1966 and its report was personally squelched by the president in 1967. The Advisory Council on Executive Organization was appointed by President Nixon in 1970 under the chairmanship of Litton Industries executive Roy Ash. Both groups worried about the lack of central management over the burgeoning field of federal domestic programs. The Heineman Task Force called for new coordinating mechanisms centered in the Bureau of the Budget, but the president refused to take action that could seem to confirm criticisms of weak administration in Great Society programs. The Ash Council had a greater lasting impact. A new Domestic Council for policy development was created in the executive office of the president and the Budget Bureau was renamed and tied more directly to the White House as the President's spokesman for management and budget issues. But the Ash Council's larger plans for centralized presidential control over the departments were quickly shelved under the impact of Watergate. The Domestic Council staff took on a variety of noninstitutionalized forms depending on the personalities involved. The management side of the Office of Management and Budget has been notable chiefly for its succession of unrelated initiatives led by short-term appointees with little discernable impact on real-life government management.

The latest foray into rethinking the executive office of the president occurred early in the Carter administration. In 1977 a major reorganization study was initiated by the new management staff that came into the Office of Management and Budget with the new president. The studies produced some of the first data about the functioning of the executive office as a whole, but it is also fair to say that the studies were innocent of any historical knowledge of the office of the president and lacked any serious political support. The major change that resulted was the creation of an Office of Administration.[12] This office provides common administrative services (personnel, bookkeeping, library, and computer center) to all organizations in the executive office of the president, but the bulk of its time is taken up with services supplied to the office of Management and Budget and the White House Office.

Resulting Trends

The record of attempts to think through new and enduring arrangements for the executive office of the president as a whole is a record of failure with assorted pieces (Council of Economic Advisors, Domestic Council, Office of Administration) left in the wake. There are three basic reasons for this failure.

The White House Perma-Crisis. Whatever one's organizational theory, administrative management in the presidency is a crisis-driven phenomenon.[13] Ever since FDR's original order creating the executive office of the president, problems requiring immediate decision have tended both to displace presidential attention from less urgent matters (such as management of the executive office) and to disrupt whatever pre-existing control system may have been in place. Not the least of these recurring emergencies is the arrival of new presidents and a constant turnover of staff with little knowledge of or interest in a predecessor's methods.

The need to deal with a constant flow of urgent situations scours a gulf between what seems relevant inside the White House and whatever grand design one can imagine for the executive office of the presidency. To deal with this reality, FDR and all his successors have demanded flexibility, and this has tended to undercut efforts at orderly central staffing arrangements within and between administrations.

External Political Constraints. Contrary to public impression, the president is not in a position to control his own executive office structure. In part this is because of statutory requirements, but the larger reason has to do with the anticipation of adverse political reactions, particularly in Congress. All recent presidents have been under strong public pressure to hold down the size of White House staffing, whatever the needs of the office. Likewise, knowledgeable presidential advisers, persons who might have been expected to favor a more rationally ordered system of central staffing, have generally argued over the years that arrangements should be kept informal, flexible, and above all nonstatutory. They have done so with one eye on the need to suit variations in each president's operating style but, no less important, the other eye on the danger of creating formal organizational handles which Congress would be tempted to try and control.

Presidents are not masters of their own house, but then neither is anyone else. Advisory systems that Congress tries to stipulate (such as the NSC or CEA in their original forms) can easily circumvented by the informal ways presidents choose to consult with advisors. But these informalities are a recipe for haphazardness and a lack of continuity that presidents cannot allieviate without inviting congressional interventions on executive office of the president organization. Thus the line runs straight and true from FDR, who worried in 1937 that to formally designate one of the new aides as a central coordinator would concentrate troublesome political attention on the man—to Jimmy Carter, who predicated his reorganization of the executive office of the president on a commitment to certain congressmen and the public that total employment in the executive office would be reduced.

Internal Bureaucratic Politics. Any full history would show that in each major period of attempted reform, action has been constrained by the desires of existing units of the executive office of the president to protect their organizational interests. This observation applies with special force to the largest unit, the budget agency, but the same tendency can be found in every small corner of the White House and Executive Office Buildings where people with very healthy egos are carrying out their own version of the president's mission. Turf protection among presidential staffs constrained creative handling of the future of the Office of War Mobilization and Reconstruction in the mid-1940s just as it inhibited major reform in the Carter administration's reorganization studies.

To say these things is not to doubt the public spirit of the people involved. It is to say that every attempt at significant change has encountered assistants and organizations in place who are confident that they are doing their best and are capable of gutting the entire enterprise of reform of the executive office. Another way of saying the same thing is to observe that, short of presidents themselves, there is no client with a continuing stake in the successful operation of the executive office as a whole. And because of the press of emergencies and external politics, each president is a problematic client within his own administration—much less one with any compelling reason to worry about the state of the executive office for his successors. Given the same system of incentives I expect that all of us would behave in about the same short-sighted way.

It follows from the largely unsuccessful attempts to rethink the executive office of the president and from the three powerful forces that have produced this record of frustration that the actual trends in management and organization of the office are unlikely to have been the result of very much forethought or conscious design. The trends are mainly a by-product of various piecemeal adjustments to circumstance within separate niches of the executive office. Some circumstances can be identified with particular initiatives of a president and his close advisers. Others stem from pressures in Congress or interest groups to create special advisory units. Still other circumstances have to do with the momentum of business in existing units of the executive office of the president. All contribute to the confusing organizational picture presented by today's executive office. In the space available I would like simply to headline what seem to be the most important trends.

1. *Structural Instability.* The executive office of the president grew from six unis in 1939 to a total of thirteen in 1983, and it did so with an immense amount of chopping and changing in the interim (table 8–1). So far as I can tell only two of the last twenty years (1965 and 1968) have passed without some change in the composition of the executive office. It is doubtful if any other Western nation can match this record of formal organizational change at the highest levels of government. During the first two decades after 1939, the changing composition of the executive office of the president tended to focus on national security concerns and creation of units in the president's official family tended to shield activities from public view. In the second two decades, additional units were more closely identified with social and economic problems and the status of the executive office was often used to heighten outside attention to the matter at hand.

2. *Elements of Continuity.* Viewed organizationally, the executive office of the presidency has a core composed of two large bodies—the budget agency with 40 percent of its total employment and the mosaic of White House office staffs with about 33 percent of the total—plus three special purpose policy staffs (NSC, CEA, and a regularly renamed domestic policy unit) and a housekeeping unit (the Office of Administration). The continuity that exists is in terms of segments and functions, not in terms of general structure and staffing.

3. *The Illusion of Bigness.* During the past thirty years the number of permanent positions in the executive office of the presidency has increased by a little over 50 percent, from around 1,100 to 1,700 persons. Another 300 to 400 persons are typically present in the executive office as temporary consultants or on detail from other executive branch agencies. The conventional wisdom is that American presidents have very large staffs compared with the leading political executives of other Western democracies.

The executive office's employment growth rate is largely in line with that of general federal employment and well below the rate of change that has occurred in federal government responsibilities in the past thirty years. What presidents have in the executive office of the president compared with central governments elsewhere are large numbers of personal aides, specialized staff

Table 8–1

Composition of the Executive Office of the President, 1939 to 1983[a]

Office or Unit	Initiative	Duration
Executive Office of the President	Public Law	1939–
White House Office	Public Law	1939–
Bureau of the Budget/OMB	Public Law	1939–
National Resources Planning Board	Public Law	1939–1943
Office of Government Reports	Exec. Order	1939–1948
Liaison Office for Personnel Management	Exec. Order	1939–1945
Office of Emergency Management	Exec. Order	1940–1943
War Agencies (OWMR, etc.)	Exec. Order	1943–1946
Council of Economic Advisors	Public Law	1946–
National Security Council	Public Law	1947–
National Security Resources Board	Public Law	1947–1953
Office of Defense Mobilization	Exec. Order	1952–1958
Office of the Director for Mutual Security	Public Law	1951–1953
Telecommunications Adviser	Exec. Order	1951–1953
Operations Coordinating Board	Exec. Order	1953–1961
President's Advisory Committee on Government Organization	Exec. Order	1953–1960
President's Board of Consultants on Foreign Intelligence Activities	Exec. Order	1956–1961
National Aeronautics and Space Council	Public Law	1958–1973
Office of Civil and Defense Mobilization	Exec. Order	1958–1961
Office of Emergency Planning (Preparedness)	Public Law	1961–1973
Office of Science and Technology	Public Law	1962–1973, 1976–
Office of the Special Representative for	Exec. Order	1963–
Trade Negotiations	Public Law	1974–
Office of Economic Opportunity	Public Law	1964–1975
President's Committee on Consumer Interests— Office of Special Assistant for Consumer Affairs	Exec. Order	1964–1966
National Council on Marine Resources and Engineering Development	Public Law	1966–1971
President's Council on Youth Opportunity— Office of Special Assistant for Youth	Exec. Order	1967–1971
Council of Urban Affairs	Exec. Order	1969–1970
Office of Intergovernmental Relations	Exec. Order	1969–1972
Council for Rural Affairs	Exec. Order	1969–1970
President's Foreign Intelligence Advisory Board	Exec. Order	1961–1977, 1981–
Council on Environmental Quality	Public Law	1969–
Office of Telecommunications Policy	Public Law	1970–1978
Domestic Council/Policy Staff, Office of Policy Development	Public Law	1970–
Cost of Living Council	Public Law	1971–1974
Council on International Economic Policy	Public Law	1971–1978
Office of Consumer Affairs	Exec. Order	1971–1973
Special Action Office for Drug Abuse Prevention	Exec. Order	1971–1975
Federal Property Council/Property Review Board	Exec. Order	1973–1978, 1981–
Energy Policy Office	Exec. Order	1973–1975
Council on Wage & Price Stability	Public Law	1974–1981
Presidential Clemency Board	Exec. Order	1974–1975
Economic Policy Board	Exec. Order	1974–1977
Energy Resources Council	Exec. Order	1974–1978
Office of Drug Abuse Policy	Public Law	1976–1978
Intelligence Oversight Board	Exec. Order	1976–
Office of Administration	Exec. Order	1978–

[a]Presently existing units are in italics. This table does not include the Office of the Vice President which, since the 1960s, has been increasingly formalized and included as a component of the Executive Office of the President.

(often operating well outside areas of direct presidential interest), and inexperienced helpers. What they do not have is a significant core of senior officials experienced in government and working closely with the chief executive on the full range of presidential policy business.[14] One current estimate puts the number of such officials working for prime ministers in Britain or Canada in the range of fifty to sixty persons.[15] My own guess for the Reagan administration would be perhaps a dozen; for Jimmy Carter I expect the number would have been closer to two or three. The presidency cuts a big political figure but a pinhead of an institutional figure in the executive establishment.

Implications

In view of the frustrating record of attempts to think seriously about the executive office of the president, I would be foolhardy to suggest some grand new design. My frank view is that the political forces favoring inertia are far too strong to be overcome by some bright new idea. But it would be worthwhile to nurture any tendencies that have the effect of making the executive office of the president an instrument for serving a succession of presidents and not simply catering to the personal entourage of the president of the day or mindlessly pursuing its own bureaucratic agenda. "Always serving, never servile" should be the motto of the executive office of the president.

If one accepts the strategy of building where there are already foundations, then there seem to be several promising lines of development. One is the Office of Policy Development under Reagan. For the first time the small nucleus of a domestic policy staff has been assembled and played roughly the facilitating and coordinating role that Brownlow had envisioned in his report to FDR in 1943. We should be looking for ways to organize the career lines of that staff and cross-fertilize personnel with the staffs of the National Security Council and Council of Economic Advisers.

A second line of development lies with the Office of Administration, an office that survived early doubts during the succession from Carter to Reagan and that is replacing contract personnel with permanent government employees to operate the White House and the Computer Center of the executive office. It would be wise to reserve the directorship of this office to career civil service officials. I would make the office responsible for authorizing the use of all detailees to the executive office (a hidden process that congressmen are forever trying to probe and that should be opened to the light of day). Put in the right hands, the small change of administrative housekeeping could have a large effect on the institutional life of the executive office.

Many other suggestions could be made along similar lines. By now I have probably already said enough to elicit the charge that my agenda calls for an even greater bureaucratization of the presidency under the guise of outmoded civil service concepts. And I must admit that, if forced to choose, I would rather see the executive office of the president bureaucratized with civil servants than by the customary layers of governmentally inexperienced short-timers. I say this because most of the real world pressures in the presidency constantly converge to drive out longer term institutional perspectives.

But we should not have to choose between a government of tyros or of mandarins. The challenge is one of finding appropriate relationships and—no less important—of sustaining an appreciation for what is appropriate across the flow of personalities and events. Viewed through the lens of the executive office of the president, the unchanging nature of the problem becomes a little clearer. The president is a person; the presidency is an office. To speak of a president's job is to consider what he (or someday she) as a person can or should do. To speak of the presidency is to consider what things can or should be done centrally in the executive branch. These two things are not the same and how to ensure their proper distinction and relationship is the essential puzzle.

The content of the president's job, the things *he* must do, seems stark and clear. He must deal with the particular issues affecting the nation's physical survival against foreign threats. Since international survival also depends on strength at home, a president must deal with major issues addressing the health of the national economy. Likewise, he must respond to those urgent situations that threaten our domestic order as a nation. Coping with the constant flow or particular issues affecting our peace, prosperity, and domestic order is the indispensable core; everything else about a president's job is secondary.

And yet this job of each president does not exhaust all those things that it is useful to have done centrally, that is to say, in the presidency. The time frame for significant policy changes and for learning from experience is likely to extend beyond the life of any particular administration. While the president lives moment to moment in the flow of events, the attention span of the presidency needs to extend to decades. And somehow the two perspectives need to be related. Without conscious effort and staffing to the contrary, it is always the former perspective that drives out the latter in the executive office of the president.

In addition to elongating the time perspective in the president's own job, there are more routine things that it is useful to have done centrally above the level of operating departments. These things have to do with the coordination of policies and management issues that cut across departments. Coherent action is unlikely to result if departments and agencies are left to their own devices, but such central government work is not particularly crucial to a president's doing his job. Nevertheless, to say "central" in the executive branch is, under our system of government, also to say presidential. There is no realistic possibility that executive office work will be taken seriously elsewhere except as it is done in the name of the man who—for a moment—embodies the office.

The puzzle of this non office called the executive office of the president will become more interesting in the years ahead. The need for a longer attention span and broader coordination in the presidency is likely to become greater not smaller. I am struck by the fact that despite their personal differences, all of our recent presidents have returned to the problem of what to do about the executive office of the president, typically in their second terms. I am also struck by the fact that the Reagan administration has done more than any of its recent predecessors to centralize domestic policy processes, executive budget decisions, and other forms of coordination. If this is what has happened with an antigovernment party in power, the aspirations of the executive office of the president founders may not be so archaic after all.

Notes

1. The sustained attention to the executive office of the president, such as it is, occurs mainly in the interchanges annually between an appropriations subcommittee of the House (the Senate committee rarely pays any attention to the matter) and a handful of executive office witnesses. See for each fiscal year the *Hearings before the Subcommittee on the Treasury, Postal Service, and General Government Appropriations,* of the Committee on Appropriations, U. S. House of Representatives. Appropriations for the various accounts of the Executive Office of the President are subsumed under this "General Government" category.

2. Robert E. Sherwood, *Roosevelt and Hopkins* (New York: Harper & Brothers, 1950), p. 209.

3. George B. Cortelyou rose from being a stenographer and executive clerk for Grover Cleveland to serve as McKinley's right-hand assistant, President Theodore Roosevelt's secretary and from there to serve successively as TR's head of the newly created Department of Commerce and Labor, Secretary of the Republican National Committee, Postmaster General, and Secretary of the Treasury. He spent his remaining thirty years as head of the nation's largest utility, Consolidated Edison.

4. In other major physical changes, the West Wing of the White House was reconstructed in 1930 following a fire in 1929, expanded and air-conditioned under FDR in 1934, and enlarged again during 1947–48.

5. Ira Smith with Joe Alex Morris, *Dear Mr. President* ... (New York: J. Messner, 1949).

6. A forthcoming book by James Sterling Young shows, by counting aides outside the White House, how large FDR's staff really was.

7. FDR Office Files, 1934, Hyde Park Library.

8. The standard secondary sources are Richard Polenberg, *Reorganizing Roosevelt's Government 1936–39* (Cambridge, Mass., Harvard University Press, 1966); and Barry Dean Karl, *Executive Reorganization and Reform in the New Deal* (Chicago: Chicago University Press, 1980). I have been influenced in my interpretation by Barry Karl's recent paper, "In Search of National Planning: The Case for a Third New Deal," a paper presented at the meeting of the organization of American Historians, April 6–9, 1983 (reproduced).

9. The minutes of FDR's discussions with the Brownlow Committee suggest that he took the plans seriously, although he clearly did not want formal public statements about detailed organization of the executive office nor about the duties of his administrative assistants. But he does appear to have desired—before the press of events following the outbreak of war in Europe—an informal designation of continuing subject matter assignments for his administrative assistants and an in-house coordinator of their work. So much was this the case that at one point in the spring of 1939, Brownlow was led to cite FDR's own 1919 testimony (as assistant navy secretary) against such clear assignments.

10. As Brownlow described the purpose, "... it is to lock all interested department heads together in a room until they knock their heads together and come out with an agreement. The something that has been added is the presence of a neutral moderator who may insist on their reaching an agreement, and, once it is reached, get it up to the boss." FDR's comment after reading Brownlow's 1943 report was, "He has not got the answer yet. I don't think anyone has. I am a bumblebee. I am going to keep on bumbling." FDR Office Files, Appendices, "Power of the President, 1941–45," OF101 and 101b, Hyde Park Library.

11. A fuller account would include the work of the Hoover Commissions, although I am not convinced that the Hoover study ever seriously penetrated the subject of the executive office of the president.

12. With some fanfare, the new president also eliminated several already inactive units of the executive office of the president and reassigned the activities of others. For example the Economic Opportunity Council, which had not met for years, was abolished. The Domestic Council—basically a cabinet committee—was abolished, but its staff retained under a senior presidential aide. The Office of Drug Abuse was abolished, but its functions were transferred to another White House aide and these later migrated as a largely self-contained unit under the Domestic Policy staff, renamed the Office of Policy Development under Reagan. Apart from the creation of the Office of Administration, the Carter changes were, to put it politely, mainly cosmetic and scarcely stood the test of time. In his first year Jimmy Carter made a considerable public show of reducing projected employment in the executive office of the president from 1,712 to 1,460 but after another year the personnel ceiling was revised upward to 1,662; had Carter won re-election, plans called for new staff additions for the anti-inflation program, for a new Energy Mobilization Board, and for a Central Statistical Board that would have amounted to an executive office of the president totaling roughly 2,300 persons in 1981.

13. This was the message of a lecture delivered by Congressman Steed in 1977 to a young Carter aide bubbling with reorganization plans to reduce the size of staffing of the White House and executive office of the president. After pointing out the shortsightedness of penny pinching, Steed summed up the enigma of presidential management with splendid congressional inscrutability: "... the President," he said, "doesn't have that much control over what he is going to have to do if he is going to run this country." *Hearings before a Subcommittee of the Committee on Appropriations,* House of Representatives, 95th Congress, Treasury, Postal Service and General Government Appropriations for FY 1978, part 3, p. 96.

14. Such institutional capacity, as I would call it, is certainly not all a president needs, but I think it is important and has to do with staff's experience in government and breadth of perspective. I mean to cast no personal aspersions, but by this standard it

is interesting that the executive office of the president's Office of Administration— surely one place to expect institutional routine and perspectives—under both Carter and Reagan has been headed by political aides in their thirties with no experience in the federal government.

15. Colin Campbell, *Governments under Stress* (Toronto: University of Toronto Press, 1983) p. 5.

9
Comments on Part III

Katharine Ferguson

A s important as it is to think about the presidency in institutional terms, it is equally necessary to recognize that a president's own personality and his willingness to use his personal discretion play a large role in determining how things turn out. I can illustrate this point by looking at two of President Reagan's most important personnel decisions: his choice of William Clark to replace James Watt as secretary of the interior, and his designation of Robert McFarlane to take Clark's place as chairman of the National Security Council.

Reagan chose Clark on his own. He discussed a list of close to thirty people to replace Watt with his advisors and this list was sent over to the head of Personnel for further review. The choice of secretary of interior is of the utmost concern to a wide variety of interest groups and Republican party loyalists, and therefore one might expect the choice to be made in a very cautious and deliberate fashion. While this formal selection process was going on, however, the president apparently decided on his own that he wanted Clark and he discussed the idea privately with him. He did not tell some of his top advisors about this for several days. Some did not know about it until the day of the announcement. Despite all the complexities involved, the president can still go ahead and surprise us if he wants to.

In contrast to Clark, who brought few formal qualifications to either the post of NSC Chairman, or the secretary of the interior, McFarlane has a very impressive résumé. He had served on the NSC during several different administrations. He also served as a committee staff member on Capitol Hill. McFarlane is eminently well qualified to fulfill the formal responsibility of the NSC chairman, managing the flow of information on foreign affairs that reaches the president. However, the NSC chairman is not simply a manager. He has the ear of the president and therefore is, or can be, a close confidant. However, he can only perform this role if he can establish a close personal rapport with the president. This personal quality was the great asset that Clark brought to the post. He had known the president for a very long time, having served him in a variety of posts in California and Washington. He and Reagan were close personal friends as well as political colleagues. Much of McFarlane's exquisite training and wealth of experience will be wasted if he is unable to find ways of establishing a similar kind of intimate rapport with the one man who, despite bureaucratic complexities and institutional constraints, remains in a position to say "yes" or "no" to the most vital questions involving the nation's security.

I would also like to add a few thoughts on Professor Heclo's proposal that a senior cadre of bureaucrats surround any president in place of the personal aides and political appointees now put in place. I think it is a poor idea. Or rather, I think there is already such a cadre of highly skilled professionals in place and at work in each of the federal agencies and departments.

To these professionals is added a layer of political appointees in the departments and agencies and personal staff aides brought to the White House. There is a growing group of men (and finally women!) with experience in government service who find themselves recalled to work in different administrations. George Shultz is one example of a secretary of state with previous cabinet posts behind him before he joined Mr. Reagan's cabinet. Caspar Weinberger is of course another excellent example; so too is education secretary Terrel H. Bell, who ran education programs when they were still under the auspices of the Department of Health, Education, and Welfare. This phenomenon is not limited to Republican administrations. Carter's choice of Joseph Califano for HEW and James Schlesinger as energy secretary, are good examples as well. It is possible for a president to choose men and women to carry out his political mandate, whatever it may be, while still bringing into government service individuals with experience and prior knowledge who can "hit the ground running" when sworn in. And it would be inadvisable to replace the top aides at the White House with those unknown to the president and unschooled in his or her beliefs and style.

President Reagan has been particularly well served by the men in the inner circle of the White House. Chief of Staff James Baker stands out for his ability to meld the president's ideology to the vagaries of political necessity. This president has achieved much of what he hoped to gain from the Congress. It would be wrong to believe this was true only of the first Congress he dealt with. In domestic spending, tax issues, defense spending, and foreign policy, Mr. Reagan has succeeded where his predecessor did not. And from my limited experience as a White House reporter,[1] it seemed to me that over and over again, it was James Baker, meeting with majority leader Howard Baker and ranking members of the Senate, who was able to work out a compromise. And, it was James Baker who met with ranking Democrats and Republicans of the House, including Speaker O'Neill, to bring legislation to some acceptable middle ground for both the White House and the Congress. Perhaps a person like James Baker could be found in a core of professional aides who carried over from administration to administration. But it seems to me a more workable plan to have those professionals in place at the top levels of agencies available to advise political appointees of Baker's caliber working directly for the president.

To those who argue that I have glossed over the examples where the current format does not work, I admit those examples do indeed exist. Perhaps most notable during this administration is the Environmental Protection Agency under Anne Gorsuch Burford. It is said the professional staff was "terrorized" during her tenure. Perhaps that is journalistic exaggeration, but I know from my own work it is a charge not totally without basis. It is also said the president was never "briefed" with the advice of the career people. Their advice filtered out somewhere between the agency's headquarters and Pennsylvania Avenue. In this case I would only say that the appointment of Mr. Ruckelshaus, a noncareerist who has extensive government experience, has brought balance between the president's political agenda and the Congress's desire for the agency to vigorously pursue environmental goals.

As to the question of the presidency as an institution, I would like to add a few random thoughts. The presidency is more of an institution with each succeeding administration. The White House is now surrounded by concrete barriers at various entrances and exits. Some of those were once available for a tourist's car to pass through in order to get a better glimpse of the buildings which all Americans can in some ways correctly claim as their own. Even those members of the press bearing White House credentials, many of whom have as their daily office a cubicle in the basement of the West Wing known as "the press room," are searched each and every time they re-enter the complex. Unfortunately, these security measures may truly be necessary in these days of bombings at the Capitol and intelligence reports that Libyan "death squads" are at large. And yet the imposition of each new concrete barrier (now planted in a quaint fashion with begonias!), and of each new security device, serves as yet another reminder that the president and the presidency in 1983 is to be looked at from a distance, but not touched. The president with undoubtedly the best ability to communicate to many (indeed the "great communicator") is brought to us via television and only "allowed out" on the rarest and most orchestrated occasions.

Let me disabuse you of the notion that the ability of the White House press corps to observe the president is very different from the opportunities available to most Americans. While covering the White House on a daily basis for a year and a half, it was quite often the case that I, and my press corps colleagues, would go several days without even laying our eyes on the man. The president on most days will give a luncheon address to a group of mayors; meet with members of Congress; swear in a Cabinet officer; sign legislation into law. At many of these events, Mr. Reagan makes brief remarks which the press can cover.

Here is how I most often "covered" the president. National Public Radio has a small closet we generously refer to as a recording booth. It has a sound mixer to both send reports to NPR headquarters just a few blocks away and to receive White House "feeds." Those feeds are the live transmissions of the president's remarks, made in the East Room at a luncheon perhaps. The facilities for my colleagues are quite similar. We can listen to what the president says, we can tape his remarks for later broadcast, but quite often we are nowhere near him. Now the press is usually present for the departure statement of a visiting head of state, on the south lawn for instance. And, we may join the president as he receives a guest for what is known as a "photo opportunity" in the Rose Garden. But these are highly orchestrated events and, when we are in shouting distance for a question, the president often reminds us that questions "are not allowed at photo opportunities." So when people ask me, "How does the president look to you? Does he really dye his hair? What is he like?" few understand how truly difficult those questions are to answer. I would much rather take on trade policy with Japan—a subject I know relatively little about.

To "cover" the president from a distance, even when your White House cubicle may be only a few yards from the Oval Office, makes one a very real part of the institutionalized presidency. Perhaps, with the advent of television cameras broadcasting live from the White House, there is no longer a need to rely on the personal impressions of the reporters at hand to transmit the personality and character of any individual occupying the presidency. If that is the case, it seems to me a shame.

I have colleagues who recall reading the news wires at the White House press office only to look up and find Lyndon Johnson peering over their shoulders. Even if that story is apocryphal, it is nice to believe that at one time it was permissible for a president literally to rub shoulders with reporters. I doubt this institutionalized relationship of the press corps to the president is unique to Mr. Reagan's White House. I feel sure it is a phenomenon that will become "only more so." But even this president, as keen as his speaking skills are, loses something in the translation to television. I think often it is his genuine warmth and humor as well as his genuine opinions that are lost. How odd that this should be kept at such a distance from the American public.

One completely unsolicited piece of advice: in future presidential campaigns take advantage of seeing a candidate at a small gathering. Pay particular attention to accounts of impromptu airport news conferences. Even in this era of media-managed campaigns, I feel sure after more than a year covering the White House, and once an election is over, you and I will never again get as great an opportunity to observe the individual who becomes president. Once sworn in, all we'll have to watch is the presidency.

Note

1. I left the White House assignment to cover foreign policy in January 1984.

10
Comments on Part III

Barney Frank

T he central problem with the executive office of the president is the extent to which it has expanded and has overlapped so substantially with regular government. Congress treats the executive office differently from the rest of the government. Its officials are not subject to Senate confirmation; there are more constraints when Congress questions them; they have been more able to plead executive privilege in certain contexts; what they do is more shielded from public scrutiny than cabinet actions are. The distinction Congress has made is that cabinet officers are public administrators appointed by the president to be sure, but confirmed by the Senate. They are not wholly creatures of the president, but people with separate statutory duties and with some public responsibility. We have retreated some since the Tenure of Office Act, which was used against Andrew Johnson. But still, cabinet officers are public officers of the United States as well as presidential aides. The members of executive office of the president lack that dual status. They have been conceived of and are treated politically as the president's people. In fact, what has happened is that in many areas they are virtually interchangeable with cabinet offices, except they have more ability to "stiff-arm" Congress, the press, and the public.

The national security example is a good one. There is virtual interchangeability now among the State Department, the Pentagon, and the National Security Council. William Clark was the deputy secretary of state and then he moved on to being national security advisor. Henry Kissinger moved from national security advisor to be secretary of state. Staff members go back and forth between and among these organizations. We have the irony that if you are an assistant secretary of state you are subject to Senate confirmation and are likely to be called up to testify before Congress. If you are the head of a similar regional division within the National Security Council you have virtual insulation from that kind of public scrutiny. You may in fact have more power in the latter job, where you are insulated, than in the former job, where you are available to the public. This has become a very serious problem as the executive office has expanded. This problem also exists with regard to the Office of Management and Budget. The regulatory arm of OMB that Mr. DeMuth is now running has the power to tell the Labor Department, the Environmental Protection Agency, and others that they may not promulgate a particular regulation. OMB is not covered, in practice, or, it argues, by statute, by the same rules governing administrative procedure and conflict of interest. OMB is too big and too important and too powerful to be treated the way administrative assistants to the president ought to be treated. It has important functions and in fact overrides some cabinet officers. It is much too sheltered.

I was recently involved in a situation where the Labor Department had promulgated rules for measuring the success of training under the Job Training Partnership Act, which is the successor to CETA (the Comprehensive Employment and Training Act). Under the act, the results of the training are subjected to evaluation. Are people who are being trained getting jobs? What's the percentage? The Labor Department met with the National Alliance of Business, the AFL-CIO, mayors, governors, the private industry councils who are supposed to be running these programs locally, and a national commission that had been set up to supervise it. In consultation with all of those groups it devised a set of rules whereby the states and the cities administering this program would report data in a certain form that would yield a basis for national comparisons. It allowed for differences in local populations. OMB, without having talked to any of the groups, vetoed it on the grounds that it was too much of a burden on the states.

It seemed to me there was a Rousseauan operation here. OMB was forcing the governors to be free. I asked the head of the OMB regulatory authority whether any governor had complained of this burden from which he was relieving them. He said, "no." The National Governor's Association testified in favor of this burden. He said, "No, we know better than the governors what's good for them." It's an ironic situation when the federal government says it must not unduly interfere with state autonomy, and it does not care what the states say, it is simply not going to interfere with state autonomy.

I had a hearing on this OMB veto. The difference in procedures between the Labor Department and OMB was striking. OMB did not talk to anybody. People wrote OMB letters. One presumes they were read. It was not just the AFL-CIO and the mayors, who may be seen as more ideologically opposed, who were ignored. Neither the National Alliance of Businessmen nor the business-dominated private industry councils, which by law have to be composed of 50 percent plus 1 private sector people, reported that OMB had ever talked to them.

I have no objection to the executive office of the president existing and I would give it a lot of freedom vis-à-vis executive reorganization. I think though that it tends sometimes to over-reorganize. The only years in which there was no executive reorganization were 1965–1968. Perhaps Johnson did not reorganize because he was too busy doing things. He had a great legislative year in 1965 and he was very busy with the Vietnam War in 1968. I tend to think of reorganization as a substitute for constructive activity most of the time. But, I am prepared to allow that to happen. But I think the time has come to say we cannot consider the whole executive office of the president as the same thing any more. It differs within itself. There are elements of it which hew to the old conception and where I think the president is entitled to some power.

The relationship between the president and his closest advisors ought to stay quiet. We got a glimpse of that relationship when William Clark was appointed secretary of the interior. The president felt he had to announce Clark's appointment quickly before James Baker had time to overrule him. He got it right out there and confronted Baker with a fait accompli. An interesting argument took place in which people like Robert Novak claimed that the executive office has in fact become a jailer keeping the president in chains and not allowing him to do things that he wanted to do; that is an extraordinary power relationship. The slogan was voiced, "Let Reagan be Reagan." I would have thought the Secret Service would have stepped in to stop whoever it was that was preventing the poor man from doing what he wanted.

I do think that there is an inner core of the executive office staff with whom the president is entitled to have secrecy, not just confidentiality. He is entitled to deal with them in a very personal and very private manner. But there are also operational branches of this office now, OMB and the National Security Council, which are not really distinguishable in their function from the regular cabinet except that they are probably more important. They certainly have more clout when it comes to a disagreement. Therefore the methods Congress has for exposing administrators to public scrutiny ought to be used.

I think that Professor Cronin's act I to III trichotomy is a useful one. Ronald Reagan is probably unusual in being the least act III president. The pressures that pull one toward being an act III president are nowhere clearer than in foreign policy. Anyone who predicted that Ronald Reagan would react to the shooting down of the Korean airliner in a more moderate fashion than Jimmy Carter reacted to the invasion of Afghanistan would have been disbelieved. But, while Reagan's rhetoric may have been sharper, his actions were in fact substantially milder than Carter's. Basically what he said was that if he had not already been banning the Soviets from landing here, he *would* ban them from landing here, and he hoped other people would too. That was the essence of his reaction. I think that does show that yes, there are those kinds of constraints that people in power face. It is true that when you are talking about things becoming law, you are not dealing with the cutting edge of intellectual discretion because it is virtually impossible to get the kind of majority support you need for things at the "cutting edge."

When Professor Cronin gave his list of act II people, it was basically a distinction between elected and nonelected officials; he mentioned two who in fact did hold some elective office. Both were members of the House, and I think that that's probably the role that members of the House can play. From the national standpoint it is an elective office but not one that overly impresses people in Washington so that you have some of the freedom to continue to be an advocate. Ed Markey, my colleague from Massachusetts, has been playing some of that role with regard to the nuclear freeze, using membership in the House to push an issue a little bit before the people are ready for it.

The last point I wanted to touch on concerns bipartisan commissions. There are two kinds of commissions. Those commissions which are put forward honestly to study longer range problems are useful. The Koerner Commission had a very useful impact on American policy and thought. It was very helpful in putting the coup de grace to official racism. But the Scowcroft Commission, the Kissinger Commission, the Social Security Commission—commissions that are used to put forward a solution to a pressing problem—are an abomination. The only good thing you can say about the Kissinger Commission is that if you were going to have a bipartisan commission they picked the right man, because anybody who could have supported the two candidates running against each other in 1968 has a degree of bipartisan skill not previously seen.

The Social Security Commission is the clearest example to me of an outrage. It was appointed to remove the question of social security cutbacks from the democratic process. They could not do it entirely but they came very close to doing it. Literally, ten people went into a back room and shut the door and made the deal. Not all fifteen members participated, but about ten people went into a back room, made a deal, and then they came out and said, "Here's the deal and you may not change it" and asked the House of Representatives to vote on it under a system by which it could not be amended. In the Senate, where the rules do not allow banning of all amendments, they use that as moral pressure to keep amendments from being entered. It was an effort simply to avoid debate and discussion. The issue was not an extraordinarily complex one, but it allowed members of Congress to vote for something and the president to support something which embodied some very important value decisions and some very controversial ones and to do so in a nondemocratic way. Similarly, the Scowcroft Commission was an effort to remove a series of competing value questions that had to be resolved in the MX missile debate from public discussion.

Neither one of these commissions was appointed in a very representative manner. I do not criticize the president for that. If Ronald Reagan is the president, then he gets to appoint commissioners. He is going to appoint people who agree with him and he has done that in every case. In the Social Security Commission, the president got five appointments, the speaker of the House got five, and the Senate majority leader got five. Well, members of Congress are more used to dealing in a compromise way. Tip O'Neill named three from his party and two from the other, and Howard Baker named three from his party and two from the other. Ronald Reagan went five for five. One of Ronald Reagan's Democrats was Joe Waggoner, who was about as right wing a member of the House as ever to serve from Lousiana and one of the leaders of the conservative coalition. So, we had a ten-to-five commission, because it was Tip's two, Baker's three, and Reagan's five, against Baker's two and Tip's three. And, it went downhill from there. The Scowcroft Commission was composed entirely of people who believed in the MX. That is perfectly legitimate. Ronald Reagan could appoint a commission if he wanted to compose it of the members of the American Security Council, but it ought not then to be used as a means of reducing debate. Now that is not Reagan's fault. It is the fault of the people who succumb to it.

The faults of these short-term presidential commissions are similar to those stemming from the operational use of the executive office. In both cases they represent efforts to diminish the extent of full democratic participation. In the case of the executive office, giving OMB and National Security Council people the aura that they are in fact just personal assistants to the president who should not be subject to any kind of scrutiny is an infringement of congressional prerogative. With regard to the commissions, Congress, or at least the majority of Congress, is a willing collaborator. Elected officials, particularly legislators, do not like to make tough decisions. They like to find ways to muffle tough decisions and avoid the consequences of having to make sharp choices. Those bipartisan presidential commissions have been used by the president and Congress as a way to throw a little sand in people's eyes and to deny the fact that they are making choices. With regard to the executive office, it is time to split it up. Those parts which really do represent an executive office composed of presidential assistants who are there to help the one person do those personal parts of his job should remain, but the more institutionalized parts of the executive office that are in fact functionally absolutely indistinguishable from the cabinet departments should be carved out and treated differently in that fashion.

Part IV
FDR

11
Going into Politics

Geoffrey C. Ward

F
ranklin Roosevelt's first job out of Columbia University Law School was not notably taxing. He was a very junior clerk in the somewhat sedate Wall Street firm of Carter, Ledyard, and Milburn. Nor did he take his work with great seriousness. A member of the firm recalled that FDR tended to "dance on the top of the hills," leaving his less nimble colleagues to hard labor on the slopes below.

The result was that he had a good deal of time on his hands. One especially slow afternoon in 1907 he and several of his fellow clerks sat at their rolltop desks in the big, cluttered office they shared, and discussed their hopes for the future. When his turn came, FDR allowed as how he didn't plan to practice law forever. No, he thought he'd enter politics and eventually become president. He planned first to get himself elected to the New York State Assembly, then win appointment as assistant secretary of the navy and finally become governor of New York. "Anyone who is governor of New York," he explained, "has a good chance to be president with any luck."

Years later, one of his former colleagues recalled that no one in the room had laughed, a fact he then solemnly attributed to Roosevelt's "engaging frankness," the sincerity and reasonableness of what he had to say.

Yet had any other twenty-five-year-old in that room expressed the same ambition—no matter how frank, sincere, or reasonable he seemed—his friends would have been at least privately amused.

The difference, of course, the thing which made FDR's vision of the future seem plausible, was that he was a Roosevelt. The heady sequence of political triumphs to which the young lawyer looked forward with such apparent confidence had already been marked out and followed by his fifth cousin, Theodore Roosevelt.

It is always impossible to say what would have happened in history had things been different. Still, it seems clear to me that if Theodore Roosevelt had not decided to break with family tradition and seek political office as a young man, it is unlikely that today we would be much interested in the achievements and personality of Franklin Roosevelt.

This chapter grew out of my research for a book I am writing on the youth and young manhood of Franklin Roosevelt, and most of it is based upon family documents in the massive collections of the Franklin D. Roosevelt Library at Hyde Park, New York.

While a sophomore at Harvard in 1901, FDR wrote a short history of his family, then much in the news. "One reason," he wrote, "perhaps the chief, of the virility of the Roosevelts is [their] democratic spirit. They have never felt because they were born in a good position they could put their hands in their pockets and succeed." At nineteen, Franklin Roosevelt was an enthusiastic Roosevelt but an amateurish historian. In actual fact the "democratic spirit" of his ancestors was hard to discern; most of them kept their hands firmly in their pockets.

The early Roosevelt patriarchs were gentlemen before they were anything else; "another sort of people," according to the diarist Philip Hone, "proud and aristocratical. ... Men could not stand straight in their presence." The obituary notices of three successive ancestors of FDR used the identical phrase to describe the departed; each had been "a gentleman of the old school." Two had held public office during the Federalist period, when governing was still thought a suitable business for a gentleman: it was then a gentleman's duty to help guide the destinies of persons less fortunate or well informed than he, just as it was incumbent upon him to contribute to charity. But with the rise of Andrew Jackson everything had changed. Electoral politics—the clamorous sweaty competition for votes—was seen as quite another matter: unseemly, unprincipled, vulgar.

Francis Grund, an Austrian nobleman who admired American democracy, visited New York during the 1830s and was astonished by the enmity the old Knickerbocker families had come to feel toward ordinary citizens. It was as if they "thought themselves beset by dogs," he wrote, "and are continually kicking for fear of being bitten." To them, he continued,

> politics was thought wholly uninteresting except to tavern keepers on election days; ... a subject unworthy of the pursuit of gentlemen, and a thing banished from people of fashion and good taste. ... Thus, "a popular candidate for office" is equivalent to "a vagabond who has no business of his own;" "popularity" means "the approbation of the mob."

Grund cautioned that

> all these significations apply only to members of the *democratic* party ... for it is easily understood why a man of property should be attached to his country; but the poor man has no right to be so, and is therefore ... suspected when he takes an interest in politics.

The early Roosevelts were rooted in this tradition. It often pleased FDR to say, "My father and my grandfather were always Democrats." Like a good many of his pronouncements about his family's past, this was at least partly wishful thinking. Family correspondence reveals that his grandfather, Dr. Isaac Roosevelt, had been first a Federalist and then a Whig. His mother's father,

Warren Delano II, was initially a Whig and then an implacable Republican, fond of saying that while not all Democrats were horse thieves, it had been his experience that all horse thieves were Democrats. James Roosevelt, the president's father, had also entered adult life as a Whig and only after *that* grand old party foundered in the 1850s did he reluctantly drift over to the Democrats. Nor did he always stay there; he was a conservative and selective member of his party, often backing the Republicans when he thought their candidates more conservative and gentlemanly than those of his own. His friend Grover Cleveland was his political hero; civil service reform, small government, and the obliteration of Tammany Hall were his issues; he thought William Jennings Bryan a shameless demagogue, masquerading as a Democrat. "I know so very well every feeling of your dear father," Sara Delano Roosevelt once reminded her son, "and I know that being a democrat never prevented his taking the right side in a contest and he would have felt very strongly about the necessity always of opposing Tammany and vice."

Politics fascinated James Roosevelt, but always from a safe distance: he contributed to campaigns, helped pick local candidates, lobbied decorously in Washington on behalf of his railroads and a canal through Nicaragua that never got built. "I have always refused to accept any nomination for public office," he wrote toward the end of his life, "[and] repeatedly refused nomination for Congress, State Senate and Assembly." He was proud of having resisted temptation; prouder still of having been asked. His first wife had feared he might succumb: "James went to a political meeting," she noted in her diary in 1874; "I was dreadfully afraid he would be nominated ... but he got home safely."

James Roosevelt Roosevelt, FDR's much older half-brother—then known to everyone as "Rosy" and now largely forgotten—edged the family one step closer to active participation in politics. Twice President Cleveland sought to persuade his father to enter government service; both times the senior James Roosevelt declined, obtaining instead diplomatic posts abroad for his eldest son. Rosy was engaging and enormously rich—he had married an Astor and declared himself a retired capitalist at twenty-three—and he was a good Democrat, but neither he nor his party ever thought him up to anything more challenging.

It was Theodore Roosevelt who first demonstrated that a member of the family might remain unmistakably a gentleman while engaged in politics— might "go into politics," in Sara Delano Roosevelt's own admiring words, "but not *be* a politician." It had not been easy. His father, Theodore Roosevelt, Sr., like James Roosevelt, had always spurned politics, and when in the interest of civil service reform he permitted President Rutherford B. Hayes to place his name in nomination for collector of customs at New York in 1877, the bitter losing struggle with the regular Republican machine that followed broke his health and hastened his early death—or so his worshipful son always believed. On his deathbed, his father had written that while he did not regret having become involved in a battle for principle, "I feel sorry for the country. ... We cannot stand so corrupt a government for any length of time."

TR took up the struggle. He would enter the lists himself, full-tilt, and run for the state assembly at twenty-three. When he told friends of his plans, he remembered, they laughed at him; "politics were 'low,' they said, not controlled by gentlemen; ... I would find them run by saloon-keepers, horse-car conductors and the like ... rough and brutal and unpleasant to deal with."

He was not discouraged. "If this were so," TR told them, "it meant merely that people I knew did not belong to the governing class, and that the other people did—and that I intended to be one of the governing class ..." If he found the professionals too tough to contend with he would quit, but not "until I had made the effort and found out whether I really was too weak to hold my own in the rough and tumble." His immediate family rallied to him, but some members of the clan never forgave him for sullying his hands. Some years after his death, according to his biographer Edmund Morris, an elderly uncle came upon workmen laboring to rebuild the brownstone in which TR was born, as a historical monument. "I don't see why you are making such a fuss," he told them; "I used to hate to see him coming down the street."

It is hard now to remember how united the Hyde Park and Oyster Bay Roosevelts once were. James Roosevelt and Theodore, Sr. were good friends, traveled abroad together, were sometimes mistaken for each other in the street. FDR's father had proposed marriage to TR's sister, Anna, after his first wife died; and it was Anna, in turn, who had introduced him to Sara Delano. TR's luckless brother, Elliott, was FDR's godfather and—had he lived—would have been his father-in-law, as well.

And when Theodore Roosevelt charged onto the political stage, championing good government and what he later called "the strenuous life," FDR's family was almost as enthusiastic as his own. TR made his maiden speech in the assembly chamber at Albany just six days before Franklin Roosevelt was born in 1882, and as the boy grew he watched the spectacular rise of the man his mother called "your noble kinsman" with pride and awe.

As a boy, FDR visited Oyster Bay, doing his best to keep up as Cousin Theodore led his tireless brood up and down a tall sand dune; the contrast with his own fond but aging father must have been vivid. The single documented instance of boyhood anger at his mother was sparked when, for some reason now lost to history, she declined an invitation for him from Sagamore Hill without consulting him. "Please don't make any more arrangements for my future happiness," he wrote her coldly.

At Groton he led the cheers when his cousin arrived to tell "killing" stories about his adventures as police commissioner of New York, and heard TR say "For a man merely to be good is not enough. He must be shrewd and he must be courageous." (This was also the message of Endicott Peabody, the energetic clergyman who had founded Groton; Theodore Roosevelt was one of his favorite chapel speakers.) FDR was "wild with excitement" when TR was elected governor of New York in 1898, and his parents were almost as pleased. "Hyde Park gave Colonel Roosevelt an 81 vote majority," his father reported, "... last spring the Democrats carried the town by 91, so we think we did very well for our cousin." In 1899 admiration turned to emulation: when an oculist urged that FDR wear glasses for his nearsightedness, he took it upon himself to order two sets of lenses, one mounted in a gold-rimmed pince-nez precisely like that the Colonel had worn up Kettle Hill; he is not known ever to have worn the other pair.

All this seems to have delighted his parents. They bought for him every one of his cousin's books as soon as they were published, and after his father's death in 1900, his mother and her family continued to urge him to look to TR as an exemplar. There were times when her zeal for Cousin Theodore exceeded even his own. When TR intervened as president in the coal strike of 1902, FDR gravely wrote home from Harvard that "in spite of his success in settling the trouble, I think that the President made a serious mistake in interfering. ... His tendency to make the executive power stronger than the Houses of Congress is bound to be a bad thing, especially when a man of weaker personality succeeds him in office." His mother would have none of it: "One cannot help loving and admiring him the more for it," she fired back, "when one realizes that he tried to right the wrong."

"I constantly hear your father's voice saying when he was ill 'only tell Franklin to be good, to be a good man,' " she wrote to FDR two years later. "He often repeated it and never until the other day in reading Jacob Riis: [biography of Theodore Roosevelt] did I know that Mr. Theodore Roosevelt's last words to *his* son were 'Be a good man.' Is that not a coincidence?" That kind of coincidence, with its unstated hint of possible succession, must have greatly pleased her son.

At Harvard, where a *Crimson* handbill proclaimed FDR "Cousin Frank, the Fairest of the Roosevelts," he joined the Republican club and marched for hours through Boston in a torchlight parade in honor of TR. Shortly after he was graduated, he sealed his early identification with Theodore Roosevelt by marrying the president's favorite niece. There was no cynicism in this: his early love for Eleanor Roosevelt was unfeigned. But his bride's closeness to the president's immediate family must have been an important part of her dowry. TR gave the bride away and afterwards complimented the new Mrs. Roosevelt on having "kept the name in the family." The young couple were guests at the White House and sat, spellbound, just behind the president's own children at his inauguration. The law would not hold FDR long; his new wife wrote her husband would not be happy until he found something that would provide him "broad human contact"—politics.

Theodore Roosevelt, the youthful reformer, had shown the way for young gentlemen to enter what Sara Delano Roosevelt called "the messy world of politics" proudly, without shame. Theodore Roosevelt, the ex-president, now provided FDR with the chance to blaze trails of his own, for in 1910, TR and his Progressive followers had riven the Republican party. Even in the tradition-ally Republican twenty-sixth senatorial district of New York, a Democratic victory seemed at least possible. And young FDR made a plausible candidate: he was the son of a widely admired local citizen; handsome, personable, and rich. The local party chieftains hoped that he or his mother or some of their wealthy friends might pay the bills for the coming campaign. But it was FDR's last name that mattered most. If a Democrat were to win, he would first have to pry Republican farmers from their ancient allegiance. Who could do that better than a Roosevelt?

FDR agreed, checking first to make sure that Cousin Ted (now *Uncle* Ted) would not come into his district to denounce him. TR thought Franklin "a fine fellow"—though he wished he were a Republican—and urged him to run "without the least regard as to where I speak or don't speak."

A word is in order here as to why FDR ran as a Democrat. His mother, I believe, would always have been happy to have had him return to the party of her father; his wife had always thought "Republicanism and respectability went hand in hand"; he had himself been a committed Republican at Harvard, and it seems odd at first glance that so enthusiastic an admirer of Theodore Roosevelt would not have joined his party. The simplest answer, of course, is that he ran as a Democrat because it was the Democrats who asked him to run. But there was more to it than that. Loyalty to his father's memory may have played a part, and at least one biographer has seen in that decision early evidence of FDR's stubborn "independence." And it should not be forgotten that TR had four Republican sons, any one of whom then seemed to stand a better chance to inherit the Great Man's mantle than an obscure upstate cousin. Only as a Democrat could a Roosevelt from outside Sagamore Hill hope to rise very high—and Franklin Roosevelt would not willingly settle for less.

There is no need to rehearse here the details of FDR's first hurrah, but throughout that race and the three years of political skirmishing at Albany that followed, it is striking how often FDR seems consciously or unconsciously to have spoken and acted like TR—sometimes to the point of caricature. A few examples will show what I mean.

Theodore Roosevelt began in politics by making his way each evening to the Twenty-first District Republican Association, a dingy club above a saloon on East 59th Street. He always wore a frock coat and top hat. Some of the regulars "sneered" at first, he recalled, but "I made them understand that I should come dressed as I chose." Franklin Roosevelt was at first just as fashionable, if less defiant. He visited the Poughkeepsie office of Edward E. Perkins, the Dutchess County Democratic chairman, three days before his official nomination for the state senate wearing riding boots and jodhpurs. Perkins looked him up and down with remarkably little enthusiasm. Roosevelt would do, he said at last, but "You'll have to take off those yellow shoes and put on some regular pants."

FDR did as he was told, then plunged into a campaign whose flamboyance and vigor owed much to his cousin's example. Spinning along the country roads in a red Maxwell bristling with snapping American flags, he deplored big city bosses of both parties, had kind words for the Progressive Republican governor, Charles Evans Hughes, and shamelessly exploited his family connection while pretending to minimize it. He sprinkled his speeches with the ex-president's favorite exclamation "Bully!" "I'm not Teddy," he told the laughing crowds. "A little shaver said to me the other day that he knew I wasn't Teddy—I asked 'why,' and he replied: 'Because you don't show your teeth.'"

As a young member of the assembly in 1882, Theodore Roosevelt had been overdressed and overbearing—"that damned dude" to his many enemies, "the Cyclone Assemblyman" to his wary allies. His reputation was built battling loudly against Tammany Hall and the Republican regulars who had tormented his father.

Twenty-nine years later, in 1911, state senator Franklin Roosevelt seemed cut to the same pattern. He delivered his first speeches in evening clothes, literally peered down his nose at everyone who spoke to him, took over the leadership of an insurgency against Tammany's nominee for the U.S. Senate, "Blue-Eyed Billy" Sheehan. He even mimicked his cousin's blustery combativeness: TR had knocked down one of his fellow legislators with his fists, and threatened to unman another. When Senator James J. Frawley, a Tammany man who had been an amateur boxer, joked that he would face FDR any time, anywhere, "In a pulpit or a rat pit," Roosevelt boasted to a reporter that he weighed "one hundred and seventy pounds, stripped" and had been "quite a boxer" at Groton. Happily for him, the fight never came to pass.

"Awful arrogant, that fellow Roosevelt," said Big Tim Sullivan of Tammany, who rarely entertained an unfriendly thought about a fellow Democrat, and even FDR himself later admitted, "I was an awfully mean cuss in those days." It is hard to reconcile this apparently self-righteous, noisy figure with the man he would soon become.

Part of his problem can be laid to the difficulties any young man of his class and upbringing would have had when first immersed in a world where breeding counted less than ability and good manners could be overcome by brute power and the ability to maneuver. But I believe there was trouble, too, in the fact that at this early stage of his political life, FDR was still in part play-acting. As a boy he had sometimes taken part in the strenuous "point to point" hikes cousin Theodore liked to organize, the Roosevelt children and their guests scurrying after the Colonel as he strode briskly toward some agreed-upon destination through the woods around Oyster Bay. The game had a single inviolable rule: obstacles were to be conquered, not circumvented; one pushed through brambles, waded streams, crawled under fences or scrambled over them, and never, never went *around* anything. Point to point was a good metaphor for Theodore

Roosevelt's style of leadership—or at least for the style he liked to advocate. Adversaries were to be met and overcome, head-on.

FDR admired his cousin extravagantly. But his basic personality was very different from TR's. The creative uses of indirection, for example, were built into him from infancy. Raised alone by loving but anxious parents who supervised almost every waking moment of his boyhood, he learned early that the best technique for getting one's way was often to do one thing while chattering pleasantly about something else.

This is an oversimplification, of course. FDR could be bold. TR was sometimes indirect. But this and other intrinsic differences between them, I believe, made FDR's worshipful imitation of his cousin impossible to sustain. That he went on eventually to outshine Theodore Roosevelt is a tribute to the steel and subtlety that underlay his elegant but initially forbidding exterior. He was simply not credible trying to seem like someone he was not. His own distinctive personality emerged slowly but steadily, and while he never stopped venerating his cousin—"He was the greatest man I ever knew," he said—he came to shed the superficial aspects of TR's personality that had never really suited his own. The mature FDR was neither shrill nor bellicose nor hyperkinetic.

When the Sheehan fight ended in qualified victory, Cousin Theodore scrawled FDR a note which must have pleased him: "Just a line to say that we are all really proud of the way you have handled yourself." But the Cleveland *Plain Dealer* may have pleased him even more. If none of TR's own four sons proved worthy of their father, it asked, "may it not be possible that this rising star may continue the Roosevelt dynasty?"

That thought did not delight the younger generation at Sagamore Hill. So long as TR lived, the two branches of the family remained officially cordial toward one another: when TR embarked on an anti-Woodrow Wilson swing through upstate New York in 1914, he gently turned down an invitation to stop for the night at Hyde Park to avoid embarrassing FDR (who was then assistant secretary of the navy in Wilson's Washington); Sara Delano Roosevelt thought this "very kind."

But TR's death in 1919, and FDR's nomination for vice president the following year, signaled the end of election year amity between the rival clans. When admirers greeted FDR as if he were actually one of the late president's sons, shouting "I voted for your old man," Theodore Roosevelt, Jr., denounced him as "a maverick. He does not have the brand of our family."

Even then, FDR insisted that he, not the sons of Sagamore Hill, was truest to the TR tradition. "In 1912," he said, "Senator Harding called Theodore Roosevelt first a Benedict Arnold and then an Aaron Burr. This is one thing at least *some* members of the Roosevelt family will not forget."

This brief chapter has concentrated on the impact of Theodore Roosevelt's political career on Franklin Roosevelt's decision to launch his own. But as this book is devoted to the presidency, perhaps I should at least list those qualities of the second President Roosevelt which I believe were at least in part the legacy of the first: an unfeigned love for people and for politics; unbounded optimism and self-confidence; impatience with the drab notion that the mere making of money should be enough to satisfy any man or any nation; perhaps, above all, an unabashed delight in the great power of his office to do good.

Franklin Roosevelt first visited the Oval Office of the White House at the age of five. There his father's friend Grover Cleveland placed his big hand on the boy's head and wearily told him it was his fondest hope that he *not* grow up to be president; the job was too much for any man.

FDR once asked his cousin how *he'd* liked the job. "Ripping!" Theodore Roosevelt replied, "Ripping!"

Which view of the presidency was closest to his own? FDR was asked. He just smiled, showing his big white Roosevelt teeth.

12

FDR and John L. Lewis:
The Lessons of Rivalry

Marc Landy

FDR was a superb political architect. He was the designer and chief engineer of the modern Democratic party. He transformed the loose coalition of 1932 into an enduring partisan institution which has exerted an unprecedented political hegemony for so long a period (1936–1980).

This chapter considers FDR's relationship with one key building block of the Democratic edifice, organized labor. His relationship to labor is particularly fascinating because labor itself was in a process of organizational transformation presided over by a brilliant political architect—John L. Lewis. These two creative geniuses experienced bitter artistic differences. FDR considered Lewis to be his most dangerous rival. FDR is reputed to have commented to Max Lerner, "You know Max, this is really a great country. The framework of democracy is so strong and so elastic it can get along and absorb both a Huey Long and a John L. Lewis."

When Lewis heard the quip, he retorted, the statement is incomplete, it should also include, "and Franklin Delano Roosevelt."[1]

The animus between the two surfaced publicly in the summer of 1937, a scant six months after FDR's triumph in the 1936 election, which had been financed in large measure by Lewis's Committee on Industrial Organization (CIO).[2]

Although FDR had aided and abetted earlier CIO organizing efforts, he refused to support the violent and disruptive strike then being waged against the so-called "Little Steel" companies. At a news conference, FDR declared a plague on both houses, "labor and capital." Lewis's retort stands as one of the greatest of all scornful public utterances.

> Labor, like Israel, has many sorrows. Its women weep for their fallen, and they lament for the future of the children of the race. It ill behooves one who has supped at Labor's table to curse with equal fervor and fine impartiality both labor and its adversaries when they become locked in deadly embrace.[3]

The depth of Lewis's rancor grew, culminating in his refusal to support FDR for re-election in 1940. In his speech endorsing the Republican, Wendell

Willkie, Lewis promised to resign as president of the CIO if FDR was re-elected. He kept the promise and within a matter of a few years lost his influence upon the mighty labor organization he had led since its inception. A study of this epochal rivalry between the two great political builders of their age can help us to understand each of them and the great organizational monuments which they bequeathed.

Comparing them one is first struck by their differences. Their backgrounds were totally dissimilar. Lewis was the son of a Welsh immigrant coal miner. He grew up in Iowa mining camps and did not quite complete high school.[4] FDR was a Hyde Park patrician, the cousin of a president, and a graduate of Groton and Harvard.[5] Their political personas were likewise different. FDR was a reformer, a Wilsonian, and a distinction-blurrer (was he a "wet" or a "dry," a collectivist or a Brandeisian?). Lewis was an autocrat, a protégé of Samuel Gompers, a brawler (the famous punch thrown at William Hutcheson during the 1935 American Federation of Labor Convention), and a schismatic. Their rhetorical styles also differed markedly. FDR spoke like a patrician cum democrat. He spoke simply, using the most commonplace homilies. He invented the "fireside chat" as a device for creating intimacy with a mass audience. Lewis spoke like a proletarian cum patrician replete with rhetorical flourishes and Shakespearean allusions.

These differences should not blind us to key similarities in their architectural approach. Most important, they shared an ability to perceive the essential elements of the design problem they faced and to devise a blueprint which addressed those problems. As Joseph Alsop has stated most powerfully, FDR's greatest accomplishment was to create a political rubric for including those who had previously been excluded from the mainstream of American politics.[6] The new Democratic party which emerged under his tutelage came to serve as the organizational vehicle for this new inclusiveness. Lewis's greatest accomplishment was likewise to bring into the mainstream of American worklife a vast segment of the population, the unskilled workers, who had previously been excluded from any sort of protection or representation. The new industrial unions organized under the CIO banner provided the institutional structure for this new form of enfranchisement.

Neither FDR nor John L. began their projects from scratch. They were both renovators faced with refurbishing weak and faltering organizations. Perhaps their greatest leap of imagination was to recognize that the existing organizational shells were too small and restrictive to enable them to enlist the loyalties of the unaffiliated groups to whom they must appeal to establish hegemony in either the workplace or the voting booth. Therefore the first task of renovation was one of creative destruction: the old shells needed to be cracked to make room for new expansion.

The pre-1932 Democratic party was composed of patronage-based city organizations, some remnants of rural progressivism, and the South.[7] FDR recognized that this shell was too restrictive to attract the workers, non-Irish immigrants, blacks, Jews, and urban progressives whom he needed to create a majority party. He needed therefore to wrest control of the party away from the defenders of the old order. At the 1936 Democratic party convention, when he was at the apex of his popularity, he made full use of his prestige to force the party to rescind the hallowed two-thirds rule which was the device by which the South and the machines had each been able to exert veto power of the choice of the party's presidential candidate. No structural barriers remained to prevent the groups FDR was trying to attract to the party from exerting a dominant influence over the future leadership of the party.

Lewis's problem was even greater. The AFL was committed to organizing workers according to craft, a method simply incapable of succeeding in organizing the new mass production industries—steel, auto, rubber.[8] Like the Democratic party barons, the leaders of the AFL preferred to maintain control over a weak organization rather than subordinate themselves in a strong one. Because he lacked the patronage available to a president, Lewis could not manage to seduce the Dan Tobins and Bill Hutchesons of the world into grudgingly accepting the new order of things. He had no choice but to launch the CIO as a rival labor organization.

The necessity of attempting these transformations is obvious in hindsight, which is to say that all important political masterstrokes are obvious in hindsight. It was an act of consummate boldness, and ruthlessness, to break with esteemed colleagues and make common cause with people of no standing— Catholics, Jews, unskilled workers.

Both men had a strategy for accomplishing their goal of inclusiveness. Lewis embraced the principle of industrial unionism, dispensing with all barriers of craft in order to bring all the workers of a given industry under the same union banner. FDR adopted the principle of economic enfranchisement. As he vowed in his Commonwealth Club Speech, he would accomplish in the economic realm what the founders had accomplished in the political realm—that is, to create a constitutional order in which everyone could lay valid claim to personal security, civil rights, and the ability to redress grievances.[9] This he accomplished through the tools of relief, old age income assistance, unemployment compensation, and "Labor's Bill or Rights," the Wagner Act.

Strategic vision was coupled to unbridled tactical opportunism. For the sake of industrial unionism, Lewis shucked his previous political persona. He abandoned first the Republican party (he had endorsed Hoover for president in 1932) and then the AFL. He forswore the principles of voluntarism imbibed from Samuel Gompers and vigorously endorsed the New Deal's intrusions into the sphere of labor relations. He abetted illegal and violent tactics such as the sit down strikes and even formed a tactical alliance with his bitterest of previous enemies, the Communists. Lewis appreciated the usefulness of the incredibly dedicated and underpaid Communist CIO organizers. By way of explaining his willingness to put up with these zealous but hard-working organizers, he is alleged to have remarked to David Dubinsky "Who gets the bird, the hunter or the dog?"[10]

FDR's opportunism was also legendary. The zigzag course of New Deal public policy, his initial diffidence toward the Wagner Act followed by his desire to take credit for it once its passage was assured, his use of the Works Progress Administration as a partisan patronage organization, and his masterful use of radio as a means for reaching directly into the nation's living rooms all attest to his willingness to adopt various, and sometimes morally dubious, means to achieve his purposes.[11]

Boldness of design, and radical opportunism were wedded to an essential conservatism of ultimate purpose. Neither man ever abandoned his fundamental adherence to individualism, liberalism, and free enterprise despite what must have been a strong temptation to raise collectivism from a tactic to a principle. As Rexford Tugwell has most persuasively argued, FDR's famous response to all questions concerning his ideology: "I am a Christian and a democrat" was not an evasion but a straightforward statement of principle.[12] Only those blind to the strength and appeal of those two creeds could so easily assume that FDR was lying. In his mind, committing himself to those two beliefs meant not adopting any other doctrinal positions which might interfere with them. To be a Christian and a democrat meant simply to be a Christian and a democrat. Steadfast commitment to those aims imposed upon him the conservative task of accommodating to the real changes in social and economic organization dictated by industrialism while trying to preserve what could be preserved of political and economic liberties and Christian virtues in the face of those realities.

Lewis was equally conservative. Although his rhetoric was full of antipathy to robber barons and Wall Street manipulators, his goals for the labor movement were unvaryingly stated in terms of providing people with the wherewithal to compete successfully in a free enterprise economy and a liberal society. At the 1938 United Mine Workers Convention, in the midst of a severe economic downturn occurring during the ninth year of the Great Depression, Lewis could still manage to boast: "Many of our former members are successful in great business enterprises."[13]

Ironically, the depth of their mutual antipathy was caused more by their similarities than their differences. Opportunists themselves, each felt genuinely aggrieved by the great success with which the other exploited him. After obtaining FDR's grudging support for Section 7a of the National Industrial Recovery Act (NIRA) Lewis had the temerity to trumpet the news to every mine shaft and steel mill that "The President wants you men to organize." Although FDR had no such intention, he could hardly afford to disavow Lewis's claim. Later FDR would return the compliment by supping at labor's table and forgetting who had the tab.

More important than personal pique was the recognition that neither could afford to acknowledge fully the debt owed the other. The closeness of the relationship which had developed between party and union jeopardized the vision which each held of what their organization ought to be. Lewis feared labor co-optation; FDR feared labor dominance.

FDR's conservatism required subordination of labor's role. Labor must remain a constituent of the party, not the central element. Consciously or unconsciously, FDR sought to ensure that the Democratic party did not develop along the lines of Great Britain's Labor party. Labor power must be curbed in order to keep it subordinate to partisan power. FDR recognized that Lewis could not play the subordinate's role. Perhaps FDR saw too much of himself in Lewis and realized how poorly he, FDR, would serve sitting in the second violinist's chair.

Although Lewis is usually cast in the villain's role (history bring written by the winners), it was FDR who fomented the split between the two men. FDR's behavior in the Little Steel Strike itself constituted grounds for a crisis in the relationship, if not outright divorce, coming as it did a mere matter of months after his denunciation of the "malefactors of great wealth" and his election crusade for the common man. However, more serious slights to Lewis were to follow. As he had previously done to Huey Long following the 1932 election, FDR rewarded Lewis's election assistance with a calculated series of personal snubs. He did not consult Lewis concerning key Labor Department appointments and in fact cut the labor chief out of the patronage picture entirely. Most infuriating of all, FDR denied Lewis his place as labor's spokesman within the councils of the administration. This coveted role was given to Lewis's second in command at the CIO, Sidney Hillman. In May 1940, as the war in Europe was raging, FDR appointed Hillman to be labor's representative to the National Defense Advisory Council.[14] He thus placed Hillman as serving as the voice of Labor in the war effort without even consulting Lewis in advance. Such a slight would have proven intolerable even to someone who lacked Lewis's massive impression of his own importance.

If FDR's philosophic conservatism explains the outbreak of the feud with Lewis, the resolution of that conflict is best understood in terms of Lewis's philosophic conservatism. Although the denouement came in 1940, the die was cast in 1936. Lewis's greatest contribution to FDR in that election was not monetary but symbolic. By wholeheartedly adopting FDR as the friend of labor, Lewis allowed FDR to emerge from that election as the workingman's hero, rendering the later attempt to defeat him quixotic. FDR's re-election in 1936 was foreordained but his success in using it as an opportunity to transform his loose coalition into an enduring partisan phalanx was not. It depended upon his ability to rhetorically cast himself in the role of the common people's friend by virtue of his service as their champion against the forces of darkness—

speculators, bankers, and bosses.[15] FDR's depiction of Andrew Jackson serves as a succinct description of his own accomplishment in this regard.

> The beneficiaries of the abuses to which he put an end pursued him with all the violence that political passions can generate. But the people of his day were not deceived. They loved him for the enemies he had made.[16]

American business rose to the bait provided by Roosevelt's campaign rhetoric perfectly. Blistering attacks from the business community cemented the notion in the popular mind that Roosevelt was their champion. The proof of that was simply that the "malefactors of great wealth" hated him so much. Only the acknowledged leader of the new American labor movement was in a position to challenge the image that FDR was so brilliantly seeking to create. Lewis could have reminded workers of FDR's unwillingness to materially assist the passage of the Wagner Act and of his acquiescence to the probusiness tilt given to the administration of National Recovery Administration. In short, he could have tried to deny him the capacity to make such politically attractive enemies. Halfhearted worker votes would still have won FDR the election, but the stage might have been set for significant worker defections during the ensuing four years culminating in serious left-wing opposition in 1940 conducted by that brilliant political orchestrator, John L. Lewis. If the 1936 victory had not so brilliantly succeeded in riveting worker loyalty, one can imagine how skillfully Lewis might have exploited FDR's subsequent "evenhandedness" toward labor disputes, as well as the devastating impact of the 1938 recession and workers' fears concerning FDR's interventionism in Europe, to crack the shell of the New Deal coalition.

Such a strategy would have entailed great risks for Lewis and the labor movement. In the absence of unqualified labor support, FDR would presumably have been less willing to do labor's bidding than he proved to be. However, one must grant the capacity of great opportunists to sniff out one another, Lewis was capable of recognizing that, regardless of how much labor gave to the cause, FDR would do exactly as much for labor as he deemed politically prudent, and no more. He chose to back FDR so forcefully because of his own commitment to liberal government. To attack FDR from the left would have meant unleashing radical forces in the polity which he could not necessarily control. It would have created a revolutionary potential compatible perhaps with his ambitions but not his convictions. One has only to imagine how a Lenin would have responded to the opportunities provided by the sit down strikes in Flint, Michigan, and elsewhere if he had first been able to paint a picture of the president as a feckless Kerensky.

The rivalry between FDR and John L. Lewis reveals the debt which protagonists may owe to each other. The restraint which Lewis displayed enabled FDR to establish the unique relationship between the labor movement and the Democratic party which has existed to this day.

Notes

1. Melvyn Dubofsky and Warren Van Tine, *John L. Lewis: A Biography* (New York: Quadrangle/New York Times Book Company, 1977), p. 323.

2. After the full break with the American Federation of Labor, this organization changed its name to the Congress of Industrial Organizations.

3. Dubofsky and Tine, *John L. Lewis*, p. 327.

4. Although I severely disagree with it in many matters of interpretation, Dubofsky and Tine's biography remains by far the best source of information about all aspects of Lewis's career.

5. Among the welter of biographies of FDR, the most penetrating discussion of the impact of his background upon his political character appear in Rexford Tugwell, *The Democratic Roosevelt* (Baltimore: Pelican, 1957); see also Geoffrey Ward, in this book.

6. Joseph Alsop, *FDR: A Centenary Remembrance* (New York: The Viking Press, 1982), pp. 10–13.

7. The best source on the Democratic party in the years just prior to 1932 is David Burner, *The Politics of Provincialism: The Democratic Party in Transition, 1918–1932* (New York: Knopf, 1968).

8. On the state of the labor movement just prior to the formation of the CIO, see Philip Taft, *The A.F. of L. from the Death of Gompers to the Merger* (New York: Harper & Brothers, 1959); and Walter Galenson, *The CIO Challenge to the AFL* (Cambridge Mass.: Harvard University Press, 1960), pp. 3–75.

9. *The Public Papers and Addresses of Franklin D. Roosevelt,* edited by Samuel Rosenman, 13 vols. (New York: Random House, Macmillan, Harper & Brothers, 1938–1950), hereafter referred to as *The Roosevelt Papers.*

10. Dubofsky and Tine, *John L. Lewis*, p. 289.

11. On FDR's experimentalism, see Rexford Tugwell's "The Experimental Roosevelt" in his *In Search of Roosevelt* (Cambridge Mass.: Harvard Univ. Press, 1972), pp. 279–310.

12. Ibid.

13. Dubofsky and Tine, *John L. Lewis*, p. 291.

14. On Sidney Hillman and his relationships with both FDR and John L. Lewis, see Matthew Josephson, *Sidney Hillman: Statesman of American Labor* (Garden City N.Y.: Doubleday, 1952), pp. 381–502.

15. On the role of rhetoric in altering the nature of the 1936 campaign, see Samuel H. Beer, "Two Models of Public Opinion: Bacon's 'New Logic' and Diotima's 'Tale of Love,'" *Political Theory,* May 1974: 174–178.

16. *The Roosevelt Papers,* vol. V, p. 197. I am indebted to Anthony Corrado for showing me this revealing quotation.

13
Comments on Part IV

Samuel H. Beer

F ranklin Roosevelt was born one hundred years ago. I came of age during the summer of the year he first ran for president. In 1932 I could have cast my first vote for Roosevelt, but I did not. I did not vote at all. I tried to make up for that gross failure by voting for Roosevelt every four years since.

There was nothing original in my failing to vote at that time. I belonged to the huge pool of eligibles who did not vote in the 1920s and on through 1932, but who were mobilized by FDR. Insofar as those nonvoters were like me, they were smartalecky college graduates who felt themselves superior to the whole ridiculous business of politics, at least in part because they had been reading so much H.L. Mencken. There were others too. We would be called alienated nowadays. And yet we became incorrigible followers of Roosevelt and the New Deal, and we made the Democrats into the dominant majority party for many years. Only death, not even taxes, can destroy our allegiance. We were a true political generation.

The pollsters have identified this stratum of nonvoters who were then suddenly precipitated into the arena, and they have identified the same kind of stratum today. Recent events in mayoral elections in Chicago, in Philadelphia, and not least Boston, suggest perhaps there may be a new wave of participation upon us. At any rate, what was the source of our commitment, and what did the New Deal mean to us? As various scholars have shown, the New Deal was not a social revolution. It did not bring full employment; rearmament did that. It did not bring any significant redistribution of wealth; again it was World War II that did that; and, it did not set the country on the path of economic growth. The New Deal was not a social revolution.

In the winter of 1931–1932, the Depression was setting in bitter hard and seemingly invincible; unemployment was mounting toward 25 percent. I happened to be taking the bus back to college at Ann Arbor from my home in Ohio. As we went through Toledo, a city devastated by unemployment, we passed through an industrial section and saw big crowds of people in the street. What were they doing? They were not waiting for a handout; they were not in a soup line; they were not picketing, or rioting, or organizing. They were doing nothing; rather like Mr. Hoover at the same time and for much the same reason. They did not think government could or should do anything for them, and they did not expect it to try. Nearly everywhere, the country accepted the blows of the Depression with extraordinary passivity. I remember this and Frank Friedel has documented this in one of his volumes. Only the farmers spilled some milk and occasionally faced down foreclosures with shotguns.

Three years later, I got back to the United States from studying abroad and got a job in Washington. By day I worked for Rexford Guy Tugwell as a kind of junior ghostwriter in the Resettlement Administration and by night I worked for Thomas Gardiner Corcoran, then a rising Brain Truster who would farm out to me bits of the speech writing that he was doing for Roosevelt. I vividly recall our overriding preoccupation. That was to persuade people to look to Washington for help. To convince them, against the great weight of the American tradition, that government was the solution. This was echoed, in reverse, in a recent presidential inaugural address. We succeeded. We did indeed.

That revolution in political expectations was the main achievement of the New Deal, and one principal source of the lifelong attachment of our generation to it. There were material benefits, what President Reagan calls the social safety net, and they were not unimportant. There was also the symbolic aspect of them, which was perhaps even more important: including those excluded. As de Gaulle said, "Citizens with a full share." The symbolism of the material steps themselves and the experience of political combat for a new view of positive government were crucial.

Positive government for what? This brings up the question that Marc Landy refers to: Why did the New Deal go the way it went? FDR came in with an idea, an image, "the forgotten man at the bottom of the economic pyramid," a phrase he had used in a radio address in April of 1932. But, the forgotten man was a familiar figure everywhere in the politics of the industrialized countries then in the throes of the worldwide depression. These nations met the challenge in different ways. One possible way, which some looked to, was the way the Progressives attempted to deal with it, by turning back the clock to Thomas Jefferson's day, breaking up the trusts, and breaking up the political machines and returning to that innocent individualism. Another possibility was embodied in the corporatism of the National Recovery Administration. The most common strategy in other countries was the creation of some kind of social democracy or socialism through a labor party. Why not a labor party in the United States? We did have one for a little while. It was so impotent that it was taken over by the Communists and soon vanished. But why didn't it happen here? The social basis for it certainly existed, particularly once the New Deal got going.

As the Wagner Act took hold, and trade unions set out to organize the workers, particularly in rubber and automobiles and the other big industries, class war swept through the industrial regions of the country. Membership in unions quadrupled in a decade. I remember the pictures of the "Battle of the Underpass" outside the River Rouge plant near Detroit, and Walter Reuther with the blood coming down his face after being beaten up by Henry Ford, Sr.'s goons. How different this was from the atmosphere prevailing at a lunch that Dean Donald White of Boston College sponsored recently attended by a vice president of Ford (he had been a member of the faculty of the Boston College School of Management) who reported on a recent pact between the automobile workers and the Ford Motor Company in which certain odd things such as EI figured. EI stands for "employee involvement." (Can you imagine Henry, Sr. fancying a thing like employee involvement?) And after the luncheon I said to Dean White: This is certainly a long way from the Battle of the Underpass.

The men of Toledo and Chicago, and Detroit and elsewhere, empowered by law, did act and the balance of economic power in the country was irreversibly altered. Although there was class war, however, there was no class ideology. A principal reason for this was Franklin Roosevelt; his philosophical conservatism, his adaptability, or just his plain good sense. The term he used obviously wasn't social democracy, socialism, or progressivism, but *liberalism,* an unusual term in American political vocabulary at that time. It was found in what Westbrook Pegler liked to call "the butcher papers," periodicals such as the *New Republic* and the *Nation.* Roosevelt made "liberalism" a term of common discourse. He picked the word up quite deliberately from British politics, but the meaning he gave to it arose out of the circumstances of events and programs in the United States.

I thought often that the idea began to crystallize and take form in the midst of what's called the Second New Deal. An illustration is FDR's acceptance speech at Franklin Field in Philadelphia after his renomination in 1936. Lily Pons sang the Star Spangled Banner. A symphony orchestra played and all those great patriots, Boss Hague, Boss Curley, and Boss Pendergast, in serried ranks those great idealists, bathed in these great Klieg lights. It was a wonderful sight and a grand speech with that great metaphor of "economic royalists." I worked on that speech, and I just wish I'd had some hand in those subversive methaphors, but alas, everything I produced was thrown out. Roosevelt's speech was hyperbole—it was great hyperbole, swollen even by American standards, and abrasive: "the privileged princes of these new economic dynasties thirsting for power"; "a new despotism"; "this new industrial dictatorship"; "the resolute enemy within our gates." Those are the phrases with which Roosevelt developed the parallel with the past, with 1776, as he lashed his opponents and roused his supporters. He summarized his message in a phrase that became one of the most quoted items in the Roosevelt demonology "economic royalists." He said:

out of this modern civilization economic royalists carved new dynasties. New kingdoms were built upon concentration of control over material things. Economic royalists complain that we seek to overthrow the institutions of America; what they really complain of is that we seek to take away their power.

The president was very fond of that phrase suggested by Stanley High (Tommy Corcoran said it was Bill Bullitt, both were writing speeches for him): "economic royalists"; he rolled that phrase off in great style. It is a metaphor; it has the compactness and the power of emotional arousal that a metaphor has, and also the ambiguity and lack of clarity. But I think it set him on his way to this curious semi-instinctive adaptation of the American political tradition and some of its most familiar rationales to the problems of the times, unthought of in any program ahead of time. Moving from that metaphor to a concept took some time. It was almost twenty years later when John Kenneth Galbraith seized on the rationale indicated by this metaphor in his phrase "countervailing power." He talked about how this was a rationale which was common to the major New Deal programs: the Wagner Act, the agricultural program, minimum wage, securities regulation, and so on. The principal was that by these acts of government increase was given to the economic power of the numerous disadvantaged people against the small, advantaged group. It was very Madisonian, but it was not a self-conscious program.

Roosevelt certainly did not come into power with a program. Yet he ultimately did produce a new public philosophy which could be drawn on for further programmatic specifications, as Harry Truman did in his Fair Deal. It had an inner life and a cohesive social base, pluralistic as it may have been. With it he did not create a new social order, but he did very considerably change one. The life of the working stiff has never been the same since then.

What relevance has this experience for today? The presidency, the main institution by which this transformation was brought about, is still with us. There have been, in recent years, laments about its decline, fears of its weakness. I think it was President Ford who said not long ago, "The Presidency is not imperial, but imperiled." There is even a committee, financed by a rich Democrat, advocating that we adopt parliamentary government in order to strengthen government. This impression of institutional decline ceased when Ronald Reagan became president. His priorities are not my priorities. However, he showed that he is a president all right, particularly during his first year. He refuted all that gloomy talk about the vacuity and imbecility of the presidency.

Reagan restored authority to that office, not the way Roosevelt did, but by being even more of a populist. I think of him as a kind of Sockless Jerry Simpson, like that hero of the Populist era walking around among the people, continually looking down as if to see whether he has his socks on. And he was not chosen by peer review, which is the latest fad for choosing presidential nominees. The first president I remember meeting who was chosen by peer review was Warren Harding, an extremely nice man. He was really chosen by the elite of the Republican party, with zero public participation. At any rate, Ronald Reagan was not chosen that way (Ford would have been chosen if his peers had had their way). Reagan was probably regarded as unelectable, a phrase we hear often nowadays. Yet he restored authority to the office not seen since Roosevelt, particularly in that incredible Omnibus Reconciliation Act of 1981. Reagan's luck, I'm happy to say, has eroded a little bit. One trouble is, he may be the man, and he has the office, but he lacks the idea. The idea, not only in the material sense but in the symbolic sense, that gives people the feeling they are going somewhere with him. Still, the office is there waiting for the occasion, the idea, and the person; and, my hunch is that the three will appear sooner than we think.

14

Comments on Part IV

Edward F. Prichard, Jr.

After these two elegant and almost perfect chapters, and after Sam Beer's inspiring response, I feel that there's very little left for me to do except to offer the benediction. But I shall risk a few remarks. As far as Geoffrey Ward's chapter is concerned, I think he has nailed almost everything down that one could find or discover. I think he is perfectly correct in saying that Franklin Roosevelt was impelled toward politics by his admiration and enthrallment with this cousin, Theodore. The question remains, How and why did their paths begin to diverge? Possibly it was because the Democrats were the first ones to offer FDR a chance to run for office. No one ever accused President Franklin Roosevelt of a lack of opportunism. It may have been that he took the first chance that came. Having made the commitment and having come into politics at a time when the Republican party was being torn apart, he realized that the Democratic party appeared likely to benefit from those divisions. The Progressive movement started as a kind of rebirth of what had been lost in the Populist movement of the late nineteenth century, a rebirth in more urban and urbane terms; as that movement came along, perhaps he saw it running into difficulty in the Republican party, and coming into greater ascendancy in the Democratic party. Perhaps, he saw the Progressive movement in broad terms as being the wave of the future in his day and generation. Those considerations reinforced him in his direction toward the Democratic party.

Once that die was cast, and I believe it happened long before the death of Theodore Roosevelt, the division, discord, disharmony, and even hostility and enmity between the two branches of the Roosevelt family became acute. In the last years of his life Theodore Roosevelt changed quite a bit. He became something of a militaristic right-wing demagogue who compared President Wilson to a Trotskyite, and called Felix Frankfurter a stooge of Lenin and Trotsky when he wrote the famous report on the infamous Bisbe deportations. In those circumstances, I think it was unlikely that there would be any real reconciliation between Franklin Roosevelt and the Theodore Roosevelt family despite the fact that Eleanor was the president's niece.

I can remember, in the 1930s, a party at Joe Alsop's house, where the elegant, brilliant, and ascerbic lady whom we always called Cousin Alice was present. The name of Eleanor came up, and, in a few minutes, she walked out to the pantry, returned, and had peeled an orange and carved the orange peel into the shape of seven large teeth which she inserted under her upper lip and did a savage imitation of her cousin Eleanor which I shall never forget. So there was more than coolness; there was active hostility between the Sagamore Hill Roosevelts and the Hyde Park Roosevelts, which did not seem to disturb Mrs. Eleanor Roosevelt very much. Her connections with the Sagamore Hill family continued, but she remained loyal to the politics and the political ideologies and inclinations of her husband. In that respect, if you talk about the New Deal, it may be said that Eleanor was more Catholic than the pope because she probably had a commitment less free of the charge of expediency than did her husband, and probably acted in some respects as not only his eyes and ears, but his conscience in the matters relating to the social and liberal content of the New Deal.

Mr. Ward has given us a very fine and, I think, definitive delineation of those family influences which did propel Franklin Roosevelt into politics. Although I think there are some unanswered questions about how he got so actively into the Democratic party, questions that may never be answered because they depend on some things that went on in his mind, and he was not always very prone to reveal his inner thoughts. He knew how to conceal what was going on in his mind.

Marc Landy's chapter about John L. Lewis and President Franklin Roosevelt fascinates me because both men fascinated me. I met John L. Lewis before I ever met Mr. Roosevelt. In fact, I was swollen and puffed up beyond measure the first time I met him, because he recognized me. I was at a reception at the home of Mr. and Mrs. Eugene Meyer when I came as a law clerk to Washington. Mr. Lewis was standing in a corner receiving the homage of the multitude—I don't think he moved one step from where he stood. I was taken up and introduced to him, and he looked down at me and my heart leaped and my soul thrilled as he said to me: "Mr. Prichard, your reputation has preceded you." Now what he meant by that I don't know. But I had always been fascinated and enthralled by that thunderous voice and that rotomontade of rhetoric of his.

I will never forget what I read in the newspapers when I was probably sixteen or seventeen years old about an encounter that occurred between John Lewis and former secretary of war, later ambassador, Patrick J. Hurley, the Commanche Indian who sat in Mr. Hoover's cabinet. General Johnson was holding a hearing about a National Recovery Administration code. (By the way, wasn't the NRA the first industrial policy we ever had in this country? You hear everybody talk about industrial policy—that is nothing in the world but the NRA. We may have it again, and I hope it does better than it did that time.) General Hurley was representing the coal operators from the western states and he told the administrator with great eloquence that he had been, as a young man, a coal miner, had been a card-carrying, dues-paying member of the United Mine Workers of America. When he finished his argument, he sat down, and Mr. Lewis rose to argue the case for the Mine Workers. I can recall as if it were only yesterday those words that I read in print, but which, having met him, I can hear:

> Mr. Administrator, it is a matter of great pride to the United Mine Workers of America when one of its former members goes into the world of industry or the professions and achieves the summit of professional and financial success. But, it is a matter of profound shame to the toiling miners of this nation when a former member of their organization is willing to betray the union of his youth for 30 lousy pieces of silver.[1]

General Hurley's face flushed, and he rose to protest and he said, "Mr. Administrator, I resent this personal attack and I ask for an apology." Mr. Lewis rose again and replied: "Very well, Mr. Administrator, ask the reporter to strike the word lousy."

So, I remain forever fascinated by John Lewis. I think that some of the things that Mr. Landy has omitted may perhaps be a part of his history, which has sometimes gone into oblivion. We remember the Herrin massacres that occurred in Illinois, when members of a rival union were brutally killed, allegedly under Lewis's direction. Perhaps he and Franklin Roosevelt are living illustrations of Lord Acton's aphorism: "Great men are seldom good men." Both have their flaws and their moral obliquities, as will all others who occupy their places. Lewis practiced the most rampant nepotism in the control he had of the Congress of Industrial Organizations and the United Mine Workers. He had his brother-in-law on one payroll, and his brother on another, and his daughter on another. He allowed no democracy in the miners' union. It was the most autocratic and dictatorial union of all the great unions, even the Teamsters union.

Also, Mr. Landy, in pointing out the indispensability of Roosevelt and Lewis to each other, has perhaps underestimated slightly the degree to which Mr. Roosevelt, in framing the labor coalition that was to become an integral part of the New Deal, was compelled to deal with those parts of the labor movement which were not loyal to John L. Lewis, not affiliated with CIO. Mr. Roosevelt's coalition was broad enough to contain not merely the CIO—including Sidney Hillman, Philip Murray, and John Lewis—but also those elements in the American Federation of Labor which remained very loyal to Mr. Roosevelt and very much a part of his political coalition, and who probably got more of the patronage and more of the political recognition than John Lewis. This included Dan Tobin of the Teamsters Union; Dan Tracy of the International Brotherhood of Electrical Workers, who was assistant secretary of labor; and Joe Keenan, who came, I believe, from Chicago from the Electrical Workers and was very much involved in the War Production Board as a labor representative. And then, of course, Mr. Roosevelt did have Sidney Hillman as his close ally, and Walter Reuther.

So, it seems that in this struggle to control, frame, and formulate this coalition, Mr. Roosevelt and Mr. Lewis played a sort of political game, a game of some hostility, and Mr. Roosevelt won the battle. He took Sidney into camp. "Clear it with Sidney," he said in 1944 at the convention; not: Clear it with John, but: Clear it with Sidney. And Walter Reuther emerged as a dominant factor in the United Automobile Workers, much free of the Lewis domination. And in a sense Mr. Roosevelt succeeded in isolating Mr. Lewis in the labor movement; isolating him alone with his Communist allies—if not allies, I might say of them as Mr. Lewis said of one of them after he broke with him. Asked if the man was Communist, John Lewis said, "No, I think he cheats the party of its dues." But at any rate, Lewis was left alone with the left-wing unions. And then, Phil Murray purged the left-wing unions and Mr. Lewis once more was back with the United Mine Workers as a solitary organization, which it has remained since.

To some extent, the tragic plight of the mine workers must be traceable to the heritage of John Lewis, the heritage of undemocratic procedures, of nepotism, of dictatorial methods. And I say this not to denigrate him, because I do think he was in many ways the greatest labor leader we've produced in the twentieth century, unless perhaps Walter Reuther could lay claim to that. I had such a love for Walter that I may be a little sentimental about him. Mr. Lewis I stood in awe and fear of; Walter I thought of as an enduring friend. But, I do think the heritage of Mr. Lewis has been a paradoxical one, and that much that Mr. Landy says is true, but there are other things that need to be considered.

I don't want to reminisce. But I will tell a story. When I was working in the White House I received an urgent telephone call from Justice Frankfurter. It was, "Prich, come to my chambers at once." Well, I got one of those White House cars which the Treasury furnishes after it confiscates them from dope peddlers and people like that, and was driven by chauffeur up to the Supreme Court and I rushed through the marshall's office and I said, "Justice Frankfurter and Secretary Knox are waiting for me." The marshall escorted me into the chambers where Justice Frankfurter and Secretary Knox were seated at the luncheon table. Justice Frankfurter got up and grapped my arm and said, "Prich, Prich, I want you. It's very important. Will you please do your imitation of John L. Lewis?"

I will tell one more story about John Lewis. During the early part of World War II the president was having a great problem trying to fend off hostile antilabor legislation: prohibiting strikes, outlawing the union shop. So, he convened a conference of the leaders of management and labor to meet at the White House and try to work out what would now be called a social contract, by which labor-management relations could be controlled through collaboration and without the necessity of hostile and repressive legislation. They asked me to be secretary of the conference, a very humble position. The chairman of it was William H. Davis, then chairman of the War Labor Board, a very distinguished and lovable public servant. The leaders of the American Federation of Labor and the CIO were on one side of the table, and the Chamber of Commerce and the National Association of Manufacturers were on the other.

I was mostly making notes and little arrangements and playing no significant part in the deliberation, but the time came for lunch the first day and they sent word to me to announce that lunch would be served in the White House dining room at 1:00 P.M. So I got up and rang a little bell and said, "Lunch will be served at 1:00 in the White House dining room." Well, none of them paid a bit of attention to me and the chatter kept on, and the arguments kept on, so I took a little gavel and rapped it down and said, "Gentlemen (of course, there were no women there), luncheon will be served at 1:00 P.M. in the White House dining room." Mr. Lewis looked down with those heavy eyebrows at me and said, "Young man, are you by any chance studying to become a Pullman porter?"

Part V
Eisenhower

15

Eisenhower's Presidential Leadership

Fred I. Greenstein

I want to give a sense of the personal experience that led me to study and write about Eisenhower. It was an experience of being startled, surprised, and fascinated when I found evidence that demolished the assumptions I had long taken for granted about Dwight Eisenhower and the way he went about meeting the responsibilities of chief executive. This evidence led me to write a book that is partly about Eisenhower the man, but mainly about problems in conducting the presidency.

In the book, I ask two related questions. One we can call the presidential support question: How can American presidents command sufficient public backing to carry out their job successfully? The other I will call the Eisenhower question: What can we learn about winning public support and other aspects of presidential leadership from the man who filled the presidency from January 20, 1953 to the same date in 1961?

If you had asked me the Eisenhower question during his administration, or even as recently as the first half of the 1970s, I would have taken it for granted you were joking. The notion that Eisenhower *had* exercised leadership, much less leadership we might learn something from, would have struck me as a contradiction in terms. Like other observers of American politics, I assumed that Eisenhower did not *know* how to do what is called for in effective presidential leadership. In the 1950s and long after, I took it for granted that there had been *no* Eisenhower presidential leadership. Rather, I took the 1950s to have been a period of national drift under an amiably ineffective chief executive.

In 1952, as a twenty-two-year-old undergraduate political science major, I confidently voted for Eisenhower's opponent, Illinois governor and Princeton alumnus, Adlai Stevenson. I had no doubt that I was voting for effective presidential leadership. Stevenson had been in government, I reasoned. Eisenhower was a mere general without political experience. Most political scientists would have agreed with me.

By 1956, as a political science graduate student, like most of my fellow graduate students and virtually all of my professors, I again cast a non-Eisenhower vote. By that time I lived in a world in which everyone I would have considered to be knowledgeable about the presidency thought Eisenhower was the very model of a nonleader. He spoke in simple language, evoking the imagery of the *Reader's Digest* more than that of the great political philosophers. He didn't even speak in complete sentences in his press conferences. And he often confessed to the press that he simply hadn't heard about some event that was filling up the pages of the *New York Times*.

He did have the magnetic grin and open-faced heartiness that we knew was compelling to the American people, since they voted for Ike rather than our preferred candidate. But to us this simply seemed a sign that he was a symbolic figurehead—a kind of beloved constitutional monarch who reigned rather than ruled. Behind the grin, we thought, there was nothing apart perhaps from anticipation of his next golf game.

His golf didn't bother the public. But we academic presidency watchers took it as a symbol of a larger indifference to the tasks of leadership. Hence in 1960, we voted for John F. Kennedy, a young man who spoke with *vigor* about how he would get the nation moving. And we were not surprised in 1961 when a panel of scholars asked to rank presidents in terms of how well they had performed placed Eisenhower very low, twenty-first among thirty-one presidents, tied with Chester Arthur.

In that era people like me enjoyed jokes about how he could not lead, or would not lead. For instance, there inevitably was a golf course joke. A foursome at Washington's Burning Tree Golf Course, the story went, was asked by the Secret Service whether the president could play through. Why? War had just started and he wanted to finish his game in order to get back to the White House.

The most often told Ike joke by political scientists enables me to turn to how his presidency really worked. From 1953 to 1958, the press was especially fascinated with speculating about the influence of Eisenhower's official head of his White House staff, the brusque, hard-working former New Hampshire governor Sherman Adams. People questioned whether it was the aide who *really* ran the country, setting policies and merely giving the president the ceremonial responsiblility of announcing them.

The Adams story takes the form of a dialogue, obviously between liberal Democrats who had no love for then Vice President Richard M. Nixon. Person One says: "Wouldn't it be awful if Ike died, then we'd have Nixon as President?" Person Two counters: "But it would be even *worse* if Sherman Adams died. Then Eisenhower would be President."

This story captures perfectly the impression of many 1950s political observers that Eisenhower did not lead—he let his aides lead him. Adams was believed to have done this in domestic policy and John Foster Dulles in foreign policy.

I began to transform my view of Eisenhower in 1976, at a time when it was becoming overwhelmingly clear that presidents find it extraordinarily difficult to win and hold the support of the American public. In the very week when

Gerald Ford became the first incumbent president since Hoover to be defeated for re-election, I was working in the barren wastes of Abilene, Kansas, exploring the archives of the presidential library located in Eisenhower's home town. The inner files of his presidency, the ones that had been kept in his Gettysburg home for writing memoirs, had just been made available by the Eisenhower library to scholars. The files are a remarkable find. They include minute-by-minute appointment logs of what prove to have been very busy presidential workdays. They include summaries of his phone conversations, taken by a secretary who was at a blind extension; minutes of his private meetings; and even secret recordings of his one-to-one meetings in the Oval Office. I was especially struck by his many long, personally dictated letters, which are models of crisp, logical prose. In them he clearly analyzed national problems and explained how he was dealing with them. I discovered in these files a startlingly different man from the one I thought I had seen in the 1950s.

Eisenhower's papers show him to have been politically astute and well informed. He was highly intelligent and incisive. *He,* not his aides, ran his presidency. And he ran his presidency with a clear and an *original* conception of how to make that office work. His conception of how to be president is especially interesting in the 1980s, because his successors have had such a difficult time.

Carter, of course, shared Ford's fate. Their two predecessors were in effect forced from office. Nixon resigned, facing sure impeachment and conviction. Johnson dropped his re-election plans, knowing he was profoundly unpopular. And just a year before his 1984 spurt, Reagan was running behind likely Democratic contenders in Gallup poll trial heats.

Eisenhower turns out to be the *only* president, since we ratified the Twenty-second Amendment and confined presidents to two terms, who actually served and completed a full eight years in office. And he managed to stay above the 50 percent approval mark in the Gallup poll for all but two months of those eight years.

Eisenhower's success in dealing with what I earlier called the presidential support problem was enchanced by his highly original solution to a dilemma the Founding Fathers built into the job of the American presidents. In most democracies different people carry out the two major executive tasks—those of head of state and of political leader. A striking example is England. As Prime Minister, Mrs. Thatcher does the politics, and she often gets complaints about how she does it. Queen Elizabeth represents the nation. She is a popular rallying symbol for feelings of unity and patriotism.

In the United States we combine the roles of political leader and head of state in one. They mix poorly. As national leader he has to trudge through the swamp of political reality. If he plays chief of state and does not lead, the country goes to pot and he is held to blame. If he plays politics intensely, he loses his luster as a unifying symbol. And he is also visibly tied to the success and failure of policies that often fail. So either way he is likely to be shot down.

Ike's approach to leadership was to play *up* his status as chief of state. At the same time he worked hard, *without publicity,* at political leadership. Since he did not take the credit for his private politicking, political scientists thought he was an inept president. What we forgot was that he also did not take the blame for being a manipulator. This was one reason why the American people gave him the support that few other presidents have been able to command.

Here are some Eisenhower operating rules for being what we can call a private prime minister and public chief of state.

The first is *hidden-hand leadership,* the phrase from which I took the title of my book. When there were messy political jobs to be done, he often farmed them out. I have devoted a long chapter to how he used middlemen to help undermine McCarthy. He worked indirectly out of the conviction that he would lose, and McCarthy would gain, if he tangled directly with a political gutter fighter.

The second rule I call *instrumental use of language.* He used words to solve problems, not to sound good. His press conference replies often were vague. The minutes taken of the planning meetings he held just before the press conference, however, show that he deliberately ducked, or even confused issues, if he thought airing them would cause trouble and interfere with solving problems. Here is an example from his own memoirs. His press secretary, James Hagerty, relayed a message from the State Department urging him to refuse to answer questions about a touchy issue. The issue was whether the United States would reply with force if there were an attack from mainland China on the Nationlist held offshore islands of Quemoy and Matsu. "Don't worry, Jim," he told Hagerty, "if that question comes up, I'll just confuse them."

The question did come up. Joseph C. Harsch of the *Christian Science Monitor* asked what the United States would do if the offshore islands were invaded. Eisenhower summarized his answer this way:

> I said that I could not answer that question in advance. The only thing I knew about war was two things: the most unpredictable factor in war was human nature, but the only unchanging factor in war was human nature.
>
> And the next thing, I said in answer to Mr. Harsch, is that every war is going to astonish you in the way it occurred, and in the way it is carried out.
>
> So that for a man to predict, particularly if he has the responsiblility for making the decision, what he is going to use, how he is going to do it, would I think exhibit his ignorance of war; and that is what I believe.
>
> So I think you just have to wait; and that is the kind of prayerful decision that may some day face a President.[1]

If this answer confused the reporters, I should add, it undoubtedly served his purposes by confusing the Chinese Communists even more. Ike probably would *not* have fought for those fly speck islands just adjacent to China. But it would have been costly, in his view, to lose them. So it was in his interest to leave the Chinese uncertain of whether taking the islands would be a painful enterprise. And this did not mean the American people were confused. They knew *he* was not ignorant of war. They were reassured that *he* was in charge. They accepted him as the best man to make such a prayerful decision.

On the off-the-record, prime ministerial side of Eisenhower's leadership, I'll mention one more element in his operating principles. This is his skill and subtlety in delegating power. The records show Sherman Adams to have become a super office manager, not the boss. They show Secretary of State Dulles to have been Eisenhower's spokesman, and not the designer of the administration's foreign policy. Eisenhower stayed in charge, but he did not try to do everything himself. He was gifted at conveying *general* policies to his subordinates and then allowing them much leeway for the specifics.

He also had the gift of delegating in ways that protected his public support. Especially if his policies were controversial, subordinates normally announced them. Precisely because Ike was assumed above politics, the subordinates, not he, got the blame, as well as any credit. Listen to this quotation from Press Secretary James Hagerty:

President Eisenhower would say, "Do it this way." I would say, "If I go to that press conference and say what you want me to say, I would get hell." With that, he would smile, get up and walk around the desk, pat me on the back and say, "My boy, better you than me."

Eisenhower maintained his broad, noncontroversial popularity as a chief of state, in part, by not showing his hand as a politician. But we also remember the image of confidence and optimism he conveyed. The image was so buoyant, we take it for granted that he aroused public enthusiasm without any effort or planning.

This was not the case. I derived an unusual insight into how he saw it as part of his job to work at inspiring the public from the unpublished draft manuscript of his World War II memoirs. I found an introductory chapter which he chose to omit from the final book. In it he described the tense period he spent in the tunnels of Gibraltar waiting to start the invasion of North Africa in 1942:

> During those anxious hours, I first realized how inexorably and inescapably strain and tension wear away at the leader's endurance, his judgment and his confidence. The pressure becomes more acute because of the duty of a staff constantly to present to the commander the worst side of an eventuality ... and the commander inherits an additional load in preserving optimism in himself and in his command. Without confidence, enthusiasm and optimism in the command, victory is scarcely obtainable.

Realizing, as he put it, that "optimism and pessimism are infectious and they spread more rapidly from the head downward than in any other direction," Eisenhower noted that he "clearly saw the dual advantages to be obtained from a commander's cheerful demeanor and constant outward optimism." He went on to say:

> The habit not only tends to minimize potentialities within the individual himself, but it has a most extraordinary effect upon all with whom he comes in contact. With this clear realization, I firmly determined that my mannerism and speech in public would always reflect the cheerful certainty of victory—that any pessimism and discouragement I might ever feel would be reserved for my pillow. To translate this conviction into tangible results ... I adopted a policy of circulating through the whole force to the full limit imposed by physical considerations. ... I did my best to meet everyone from general to private with a smile, a pat on the back and a definite interest in his problems.

Eisenhower was just as committed to inspiring morale as president as he had been when he was supreme commander. He once wrote that at the end of a motorcade he felt as if his smile was frozen on his face. Privately he made clear that he did not consider the motorcade a comfortable mode of travel. The important thing was not his comfort, however. It was holding and winning support.

He often urged other leaders to follow his own practice of taking actions that project a sense of a warmth and optimism. As one aide remembers,

> I moved around with him a great deal and I've heard him tell professional politicians: "Now here is what you do. Get out there. Do not look so serious. Smile. When the people are waving at you wave your arms and move your lips, so you look like you're talking to them. It doesn't matter what you say. Let them see you're reacting to them."[2]

The Eisenhower leadership style cannot be directly copied by other presidents in a later era. Nevertheless it is a prime source of clues for presidents who recognize that, unless they can maintain support for themselves and their office, they will contribute to the increasing national and international sense that American government is hopelessly volatile and incapable of maintaining sustained direction.

Notes

1. "The President's News Conference," March 23, 1955. *Public Papers of the Presidents: Dwight D. Eisenhower, 1953-1961* (Washington, D.C.: U.S. Government Printing Office).

2. "Gabbing with (Bryce) Harlow," by John Osborne, in his column "White House Watch," *New Republic* May 13, 1978, pp. 12–14.

16
Eisenhower Revisited

Kenneth S. Davis

My personal contact with the Eisenhower family was through Milton Stover Eisenhower, the youngest of the six sons of David and Ida Elizabeth Eisenhower who grew to maturity in Abilene (one son died in infancy).

As I'm sure most of you know, Milton, though ten years younger than Ike, had become something of a national figure, and famous in his home state, a dozen years before Ike was thrust abruptly into world fame. Roosevelt recommended and used him as a topflight federal administrator, one of the most brilliant in Washington, long before he ever heard of Dwight. Indeed, the first words Roosevelt ever addressed Dwight when the latter was introduced to the president by George Marshall had to do with Milton. "I'm having a lot of trouble with your brother Milton," he said to Ike, who was taken aback until Roosevelt went on to say, "Four different government agencies want him and I have to decide where he is to go." This, however, was said on the last day on which Milton's fame exceeded his older brother, for on the next day, June 25, 1942, a War Department communiqué announced that a theretofore wholly unknown Major General Dwight D. Eisenhower had been named to command a newly created European Theater of Operations for U.S. Armed Forces in the then-raging Second World War. In the following spring, having organized the Office of War Information and functioned as its actual administrative head, under journalist Elmer Davis, for a year, Milton resigned from government to accept the presidency of Kansas State College, his alma mater, as it is mine.

And I happened to move back to Manhattan, Kansas, my home town and the home of Kansas State, in the late summer of 1943, which enabled me to see and hear Milton deliver his inaugural address as college president. I was immensely impressed by what he said, and by the man himself—was therefore immensely pleased, and flattered when he let me know that *he* was impressed by a novel I'd written (a first novel)[1] and wondered if I might not like to team up with him—a speech, maybe an article, and answers to requests for information about the Eisenhower family which then poured in from magazines, newspapers, authors. Several book publishers asked him to write a book about his brother, requests he referred to me, after flatly refusing to do such a book himself. The upshot was that, in early 1944, I abandoned for the time being a second novel I'd been writing and signed a contract with Doubleday Doran to

do a full-length biography of the general, Milton having promised full cooperation with me on the project but with the clear understanding—he insisted upon
this as emphatically as I—that the book was to be *mine,* that there'd be no
censorship of views taken or opinions expressed, and that it would *not* be a
quickie or a puffery job but a full length serious study. He kept his word. He
smoothed the way for me with introductions, enabled me to see all his brothers,
his mother, his aunt and uncle, family friends, Mamie, and so on. He provided
me with family documents. And, most important, he wrote to Ike overseas and
got me accepted personally by Ike as a war correspondent assigned to the
supreme commander's personal headquarters. I became, I think, the only war
correspondent representing a book publisher in the whole European theater.

But before I went overseas I had in hand a mass of information about the
Eisenhower family and Ike's own career, had what proved to be a substantially
valid conception of my biographical subject and of the story I had to tell. I'd
even written a considerable chunk of the book, dealing with family and social
background from which the boy Ike had emerged. "The family history fascinates me," I wrote my agent at that time. "In part it's a history of the development of that peculiarly American democratic strategy, the strategy of the
relaxed will, of controlled drift, of creative compromise. Exponents of it on the
military side in this war are Marshall as well as Eisenhower."

There was thematic significance, I thought, in the fact that Dwight Eisenhower had grown up within a few miles of the exact geographic center of the
United States; and that the Kansas of his formative years was a peculiar balance
of opposing traditions, as befitted a state poised halfway between both pairs of
national geographical extremes. A crusading Puritanism had been introduced
into eastern Kansas by immigrant New Englanders in the days of "Bleeding
Kansas"; it had been sustained by such religious colonies as the Mennonite
River Brethren, whose immigration from Pennsylvania had brought the Eisen-
howers to Dickinson County in the 1870s; and it continued to manifest itself in
a disposition to legislate the private morality of citizens. But western Kansas, a
high, flat tableland of little rain, accepted to a degree the cavalier traditions of
the Old South—a combative "code of honor," an emphasis upon the skillful
handling of horses and weapons, an insistence upon untrammeled personal
liberty—as it developed in the gambling "rugged individualism" of cattlemen,
wheat farmers, and oilmen.

In Abilene, during the years of Eisenhower's growing up, the opposing
traditions were mingled in approximately equal proportions. The town still
retained some of the flavor and, among its boys especially, many of the vital
attitudes of its wild cowtown past. The boys played cowboys-and-Indians as a
favorite game while in grade school (Ike's favorite recreational reading when I
was with him continued to be Western pulp magazines; he had them shipped to
him by the bale); and the boys' fist fights, in several of which the boy Ike was a
principal, were of a ferocity almost incredible to a later generation. But Abilene
was also a town of churches, and in the Eisenhower family home—a white,

two-story frame house at the southeastern edge of town, where the eighty-year-old and senile Mother Eisenhower still lived in the summer of 1942 (the father had died in March)—all pride of combat, bred by lawless violence, was opposed by a deeply religious pacifism. As a matter of fact, both the Eisenhower parents became Jehovah's Witnesses. They insisted that each of their sons be self-sufficient, self-reliant; they made no effort to dictate careers to them; but they could not hide their disappointment and hurt when young Dwight Eisenhower announced his decision to try for a service academy appointment. When he won his appointment, his mother reportedly went upstairs to her room and wept.

It might be expected that the professional soldier who came out of such an environment would retain a "civilian mind," that there would be in him a balanced tension of frontier pragmatism and religious idealism, and that he would have (so to speak) a psychology of "middleness" and "togetherness." There would have been encouraged in him a tendency to seek always for common denominators among diverse people and things and forces, then to employ these for the achievement of coalitions, amalgamations, homogenizations. And this of course was required for Eisenhower's success in his great new assignment. Of the very essence of his task was the discovery and cultivation of "middle grounds" where forms of active creative compromise might grow out of initial oppositions.

And there was another fact about Abilene, the Abilene of the early 1900s, which is worth stressing. There was somehow encouraged in the boys who grew up in that town during the first three decades of this century an abnormally great and potent success-anxiety, a passion for "getting ahead"—with success defined exclusively in external, materialistic terms. It is quite incredible how high a percentage of the two or three hundred Abilene boys of Ike's generation did achieve this kind of success—as bank executives, utilities executives, merchants, agribusinessmen. Thus, of the six Eisenhower sons, Arthur, the eldest, became executive vice-president of one of the largest banks in the Midwest, in Kansas City; Edgar, the next eldest, became a very prosperous corporation lawyer in Tacoma, Washington; Roy, a couple of years younger than Ike, became one of the leading businessmen of the Kansas town of Junction City; Earl, perhaps the least obviously successful, nevertheless did very well as an electrical engineer and (as I remember) owned a radio station in Illinois when he died. And the young Ike, though openly manifesting remarkably little success anxiety during his first years in the Army, kept a shrewd eye out for the main chance and took full advantage of it after he'd been convinced by General Fox Conner, during a tour of duty in Panama, that another world war was inevitable and that he, Ike, had the stuff for high command provided he prepared himself properly.

For instance, and an important instance in Ike's career, he was asked in late 1926 if he'd be interested in an assignment to the American Battle Monuments Commission in Washington, to prepare a guide (a guidebook) to the American battlefields of the Great War in Europe. It was a writing assignment, not attractive to most officers. But the work would be done under the appraising eye of General John J. Pershing, and Ike promptly accepted. He did a grand job, with considerable help from Milton, producing in 1927 a guidebook on historical principles which remains an excellent reference work on World War I. And Pershing, who had major clout in the Army, became Ike's enthusiastic supporter.

The War

I went overseas as a war correspondent in the summer of 1944, a month after Normandy D-Day. The supreme commander was still headquartered in England, and I first interviewed him in his office at Wide Wing, in a village just outside London. Actually we talked, that first time, not in his office but in an adjacent surface air raid alert—a V-1 or buzz bomb was approaching—and he told me that, since he had issued orders for all hands to take cover during such alerts, he himself must do the same. He welcomed me as Milton's friend and told his three aides to facilitate my seeing all his top subordinates at Supreme Headquarters, Allied Expeditionary Forces (SHAEF), which they did. I found myself quickly and wholly accepted as a member of his really very small close official family. I had lengthy repeated interviews with all of them, including chauffeur Kay Summersby, who, I vividly remember, told me one afternoon of the great love she had had for a British officer who had been killed in North Africa a good many months before she first met Eisenhower. One day, a Sunday as I remember it, when Ike was away somewhere, Navy Captain Harry C. Butcher, Ike's principal aide and boon companion in those years, took me down to Telegraph Cottage, which was then Ike's secret hideaway. We spent a long afternoon there, intending to drive back to London in the evening. But we had such a good time, and I was getting such marvelous stuff from "Butch" for my book, that we decided to stay the night. I was reminded of this by a clipping I found in the stuff my wife dug up for my use in preparing this chapter. In a letter to my editor, Lee Barker, I mentioned that, having no night things with me, I had spent a night in Telegraph Cottage sleeping in Ike's bed and Ike's pajamas. Lee evidently was so impressed with the closeness of approach to my biographical subject that he fed the item to gossip columnist Leonard Lyons.

When Ike transferred his personal headquarters from England to a small tent camp in an apple orchard halfway between Bayeux and St. Lô in Normandy, I was one of his party and we lived there, became quite intimately acquainted with one another, all of the few of us, for several weeks. I also flew over to Bradley's headquarters, then to Patton's, which was then near Paris (it had not yet been taken), and had lengthy interviews with each of them. My most memorable session with Ike, was one afternoon when he was nursing a knee he had injured while hopping out of an airplane. We spent hours together during which he gave me much valuable information about his theory of command, about the strengths and weakness of various field commanders, about his own view of his own role, and about the Darlan Deal and the Patton soldier-slapping incident as he saw and judged these. It is a measure of his frankness and friendliness that I dared disagree with him about the Darlan Deal, thereby eliciting a defense highly revelatory of his sense of relative values. By the time I flew back to London, in early autumn, I had masses of notes and an enormous admiration and liking for Ike, as a man and as supreme commander.

It was not a wholly uncritical admiration. Shortly after I returned to London and was hard at work at the actual writing of the book (while V-2s came in), a friend of mine who was in the Office of War Information (OWI) asked me to give a talk about the supreme commander to his staff in the American Embassy. As I reviewed by notes for this talk, and as I later wrote into the conclusion of my book, I was struck by the fact that I had held two distinct and contradictory attitudes toward Eisenhower.

Said one of the notes, written in a moment of despair: "It is almost impossible to write a biography of any depth and significant density, when its subject is a man who has no interior life. Eisenhower ... is a man whose whole mental life is involved in *external* strategy. If he cares about *meanings,* even historical ones, I am not aware of it. ... Yet he is caught up in historic circumstances. In writing about him one is impelled to carry meanings to him." Another note said: "Meaning, significance, is not rooted in him; it only *adheres* to him. His significance is all external, imposed. He drifts with a destiny he probably does not understand, and he does nothing (practically) to determine it." Still another note said: "He is in a heroic position without himself being a hero. None of that moody grandeur, depth, et cetera, which inspires men to be better than themselves. One can't imagine him leading a great historic movement. No *creative* will. There is no *beyondness* in him."

There followed a series of transitional notes through which, obviously, I'd tried to work my way toward a more positive attitude toward my subject. "Don't try so hard to understand him," said one of them, "or you'll falsify the portrait by forcing its subject into preconceived molds. Be passive. Passivity need not be negative. You have to accept before you can criticize and reject. Let him work on you." Said another transitional note:

Eisenhower is a mirror of democracy. Use Sidney Hook's neat distinction between "eventful" and "event-making" men. Ike mirrors events, colors them with his personality, but never (in the deep sense) *causes* them. ... But that's absurd. To color such mighty events as these is in itself a creative act. Moreover, SHAEF is perhaps the greatest fact of this war and SHAEF is certainly Ike's creature. ... History may yet write Eisenhower's special qualities down as determining forces in the world stream. Must avoid the intellectual fallacy—belief that if a thing is simple it is without significance, or if obvious without truth.

The final notes were all affirmative in tone. They followed thousands of words reporting my interviews and observations in France, and the admiration these final notes expressed was wholehearted. Said one of them: "Do not his vital attitudes constitute a psychological base for world-wide cooperation? Tolerance, gradualism, etc. 'The world moves forward in little steps,' as he says. Are not these attitudes possible to all mankind? Cannot they become commonly operative, part of a world-wide common mind?" Another note said that "history is a by-product of ordinary workaday effort, and you have to stand a long way back from Eisenhower to realize what an immense and a truly creative job he's done in a situation where, one would have thought, only vast killing and destruction were possible." It was on this note that I at last based my little talk to the OWI people, and I caught from my listeners a glow of enthusiasm for my subject which helped sustain me through the remainder of my long and arduous writing task.

A few weeks later I was back in Manhattan, Kansas, where I wrote the bulk of the book during the next ten months or so. The proximity of Milton Eisenhower, the fact that I could check things over with him, and that he and his wife Helen were willing and eager to read the manuscript was of enormous help to me. I find in the files my wife dredged up for me some twenty-odd pages of single-spaced typewritten notes by Milton, commenting on every phase and detail of what I'd written, correcting factual errors, commenting, often critically, upon interpretations, and more. But his overall conclusion was gratifying: "I am satisfied that you have produced a great book, one which will establish you as a significant American writer."

A Visit with Ike

I called the book *Soldier of Democracy*. It was published in November 1945 and had a considerable success, both critically and commercially. It at once appeared on best seller lists and stayed there, in the top five much of the time, through four or five months. The success was almost as gratifying to Milton, and as great a relief from anxiety, as it was to me. He had really stuck his neck out on this project, had risked acrimonious censure—and indeed got some from Mamie, who flatly demanded of me that I remove all mention of Kay Summersby from the book. ("I don't even want her in the index," I remember Mamie's telling me.)

His brother, too, was pleased. I went down from New York to Washington to see the general on the weekend of February 2, 1946, he being then U.S. Army chief of staff and I a lowly instructor in journalism at New York University. We had a brief, pleasant visit in his Pentagon office on Saturday morning and then, next day, spent a whole afternoon alone together, at his home in Fort Myer. It was for me a vividly memorable afternoon. I had brought with me a copy of my book, hoping he would inscribe it, and he promptly did so, writing out on the first title page several sentences expressive of his personal gratitude for the way I had portrayed the Eisenhower family. He had certainly read the book with care. He had written out at least one page of notes on it, had also made extensive marginal notations in his copy, and we went over these together in an animated and, for me, exhilarating conversation during which he commented freely and fully on the command problems discussed and on the personalities portrayed. He continued to object strongly to my views as to the need and consequences of the Darlan Deal, of course, but his disagreement was as friendly as it was frank, and it was offset by his approval of other things done in the book, especially the character portraits of his boyhood family, of the people on his immediate personal staff in Europe, and of Montgomery, Bradley, Patton, Tedder, and other top British and American officers who had served in or under SHAEF.

At that point I remarked, a bit ruefully, that his approval of the character portrayals was emphatically *not* shared by Field Marshall Bernard Montgomery.

Certainly the portrait I had drawn of Monty, using materials derived fully as much if not more from British officers (notably Tedder and Ken Strong) as from American, was not flattering, though I still think that, as psychological analysis, it was sound. And in the circumstances I couldn't blame Monty for being hurt by it. For the book's "acknowledgments" indicated that the Eisenhower family, including Ike, had cooperated fully with the author, and this in turn must suggest to Monty that what the book said is what Ike thought. Monty was furious. His fury was made known to English publishers who had been bidding for British publication rights to the book. They promptly withdrew their offers: the book was never published in England. Moreover Monty let Ike know *directly* what he thought of the book, in a letter Ike had received only a day or so before my weekend visit with him. He made no mention of it that afternoon. He *did*, however, express with great emphasis his personal opinion of Monty. He had the habit of getting up and pacing the floor when he wanted to emphasize his remarks, and he did so as he told me, and I quote verbatim: "Monty is a *little* man—little physically, little mentally, little in every way." And he went on to cite, and to vent his irritation over, various episodes in which Monty had displayed arrogance, egotism, touchiness, vanity.

He also let me know that afternoon precisely what he thought of Butch and the publication of Butch's diary *My Three Years with Eisenhower.* I began to feel actually sorry for Butch as Ike dressed him down in absentia, despite the fact that my book would have been a Book-of-the-Month Club selection, had not Butch's book been pending, and despite the $275,000 Butch was getting for the *Saturday Evening Post* serial rights. I even attempted a defense of Butch, saying I knew he idolized Ike and had no notion that Ike would feel as he did. But the general would have none of that. "Butch knew exactly what he was doing," said angry Ike. "There are only two things Butch cares about, (1) getting his name in the paper in a favorable way, and (2) money."

I particularly remember something he said a propos the then-recent replacement of Tory Churchill by Socialist Attlee as British prime minister. Said Ike about his own political philosophy: "I'm willing to go along a little left of center 'til it comes to socialism"—a remark which can drive you a little crazy if you think about it and which seemed revelatory of far less political sophistication, far less knowledge about the deep running political currents of our time, than I had thought he possessed.

He was much more impressive in his talk about himself in relation to the partisan politics of the moment.

During my talks with him in Normandy he had manifested an acute and accurate awareness of his symbolic role—his role as symbol as well as military architect of allied unity, his role as military hero profoundly dedicated to the making and maintenance of world peace. At one of his meetings with us war correspondents at his personal headquarters in August 1944, having spoken as he always did about the "splendid cooperation" of Allied commanders, he added that "perhaps it gives a pattern for future cooperation to keep the peace." During the triumphs given him upon his return from Europe in June 1945 he had spoken of the "absolute necessity" of peace if civilization were to survive, had stressed the need for international cooperation (adding, of course, that "we must be strong ourselves" because "weakness cannot cooperate with anything"), and had inveighed against isolationism.

His sense of symbolic function seemed even stronger in early 1946. He told me about the delegations of important people who were continually calling upon him, promising "fantastic" sums of money to finance a campaign on his behalf if only he'd declare himself "available" or, at the very least, promise not to withdraw his name when others proposed it. At that time, both political parties sought to claim him as their own, and he regarded this as evidence of a special social value he then possessed but would promptly lose if ever he entered partisan politics. The great need for American democracy in the postwar period was "unity," he said (he was thinking in terms of foreign policy and the danger of a return to "isolationism"); of that unity whereby America retained her integrity while joining in strong international organizations to keep the peace, he himself was the chief effective symbol.

"But if I became a candidate for either party, approximately half the peoples of this country would promptly be against me," he said, adding that the only circumstance in which he'd seriously consider running would be the unlikely one in which *both* parties drafted him."

He made it very clear that day that he felt he had reached and passed the climax of his career—that he thought of this career in the past tense. This came through especially strongly in the things he said when he took me over to that historic house and showed me the collection of decorations, awards, gifts that had poured in upon him these last years. There was a certain wistfulness, a mood of retrospection tinged with sadness. Weariness. "He's awfully tired, your brother," I wrote to Milton in the following week"—much more tired than he was in Normandy. ... He confesses that he's VERY tired." Later I was given reason to believe, and I *do* believe, that he was at that time passing through a profound crisis in his secret life, an emotional crisis having Kay Summersby at its heart. He mentioned her that afternoon, twice I think, when her name was not perceptibly relevant to what we were talking about. A propos Butch, he'd mentioned others who had been members of his personal staff, his orderly Mickey McKeogh and others whose names I forget, and who now "cashed in" on that association in a commercial way. "At least, Kay hasn't tried to cash in," he said—and I wondered at the time about his use of the phrase "at *least.*"

Columbia

My admiration for Ike, my faith in him as a great man, was then at its highest tide. "I wish he could get about six months off, for complete relaxation," I gushed to Milton in a 1946 letter. "It'd be horrible if they burned him out in that hotbed of Washington. He's such a great person, and the country needs him. Seems to me he keeps GROWING all the time—that he's what they call a 'bigger man' now than he was in Normandy, even—and he looked great to me then. It's a bigness of total character that he has, not merely brilliance of mind or charm of personality. It has been a great privilege to know him, even as briefly and slightly as I've known him."

This feeling about him remained at its highest tide when, in the late spring of 1947, I resigned from NYU's faculty and returned from Manhattan Island to Manhattan, Kansas, where, almost at once, I went to work full time for Milton Eisenhower. Milton's was a dual role, that year and the next: he continued as president of Kansas State College, but he was also chairman of the U.S. National Commission for the United Nations Educational; Scientific, and Cultural Organization, which was then a brand-new and excitingly hopeful venture, much in the news. The commission chairmanship was virtually a full time job in itself. I served Milton in both his roles, and we worked very closely together for these two years and for a year or so afterward. I had done and continued to do a great deal of ghostwriting for him—and I know of no better way to learn how a man's mind works, what his basic motives are, than to write his speeches and articles. We established a quite remarkable rapport. My wife was often astonished at the way he and I could convey to one another the meaning of whole sentences, even whole paragraphs, with a single word or, often, wordlessly, with a shrug or change of facial expression. This facilitated our getting through much work in a short time, under pressure. We traveled a lot together, shared hotel suites for weeks at a time at conferences in the United States and international conferences in Mexico City and Beirut. Thus, all through this time, I was enabled to watch Ike's operations very closely through Milton's eyes. I listened closely to Milton's talk, and he talked a lot, about his brother.

And all through this period, as new doubts began to enter my own view of the general, I kept comparing Milton with Ike and wishing more and more that it were Milton and not Ike who was being drawn into presidential politics. He was much the better equipped of the two for the highest governmental office. He operated from a much wider and more solid intellectual base than Ike did, had no such blind commitment to the special interests of big business as Ike began in those years increasingly to manifest. He was much more concerned with and knowledgeable about the essential meaning of the American democracy, and had some clear ideas of his own, drawn from extensive and profound experience of the workings of government in Washington—ideas about the goals our democracy should pursue, and about the way they should be pursued in the twentieth century. On the National Commission for UNESCO in those years were Archibald MacLeish, Nobel laureate Harold Urey, Nobel laureate Arthur Compton, philosopher Richard McKeon, Anne O'Hare McCormick— and these people not only accepted but enthusiastically approved Milton's leadership of their UNESCO enterprise. They would not have responded so to Ike. They would instead have responded in the negative way that a major segment of the faculty and student body of Columbia University was responding at precisely that same time to the general as university president.

My UNESCO Commission friends and I could see no good reason for Columbia's trustees to offer the general the presidency of their university—this in late 1947. (What seems actually to have happened is that the trustees, seeking a successor to Nicholas Murray Butler, asked Robert Hutchins of the University of Chicago, among others, for suggestions. Hutchins recommended Eisenhower, meaning Milton. This suggested the magic name of Ike to trustee Thomas Watson, head of IBM.) I saw even less reason for the general to accept the offer. Nothing in his earlier experience prepared him for leadership in the academic world, not even for the kind of front-man money-raising "leadership" required of most college presidents. He admitted as much to reporters who interviewed him when his appointment was first announced, doing so with a frankness which, if disarming, was also disturbing to those who cared about higher education. "I hope," he said to reporters, "to talk to various officials while I am here and get some advance inkling of what a college president is up against. I know nothing about it." Why, then, did he take it? His predecessor on Morningside Heights had been a perennial candidate for Republican presidential nomination. Was the same post now regarded by Ike, or by the big businessmen with whom he now increasingly associated, as a way station between army and Republican White House?

The question seemed finally answered in late January 1948, a few days before Eisenhower's term as chief of staff ended and he resigned from active army service. He refused to permit his name to be entered in the New Hampshire primary, in a letter to a New Hampshire newspaper publisher saying:

> The necessary and wise subordination of the military to the civil power will be best sustained, and our people will have greater confidence that it is being sustained, when lifelong professional soldiers, in the absence of some obvious and overriding reasons, abstain from seeking high political office.

Politics, he continued,

> is a profession; a serious, complicated, and, in its true sense, a noble one. In the American scene I see no dearth of men fitted by training, talent, and integrity for national leadership. On the other hand, nothing in the international or domestic scene especially qualifies for the most important office in the world a man whose adult years have been spent in the country's forces. At least this is true in my case.[1]

Abruptly, the previously loud talk of him for president died to a whisper. Abruptly, too, there was a resurgence of my own former faith in Ike's basic living wisdom, in the accuracy of his self-perceptions, his conception of his historic role, and in the integrity of his character. (I'm using "integrity" here in its precise meaning of oneness and wholeness of being—of unflawed unity.)

It was in the interim period between the end of his chief of staff term and his inauguration as president of Columbia University that Ike himself cashed in on his heroic fame by producing, under contract with Doubleday, his *Crusade in Europe*. Ken McCormick and Lee Barker of Doubleday insisted to me at the time, as of course they did to the public, that the general wrote every word of this 200,000-word tome in just five weeks, with only minor editorial assistance from Joe Barnes, at that time foreign editor of the New York *Herald-Tribune*. He dictated it, they said. Perhaps he did.

In any case, as Ike assumed his new duties at Columbia in the spring of 1948 it became necessary to judge him by standards different from those that measured him adequately during his period of supreme command, standards which gave a greater weight to purely intellectual capacities, placed a greater emphasis on intellectual honesty—and I'll never forget the disappointment, the dismay even, with which I read his Columbia inaugural address. In its dealings with academic freedom, increasingly gravely threatened in that year of developing Cold War, the address was blatantly, dangerously self-contradictory—also far closer in spirit and idea to Karl Marx than to Thomas Jefferson or any other exponent of democracy.

> to protect academic freedom the teacher must support the entire free system which, among other things, guarantees freedom for all. ... All our cherished

rights—the right of free speech, free worship, ownership of property, equality before the law—all these are mutually dependent for their existence. Thus when shallow critics denounce the profit motive inherent in our system of free enterprise, they ignore the fact that it is an economic support of every human right we possess and that without it, all rights would soon disappear. Their demagoguery, unless combatted by truth, can become as great a threat to freedom as exists in any other threat.

It was an appalling intellectual performance.

And ambiguity was compounded in a half-dozen later public speeches. Indeed, ambiguity now became of the essence of Ike as public figure. He was an educator, yet not an educator, while remaining a general, though not a general. With the publication of his book he became an author who was not an author, for the Internal Revenue Service allowed him to pay only a 25 percent capital gains tax instead of the much higher income tax on the $800,000 or so the book made for him, this on the grounds that the general was not a professional writer! He was a Republican who still might be, as some insisted he was, a Democrat—this until Truman scored his astonishing triumph over Dewey in the fall of 1948, at which point the big businessmen with whom Ike exclusively associated began to increase their pressures upon him to run as a Republican in 1952. He began to talk more and more like a Republican candidate, yet emphatically denied he was one. In one notorious utterence during this interim he insisted with great emphasis that only he could speak for himself in politics, yet went on to say that if some of his friends thought they knew him so well that they could speak and act for him, they were perfectly at liberty to do so—on their own responsibility, of course.

I find psychological significance in the fact that it was at the outset of his period as Columbia president that Ike took up painting as a pastime. It became rather more to him than a pastime. It became almost a compulsion, as I learned long afterward when I wrote the text for a very fancy and expensive, huge-format book reproducing Ike's paintings from the Eisenhower College Collection. In the White House, on his way from his living quarters, to the executive office, or on the way back, he often or generally ducked into a closetlike room in which he would set up an easel to apply some more brush strokes to canvas.

I'm sure Ike was even more relieved than were important segments of Columbia's faculty and student body when Truman asked him to return to active army duty as NATO commander in Europe. He accepted the post, going to Paris in early 1950 to establish SHAFE—the Supreme Headquarters, Allied Forces, Europe. His public role remained ambiguous: he was still technically president of Columbia University, on leave of absence while also supreme commander at SHAFE. Something of his former clarity of mind and integrity of purpose seemed again to return to him, however, as he laid the foundations of a European army and lent his enormous prestige to the proposal for an actual political federation of West European nations. Soon the fog of ambiguity closed around him again as political pressures intensified upon him, and he declined to declare himself either in or out of the 1952 presidential campaign.

All too typical of the postwar Dwight Eisenhower was the manner in which he finally entered that campaign. Senator Henry Cabot Lodge, Jr., of Massachusetts, having returned to America from Paris in January of 1952, told a press conference that the general was a Republican, that the general would accept the Republican nomination if it were offered, and that this statement would not be denied by the general. On the following day Eisenhower, besieged by reporters, made his reply. In it he did not flatly state that he was a Republican; he said that Senator Lodge's announcement "gives an accurate account of the general tenor of my political convictions and of my Republican voting record." He did not clearly approve the movement on his behalf; he said that "of course there is no question of the right of American citizens to organize in pursuit of their common convictions." He did not even clearly say that he'd accept nomination: he said that Senator Lodge and associates had a right to "attempt to place before me next July a duty that would transcend my present responsibilities" but that "in the absence ... of a clear cut call to political duty, I shall continue to devote my full attention and energies to the performance of the vital tasks to which I am assigned."[2]

The only thing wholly unequivocal in his entire statement was his assertion that "under no circumstances will I ask for relief from this assignment in order to seek nomination to political office and, I shall not participate in the preconvention activities of others who may have such an intention with respect to me."[3] Whereupon, in the late spring, he *did* seek relief from his assignment, obtained it, returned to America, and engaged in an intense campaign against Senator Taft for nomination.

Many assumed that Ike followed this course only because he feared that otherwise the Taft-isolationist wing of the Republican party would capture the government. But having won the nomination, and at the very outset of his presidential campaign, he and Taft conferred at Morningside Heights and issued a joint statement in which Ike conceded virtually every point at issue between the liberal or moderate wing of the Republican party and Taft's Old Guard.

"Taft lost the nomination but won the nominee," quipped Adlai Stevenson.

The Afterword

As I've surely more than suggested, this whole period was for me, as for millions of others, a period and process of disillusionment with Ike—only it was, for me, a far unhappier and more emotionally debilitating experience than it was for most. I had invested a good deal of such reputation as I had as a young writer in my published conception and assessment of Ike. He made me feel I had made a damned fool of myself in public. Moreover, insofar as I remained personally and professionally involved with Milton, upon whom Ike as president would certainly heavily lean, I was forced to make some career decisions in terms of this involvement. I was thus myself led by Ike into a land quandary, a quaking country of suspended judgments.

But not for long. A year after Milton's term as UNESCO commission chairman ended, he and I agreed, amicably, to disagree and go our separate ways. He resigned as president of Kansas State College in order to accept the presidency of Pennsylvania State University; I stayed in Kansas and wrote a novel.

But this did not end my involvement with Ike as biographical subject.

For inevitably, as soon as it became highly probable that Ike was going into presidential politics, Doubleday, my publishers, decided to issue with advertising fanfare a new edition of *Soldier of Democracy* —a hardcover edition to come out simultaneously with a 50-cent paperback issue by Bantam—and I was asked to write an "Afterword" to that book, reviewing Ike's career since 1945. This was neither an attractive proposal nor an easy task for me. As I've said, it was necessary to weigh educator Ike and politician Ike on scales different from those which sufficed to weigh him fairly accurately as professional soldier—and the personal affection I had for Milton, the sense of obligation I had to him and his brothers, were such as to make me reluctant to write anything that would highly displease them. But a good deal of money was involved, and I was again a freelance writer, which is to say I was financially insecure. So I took the job, and did it rather well, I thought at the time and still think. I gave Ike the benefit of every doubt, yet dealt analytically with things he'd said and done. And when I sent the forty pages or so of manuscript to my editor, Lee Barker, he was enthusiastic about them. He wired me saying so.

Then came trouble—the kind of trouble encountered by every writer who tried to write honest criticism of Dwight Eisenhower for mass media publication during the 1950s, but rare, I think, for a writer of books. The president of Doubleday in those years was Douglas Black. Douglas Black was a trustee of Columbia University, and Doubleday was the publisher of *Crusade in Europe*. Lee felt obliged to show my Afterword to Black, and Black, as the saying goes, hit the roof. Came a letter to me from Lee saying (and he put it mildly) that "Black's reaction to the last chapter was nowhere near as good as mine. ... For your information, he was one of the five trustees who voted against Eisenhower for president of Columbia, and therefore has no axe to grind in this." But, of course, he did have an axe to grind; he ground it—and he ground me in the process. One of his points was that a singularly nasty right-wing newspaper columnist of those days, George Sokolsky, who wanted Taft to become the Republican presidential nominee, would pick up on what I'd written and make headlines saying, EISENHOWER BIOGRAPHER STATES GENERAL INTELLECTUALLY DISHONEST. I personally didn't give a damn what

Sokolsky said on any subject; but amid a flurry of wires and letters I made some changes in what I'd written, correcting things Black insisted were *factually* wrong (though I doubted they actually were), and sent the revised copy back. Lee expressed abundant satisfaction with what I'd done, the Afterword went into type, and my wife and I went down to Texas to visit friends on a ranch near Fort Worth.

And there, at Fort Worth, where I was beyond the possibility of doing anything about it (publication date was at hand), I received a letter from Lee which began:

> When we got the last chapter ... in print we had another look at it, and all of us came to the conclusion [I've a pretty shrewd notion of how it happened they ALL came to the conclusion] that it would still make trouble, particularly at a time when most of the irresponsible journalists are looking for some way to injure Eisenhower [actually the number of irresponsible journalists looking for ways to injure Ike was about one-tenth the number of irresponsible journalists then engaged in glorifying him]. It's pretty obvious that someone of Sokolsky's type will jump to the conclusion that the criticisms of Eisenhower in your last chapter represent the unofficial criticisms of his publishers and that the material on Eisenhower's tenure at Columbia represents the opinion of the Columbia trustee who is also president of Doubleday and Co. It finally seemed to me best to avoid the entire problem by cutting out the long section in the After Word which takes up the question of Eisenhower's effectiveness at Columbia.

So that's what happened.

I became more and more miserable about it after the 1952 campaign began, and I discovered that some people thought *Soldier of Democracy* was a campaign biography. Ike's campaign was, from my point of view, and I think from the standpoint of intellectual honesty and a decent respect for the electorate, such a slimy, sleazy operation, what with his betrayal of his greatest benefactor, General Marshall, and his more than tacit encouragement of McCarthyism. Indeed, Joe McCarthy would probably not have won re-election that year in Wisconsin (by a mere 5,000–vote margin) if Ike had not deleted from his Milwaukee speech, upon McCarthy's demand, his praise of Marshall and then told his audience that he and McCarthy were agreed as to ends, differing only in "method." Nor could Richard Nixon have remained in public life to make the contributions he later made to our democracy if Ike had not embraced him, literally ("Dick, you're my boy!") after Nixon's nauseatingly sophistical "Checkers" speech.

A Final Disillusionment

The very last of my more-or-less direct experiences of Eisenhower occurred a dozen years later.

In discussing my visit with Ike at Fort Myer on February 2, 1946, I mentioned Ike's most emphatically expressed low personal opinion of Montgomery, and remarked that Ike had just received a letter from Montgomery complaining bitterly about my book *Soldier of Democracy*. Actually, I didn't learn about this Monty letter until the early 1960s, when I was engaged in writing a history of the United States in World War II, called *Experience of War*. While gathering material for this book I perforce read *The Memoirs of Field Marshal Montgomery*. I bought a Signet paperback edition of it. And on pages 319 and 320 of that edition I found printed in full a letter Ike wrote to Monty on February 3, 1946—the day after that very warm and cordial visit with Ike which had been so memorable in my young life.

Ike's letter opens with thanks to Montgomery for a book he had just published, entitled *El Alamein to the River Sangro*, then goes on to say:

> Your reaction to the book *Soldier of Democracy* is of course exactly what I would expect. There is nothing I deplore so much as the writing of so-called military history by people who are concerned mainly with rushing into print so as to catch a market that is still fresh. It happens that the author of this particular book dropped in to see me yesterday and I complained about the poor light in which several very great men were portrayed. He protested that their persons were brought into the book, merely incidentally, in order to illustrate some particular point and with no thought of attempting to judge their contribution to the war effort.
>
> The comments you make with respect to this book are even more applicable to one that is now being published in serial form and written by my former Naval Aide, Captain Butcher. It is called *My Three Years with Eisenhower*.

He then goes on at some length about Butch and about the immense personal admiration he has for Monty, then returns to my book, or to me:

> Incidentally, one of the defenses made by one of these authors [in context, it's clear he means me], when I taxed him with bad judgment and inaccuracy was to pull out a bunch of clippings taken from the British papers about the time of the Bulge battle. He said: "British writers did not hesitate to criticize you bitterly unjustly. Why should you be so shy and retiring?" My answer of course was that those reporters wrote during the heat of action and were motivated to some extent by fear. Moreover, in later writings they did their utmost to correct what they themselves must have felt to have been hasty judgment. This was an entirely different thing from writing deliberately from the attitude of "pure history," which these books are certainly not.

This was, for me, a final disillusionment with Ike. I had assumed that he was changed, that he'd been corrupted by the power-pressures and adulation that were focused upon him, after that period when I was last in direct contact with him. This evidence of two-faced double-dealing with Monty would seem to indicate I was mistaken.

The episode is of no historical importance, of course. But it does say something about Ike—about the kind of man he was—and it certainly confirmed me in the judgment I had made of him long before.

He had some of the elements of greatness, but Dwight David Eisenhower was not *in toto* a great man, nor even an especially good one. He lacked moral courage. He lacked intellectual honesty. He had immense capacities for self-deception, and for the deception of others. He abundantly exercised these capacities and as president of the United States he was, in my opinion, a virtually unmitigated catastrophe from whose effects, many of them, we still suffer.

Notes

1. Letter to Leonard V. Finder, published in the Manchester *Evening Leader,* Manchester, N.H., January 22, 1948.
2. New York *Herald Tribune,* January 8, 1952.
3. Ibid.

17
Comments on Part V

Robert J. Donovan

During the entire eight years of the Eisenhower administration I covered the White House for the old *New York Herald Tribune*. Thus I am familiar with the widespread contemporary underestimation of Dwight D. Eisenhower's skills as president, mentioned by Professor Greenstein. As I remember it, the viewpoint was centered in academic, literary, and liberal circles. People in general seem not to have been persuaded; in office, Eisenhower was one of the most popular and respected presidents the United States has ever had. But because of the liberal criticism and its lingering effect on historical interpretation, Fred Greenstein has performed a worthwhile service in offering a fresh and truer perspective on President Eisenhower. I like his work.

A considerable effort is being made today, it seems, to reassess Eisenhower now that a quarter century has passed since his leaving office and extensive new documents have come to light to guide historians. Without reference to any particular work, it has been my view that Eisenhower was a much better president than many gave him credit for being at the time, but not so outstanding a president as some now appear to think.

I do not regard the Eisenhower administration as having been a great landmark, as were, for example, the administrations of Wilson and the two Roosevelts. I would even include the administration of Harry Truman, if one were to focus on the historic initiatives of the Marshall Plan and NATO and postwar relations with West Germany and Japan; or of Lyndon Johnson, if one were to concentrate on civil rights and some of the Great Society programs. On the other hand, of course, Eisenhower avoided disasters, like Korea and Vietnam, that helped to destroy Truman's and Johnson's leadership.

Eisenhower deserves much credit for his part in turning Soviet-American relations from the harshness of the Stalin period to the detente that followed under Krushchev. On the other hand, Eisenhower threw away a great opportunity to lead the country into the emerging new era of race relations when he refused to support, defend, and cushion the Warren Court's unanimous decision on desegregation of the public schools. There was not a lack of decent instinct on Eisenhower's part. He was a very decent man. But he was intent on bringing about harmony in the country—harmony between North and South, between labor and management, and among political factions. Yet his brand of harmony did not outlast him. It was trampled in the political and social revolutions of the 1960s and 1970s, which he, like many others, did not foresee.

At home, McCarthyism was the scourge of the 1950s. Professor Greenstein has done the definitive work on Eisenhower's handling of Senator Joe McCarthy. Greenstein gives Eisenhower a great deal of credit, and who can deny it, for the downfall of McCarthy through tactics of operating behind the scenes against McCarthy, while refusing to engage him in open combat. Others, commenting favorably on the Greenstein thesis, have gone on to argue that McCarthy was able to rise because Truman fought back at him, only to fall when Eisenhower allowed the senator enough rope with which to hang himself.

As one who was in the thick of the Washington storms of the 1950s as a reporter, my sense of events is that the dynamics of McCarthy's rise were beyond anything that Truman could have controlled by keeping his mouth shut or playing Machiavelli behind the scenes. And McCarthy's doom was sealed not by Eisenhower's studied and majestic public indifference and secret cleverness but by the mere election of a Republican of Eisenhower's stature. McCarthy, a Republican rabble-rouser from Wisconsin, could get away very well with attacking a Democratic president. Lots of Republicans loved the spectacle. But Republicans would not have tolerated indefinite assault on the administration of their own hero of Normandy, newly installed in the White House. Eisenhower was the rock against which McCarthy was bound to be crushed.

Once in a private discussion in the White House about McCarthy, Eisenhower exclaimed, "I will not get down in the gutter with that guy!" Well and good. No friend of the President's would have wanted him to descend to McCarthy's level. But using the White House as a "bully pulpit" would have been something else. I have come to feel that Eisenhower robbed himself of a greater place in history by not making one shining speech condemning the legal and moral outrage of McCarthy and McCarthyism. The country needed a high Eisenhower statement on that issue and will need it again. At the time no one else was in as strong a position as he to have uttered it. He might have spoken words, like Lincoln and Washington, that would have echoed through history, providing guidance for dealing with future dangerous demagogues. But it seemed politically inexpedient to Eisenhower to do so, and we are left with almost no eloquent words by which to remember him—a president, ironically, who constantly preached the goal of public morality.

As it is, the speech of Eisenhower that is best remembered is the farewell address, in which he issued a timely warning against the military-industrial complex. It was a speech that remains a credit to him.

Eisenhower was a president who fulfilled the needs of the country well in many respects. In the two preceding decades the American people had been through the turmoil of the Great Depression, the Second World War, and Korea. Too long in power, the Democratic party had run down. The country was crying for new leadership. What it needed then was moderate leadership that would conserve the best of the Roosevelt and Truman reforms, while terminating old wrangles and giving the nation time to take stock of where it stood and where it wished to go. It was the kind of leadership that Eisenhower effectively offered.

One of his strengths was that his experience gave him a commanding hand with the military. Experts today extol the manner in which the early U.S. nuclear forces were designed under Eisenhower. He held the Pentagon in check on spending and on strategy. He made a very wise decision in keeping the United States out of the first Indochinese War when he refused to go to the defense of the French in the battle of Dien Bien Phu in 1954. On the other hand, Eisenhower may get a bit more credit from posterity than he deserves on Indochina.

While avoiding military commitment in 1954, he and Secretary of State John Foster Dulles refused to accept the consequences of Dien Bien Phu. They moved not only to recognize and build up the Diem regime in South Vietnam but to ally the United States with it as a way of preventing the Communists to rule all of Vietnam. Eisenhower played an important part in the evolution of the American involvement in Vietnam that led, finally, to disaster under Johnson and Richard M. Nixon. Eisenhower cannot be blamed for the Americanization of the Vietnam War under Johnson, but he did keep the United States in Vietnam at a crucial period in the 1950s.

Eisenhower's progress as president was, unhappily, slowed by three illnesses, the most serious being a heart attack while vacationing in Denver in 1955. He also had to undergo major surgery for ileitis and suffered a very minor stroke that slightly affected his speech.

Eisenhower was not a president who sought power or especially relished the political hurly burly, day in and day out. He had no strategy to guide the America of the period that was swiftly coming into being when he turned the reins over to Pressident Kennedy on January 20, 1961. Yet no witness to the 1950s can forget the trust that the American people placed in the man from Abilene. It was a faith that carried over into trust in American institutions. When will we ever see anything like it again?

18
Comments on Part V

Richard Rolling

My impression of Eisenhower was gleaned largely from the experience that Speaker of the House Sam Rayburn had. Sam Rayburn had known him well during his military career, because, of course, General Eisenhower worked in the Pentagon before he became famous and had quite a lot to do with Congress. As president, he had as one of his chief liaison officers a man named Bryce Harlow, who had been the staff director of the Committee on Armed Services of the House of Representatives, a Democratically controlled committee led by a conservative Georgian named Carl Vinson. Vinson, way back in the beginning of things, had been a rival of Rayburn's. But he was pretty good about working with Rayburn on a variety of things. Eisenhower had a team, with himself as the Chief, who had been around before, and they did a continuous job of personal public relations with Rayburn and with Johnson. So Eisenhower had quite a continuing relationship with the Congressional leadership. Yet, he left them with the complete conviction that he was just lazy and not very smart.

Eisenhower was really a very complicated man, almost as complicated as Mr. Roosevelt was in his dealings with people. But Mr. Rayburn was really sort of contemptuous after the first year of Eisenhower's presidency. He could not believe that Eisenhower was that dumb and that lazy. There were stories about how Ike would be presented with alternative decisions on pardons and he would just send the matter back and say, "You make the decision"—which is not really entirely legal.

There was one experience that I remember in particular. He issued a very nasty presidential message which contained the very clear implication that Democrats had been Communist followers. It wasn't quite *that* blunt, but it was bad enough that Rayburn got up and, quoting from the message, said in effect that Eisenhower had no business making statements like that; that he had to depend on the Democrats for votes in foreign affairs; and he certainly couldn't get away with that with him. That was very unlike Rayburn. The story that I got was that the speaker went to see the president after Eisenhower called him in shock—alleged shock—that he was so upset about the speech. Rayburn had done what you would expect him to do: He had marked the speech in red where the offensive words were and he handed the paper to Eisenhower, who replied, "Did I sign that?" You got the impression of a real bungler; and a lazy bungler at that.

From Greenstein we get an entirely different impression: That of a very calculated, very clever manipulator, who was essentially hiding his conservatism successfully while he pursued a bipartisan foreign policy. This was not all bad except that he failed to do much in the domestic policy arena. He refused to go along with us on anything except the highway program and maybe the St. Lawrence Seaway. We found that we could not do anything about education. We could not do anything about health except little things. So we turned to the highways because at least that produced some jobs. In those days you had more common labor on highways than you do now so that the highway program was of some use to people if you wanted to get jobs for them. In the book that I co-authored, *America's Competitive Edge,* we made a big point of the fact that that highway program was a significant contribution to the general economic situation of the United States.

But, when I look at what Mr. Eisenhower kept us from doing in terms of the social programs, I cannot help but believe that if we had had a wiser approach we might have prevented a great deal of the difficulty that we had in the sixties and the seventies—about civil rights, and all the things that affect civil rights, like educational opportunities and jobs for minorities. I worked from 1955 to 1957 mainly on civil rights legislation. I am a Southerner. I don't sound like one, but I grew up in North Alabama. My roots are in Virginia and North Alabama. I carried my roots around with me because my family has been involved in politics in those two areas throughout the history of the country. And, you have some kind of feeling about that kind of thing if you yourself are a politician. I felt violently that we were behind on civil rights. That it was a curse on the country, not on the blacks alone. We had to figure out some way to get something moving. So I worked with a very small group which included Clarence Mitchell, who was the head of the Legislative Department of the National Association for the Advancement of Colored People, and Hugh Scott, a more and more liberal Republican, who was in the throes of moving from the House to the Senate. Scott later became the minority leader. He was, in my judgment, one of the finest politicians that I have ever seen. He was a learned and a wise man, although, of course, I disagreed with him on a lot of issues. Sometimes we had Congressman Adam Clayton Powell with us, and sometimes he was off galavanting.

We had a very small group that worked together on a concept, on a legislative strategy. The strategy essentially was that we would try to get a bill through the House that was exclusively about voting, which Mr. Rayburn could support. It was a very simple, not very much of a bill, a voting rights bill. Perhaps, we would be able to build a coalition across the parties that would give us significant majorities and prevent what had been going on for years, where the liberal, pro-civil rights Republicans and the liberal Democrats were outbidding each other and never getting anything done. If they did pass a bill in the

House it would go over to the Senate and get killed by the filibuster. The Senate was the real target. The plan there was rather complex. A good many of us thought that if we got Rayburn, we then would have something of a leg up on Senate majority leader Lyndon Johnson. But the only way you were going to get Johnson on a bill like that, despite his later reputation, was by just raw politics. He had to be convinced if he did not support that civil rights bill, he would kill his opportunity to become president.

Eisenhower was not very helpful. And, there was a time when Joe Martin, minority leader of the House, and Richard Nixon, the vice president, had made up their minds that it was not going to be good for the Republicans if anything went through, and they thought it would be better if it got blocked. The editorial pages turned against us almost completely. If it hadn't been for Johnson's skill and relationship with Bill Knowland, who was from California and was the Senate Minority Leader, we never would have been able to get by Eisenhower. Knowland went in the back door and talked Eisenhower into the notion that it was a good idea politically to have a civil rights bill. I saw Eisenhower as a reluctant dragon, at best, in terms of civil rights and perhaps an opponent who took the conservative position that you cannot legislate morals. I do not really know his own personal position, but I thought of him as a dangerous possible opponent. We spent a tremendous amount of time using Johnson's enormous skill and ability to influence Knowland. Knowland was an honest civil right's advocate. He believed in it within the limits of a conservative. We only got Eisenhower, at the last moment.

Eisenhower, in my opinion, did a fine job on foreign policy although I'm not at all sure that his policy on Suez was right. Most people seem to think it was. I think it helped tear up our alliance and made it more difficult for us to deal with extraordinarily complicated situations, but that isn't the constant view that I have had. I have fluctuated. But in any event, Eisenhower was very much responsible for the continuation of a bipartisan foreign policy. So I think what I come out with is frank surprise that he was that clever and that much of a manipulator and that devious. I am not making any particular criticism of it because one of the difficulties with the presidency is that I do not know how you can be other than complicated.

Ike was a phenomenon, and he was a symbol, a very effective symbol. He had enormous impact on his troops. He had the capacity to be popular with his troops, and with all the services. Douglas MacArthur, who I worked with, managed to be very unpopular with practically everybody. The navy was always talking about Douglas MacArthur as "Dugout Doug." Well, he was the farthest thing away from "Dugout Doug" of any human being I have ever seen. I thought he was a little mad. He was so sure he was not going to get killed. I had set up an office in the advanced echelon, his advanced echelon, his office was right across the street. I saw him being shot at by snipers as he walked up and down his porch with a cigar in his mouth. I saw him refuse to have sandbags put around his bed when we were getting stuff through our roof, and he was getting it through his. He was not "Dugout Doug," but he just was not very popular. Eisenhower was an enormously popular figure.

Maintaining such popularity requires a lot of skill. There has to be a very slick operation in the White House and in the administration. A lot of people forget that the other legislative liaison guy that Ike had was a man whose brother was the governor of Alabama. He was a general: his nickname was "Slick." And, he was known as one of the ablest, slickest congressional relations people there was. Bryce Harlow undoubtedly had a direct connection with him because of his connection with the Armed Services Committee. So Eisenhower really had skillful people who had worked with him for a number of years since he was in the Pentagon as one of the chief planners. He specialized in one field, foreign policy, and prevented almost everything happening in the other field, domestic policy. He was a very calculating president doing some very calculating and highly skillful things, getting his way to an incredible degree, and remaining popular because he always turned over the nasty stuff to somebody else.

He did not use up anything much on domestic policy except to try to keep things from happening. The country was booming most of the time. If he had not had a bad recession in 1958 and if we had not had a big win in 1958 in Congress, he would not have had to spend as much goodwill as he did. We forced him pretty hard in 1959 and 1960. We had the most liberal Congress we had had in years. I think it was more liberal than the Congress that I first went into in 1949 and 1950. I think it may have been fifteen or twenty votes better.

We were close in the Eighty-first Congress. We could almost do some important things. But I think if you look at it historically and in terms of total overall effect, it's going to be very hard to judge fairly where President Eisenhowever comes out. I always thought he was a passive president. I did not realize that he was doing these things as actively as he was. I was listening to my friend, Mr. Rayburn, tell me stories that made him sound a fool, when I think he was clearly, deliberately misleading.

My first experience with a president was with Truman. Now, Truman didn't do badly on a reversal of Ike's strategy. He ate up the Republicans in the 1948 campaign on their failure to do anything with his domestic program, did not say an awful lot about foreign affairs, and thus preserved a bipartisan foreign policy. So maybe I'm not being fair to Eisenhower simply because I did not agree with him on policy as much as I did with Truman.

When I was doing the most dangerous thing that I did as a representative of my district, civil rights, I did not try very hard to get a lot of publicity about my position. I just tried to do everything I could to get something done. I learned that from Mr. Rayburn. Mr. Rayburn who was on our side on that civil rights bill, would probably have had to withdraw his support if it were known in his district. You do that kind of thing. I think all of us in politics are not necessarily overtly deceptive, but we are passively deceptive because we do not advertise exactly what we are concentrating on. I do not know how pious I can be about Eisenhower simply because he may have been doing this in a more calculated, deliberate way.

However, when you get an inch beyond the point where you have gotten the first thing done, then I think you have got a job of public education to do. There ought to have been an opportunity for the American people to know where their president was. That was true of Mr. Truman. You never really had any trouble looking at the record and finding out where he was, but you had a terrible time finding out where Eisenhower was, because what he did was keep things from happening.

Part VI
LBJ

19

Lyndon B. Johnson: The Last of the Great Presidents

Wilson C. McWilliams

T here was always something titanic about Lyndon B. Johnson, and he seems even more towering when compared with his successors. Almost universally, people discerned greatness in him, describing him in terms and judging him by standards outside the ordinary human range.[1] He inspired more hatred and more adoration than any president since Franklin Roosevelt.[2] That alone testifies on Johnson's behalf; with the exception of George Washington, our feelings about our presidents have been extreme in proportion to their statute.[3] Even his critics have been inclined to weigh him the scale of heroes, as Eric Goldman did by casting LBJ as the protagonist in a tragedy, ranking Johnson among the great, flawed kings.[4]

Johnson encouraged such evaluations. "He was not satisfied," William Leuchtenburg writes, "to go down in the history books merely as a successful president in the Roosevelt tradition. He aimed instead to be 'the greatest of them all, the whole bunch of them.' "[5] After toying with the phrase "the Better Deal," he substituted "the Great Society" as a description of his goals, implying a more exalted vision of the future and a more radical deprecation of the past. Like "the Square Deal," the New Deal as a slogan suggested that Americans were being treated unfairly, but indicated that this was due to defective leadership, adequately corrected by a new and just dealer. Johnson's watchword pointed to a defect in society itself.[6] In retrospect, Johnson's friends and admirers have often wished that he had thought less grandly and contented himself with smaller, more conventional goals.[7] But that was not Johnson's way, and he deserves to be judged by the more exacting standards he set for himself.

Lyndon Johnson strove to be great, but greatness is something of a puzzle. It is not philosophic virtue, but something closer to convention and opinion. Neither is it necessarily righteous, as Burke indicated when he spoke of Cromwell as one of "the great bad men."[8]

My own thinking about Johnson and the measure of presidential greatness led me to G.K. Chesterton's *Charles Dickens: The Last of the Great Men,* in part because it seemed to me that LBJ might prove to have been the last of the great presidents.[9] The old traditions and memories are unraveling, as Leuchtenburg observes, and there is little evidence at hand to support Leuchtenburg's own gentle faith in the future.[10] Such melancholy speculations temporarily aside, I found one caveat and two tests in Chesterton's book which seem apposite in evaluating Johnson's claim to greatness.

The warning consists in Chesterton's observation that greatness does not require refinement, and may—especially in its political forms—be more compatible with a certain robust vulgarity. Dickens' character, Chesterton wrote, was shaped in an environment which was "full of inhuman institutions," but also "full of humanitarian people." This early humanitarianism, Chesterton argued, is preferable to the urbane liberalism which followed it:

> it was a rough and even rowdy humanitarianism. It was free from all the faults that cling to the name. It was, if you will, a coarse humanitarianism. It was a shouting, fighting, drinking philanthropy—a noble thing.[11]

Human beings who are "sturdy enough to endure and inflict brutality," Chesterton observed, are also "sturdy enough to alter it," just as the best guardian has the skills of the best thief.[12] The existence of low impulses and vanities is, in one sense, irrelevant to greatness; what matters is the ability to govern such baseness—in others, even if one rules them only imperfectly in oneself. Greatness is a political relationship between leader and led, one which is defined by the *work*, and includes style and soul only as they affect this praxis. It is in this sense that one can be a great human being without being a *good* one.[13]

In fact, the great must not be faultless or even too excellent, since their defects bring them within the reach of our emulation. Greatness, Chesterton noted, draws a distinction of quantity between us and those we admire, but not one of *kind:* "the hero thinks of himself as great, but not as superior." There is a relation, consequently, between greatness and the "high rapture of equality," and not only because democracy opens the world to talent. Equality seeks to draw out the excellence it believes to exist in all of us:" as Christianity looked for the honest man inside the thief, democracy looked for the wise man inside the fool. ... Christianity said that any man could be a saint if he chose democracy, that any man could be a citizen if he chose."[14] Great human beings are necessary to that task; they are the models and rivals who prompt and promote our virtues. Just as greatness is a political relationship, its task is educational, and its decisive result lies not in what the great teach, but in what we learn. "The real great man is the man who makes every man feel great."[15]

The work and what is learned, however, are only the first, pragmatic test of greatness.[16] Greatness also does involve a teaching and a quality of soul, and it is this second test which defines the highest kind of greatness and establishes the order of rank among the great. As Chesterton put it in relation to Dickens, "the man who believes life to be excellent alters it most." One of the elements of greatness is the conviction that nature is fundamentally a good order. "It is not enough that he should think injustice distressing; he must think injustice *absurd,* an anomaly in existence, a matter less for tears than for shattering laughter."[17]

By the standard of the work, Lyndon Johnson was a great president, although that judgment is precarious. In many ways, he failed as a political educator, especially since he neglected or scorned public speech and deliberation. His best words and teachings were laws and policies, and for his civil rights legislation alone, he deserves a warm place in American memories and an honored one in our history. He played a decisive role in setting America to the task of eliminating racism, and in the process, encouraged any number of humane currents and protests against injustice.[18] Johnson's presidency was troubling and disorderly because, often unintentionally, his policies made us aware of so much that was, and is, inexcusable in American life. Many Americans resent Johnson because he cost them their innocence, but that loss is pure gain.[19] Vietnam is a special case, but even that failure, I will argue, says something creditable about Johnson's leadership. Yet Lyndon Johnson shied away from any direct confrontation with the most threatening aspects of American political life, and the opportunities he refused will not easily be recovered.

His greatest shortcomings were rooted in defects of soul. At his best, Johnson had some of the comic vision that Chesterton described. He was matchless in opposing Jim Crow, for example, because he thought it a kind of foolishness, and he refused to accept the notion that sensible human beings could not be persuaded to abandon it. Fundamentally, however, Johnson's view of human life was serious if not grim. It was not a doctrine which suited him. Like Glaucon, the advocate of the "great society" in Plato's *Republic,* Johnson was an erotic man, tempted by sensuality but moved beyond it by great longings, sensitive to beauty and above all, yearning for love.[20] Yet although his character resembled Glaucon's, Lyndon Johnson adhered to a severe moral creed, similar to the tough austerity of Glaucon's brother, Adeimantus, and Johnson's doctrine was at war with his basic temperament.[21] As a result, Johnson lacked Glaucon's lighthearted and playful qualities, and of course, LBJ met no Socrates equal to the task of teaching him that virtue can be a joy. Johnson's beliefs and his inner experience agreed in denying that the passions can be taught and in insisting that the desires can only be dominated or gratified. This notion, projected into and onto politics, decisively affected—and wounded—Johnson's political thought and practice. Yet paradoxically, his conviction that the passions are unteachable was in large measure the result of the teachings which had shaped Lyndon Johnson's soul.

There was a harshness in the ways of hill-country Texas. Socially, "amiable country values" prevailed and personal relationships mattered; "They know when you're sick," Johnson's father said at the end of his life, "and care when you die."[22] Economically, the world of Johnson's early life was often stark and always insecure. Poverty was never far away, and more important, indignity was a constant in economic life, only concealed or palliated in flush times. Farmers, and the communities which depended on them, were subject to the swings of a market they could not hope to control. In 1921 cotton prices fell from forty cents to six, even though "We had fought the boll weevils to grow it. We sweat the same amount of sweat to hoe and pick it," and the Johnsons lost their home.[23] Work often went without its reward, and events treated human attachments and purposes with bleak indifference.

"The race is not to the swift," *Ecclesiastes* had taught, "... eat thy bread with joy and drink thy wine with a merry heart, for God now accepteth thy works"; but Johnson's fellow Texans were sterner stuff, not ready for the Preacher's reconciling resignation.[24] The external world could not be mastered or trusted, but one could reduce its power to hurt and humiliate by falling back on the fortress of the self. Dignity seemed to demand an adamantine self-discipline capable of dominating the body and its needs and even the social attachments and affections, so likely to give hostages to fortune. Even in words, a confession of economic, emotional, or social need undermines the inner defenses, and it is not surprising that such avowals came to be dreaded in an environment so overwhelming. In order to safeguard dignity, people were driven to make the self into a kind of prison; small wonder that Johnson once referred to the hills as "lonely."[25]

Debt was a horror. In the first place, indebtedness was the greatest threat to a farmer's position, since it burdened him with fixed costs while leaving him vulnerable to the market. Second, debt suggested self-indulgence, an undisciplined failure to live within one's means, a primrose path leading to the equivalent of slavery. "Benefits oblige; and obligation is thraldome; and unrequitable obligation, perpetual thraldome; which is to ones equall, hateful."[26]

Hospitality and generosity, so much a part of the culture of Johnson's Texas, were more than usually competitive. Giving established one's social ascendancy and freedom from need; receiving, at least temporarily, put one into debt. Dignity demanded that any favor be swiftly repaid, and debts which could not be repaid in more material coinage called for the currency of the soul—gratitutde, admiration, and allegiance. Searching for an argument to persuade his constituents to support Roosevelt's Court Plan (and his own reelection), Johnson appealed to the gratitude owed to FDR because such an obligation—the very foundation of dignity—takes precedence over all other scruples: "Mr. Roosevelt is in trouble now. When we were in trouble he helped us. Now *he* needs help. Are we going to give it to him?"[27] The giver of great gifts reaps a double benefit: he wins superior rank while creating a claim to be loved. Benevolence on the grand scale, custom whispered, promises love without the acknowledgment of need.

Religion's nobler teaching spoke to much the same purpose. The militant Protestantism in which Johnson was raised taught that self-seeking is sin and that the way to the best life lies through service and self-renunciation. In principle, the churches held that love, especially God's redeeming love for us, *enables* human beings to experience apparent sacrifice as a higher fulfillment. In practice, church teaching and preaching tended to imply that self-sacrifice would *lead* to love. In any case, this "inner-worldly asceticism," in the churches Johnson frequented, did not yet point in the direction of capitalism.[28] Whatever one thinks of Max Weber's famous thesis, capitalism was not much admired in what was still an agrarian region. Moreover, while capitalism teaches self-discipline, it does so in furtherance of self-interest; it serves others only by accident and its real aim is private fortune. At best, the bourgeois virtues are second-rate decencies unable to pass evangelical scrutiny. Johnson's religion taught him that public service—through preaching and teaching, on one hand, or through political leadership on the other—is a truer calling, worthy of genuine honor.[29]

In Johnson's family, moreover, the teachings of regional custom and religion took on a distinctive form and force. His mother, always the personification of love and tenderness for Johnson, practiced, inculcated, and demanded a genteel version of self-control and self-denial. Supremely ambitious for her son, she thought in terms of service to God and country, and she fixed in Johnson's mind the conviction that love is won by self-mastery and by doing good grandly.

By contrast, Johnson saw his father as essentially undisciplined and self-indulgent. His father's generosity was too uncalculating and his behavior too impulsive to permit him to achieve great things. Ronnie Dugger, among others, admires Samuel Ealy Johnson for his decision, in 1907, to demand an investigation into the speculations of Senator Joe Bailey, a daring act which helped to keep Sam Johnson out of the legislature for a decade. For Dugger, Sam Johnson acted courageously, and he regrets that Lyndon did not emulate this moment of principled politics.[30] But LBJ undoubtedly saw his father's act as quixotic, paradigmatically self-indulgent: Sam Johnson's defiance may have felt good, but it did not hurt Joe Bailey. Sam Johnson's venture into principled indignation was like his drinking, a self-inflating gratification which was ultimately self-destructive. (By contrast, Lyndon Johnson admired his father for supporting civil liberties in a way which was compatible with his self-interest.) To his son, Sam Johnson was too easygoing, too content with the warm satisfactions of local celebrity and community; if he hoped for greatness he lacked the dedication to achieve it. And since Lyndon Johnson's greatest passion drove him toward great achievements, his father's example confirmed the need for single-minded devotion.

Of course, LBJ did not passively adopt his mother's views. He had his brief, rebellious period of "helling around." More important, he decided to reject the intellectuality he associated with his mother. It is easy to be amused by Rebekah Johnson's literary pretensions, but Lyndon took them dead seriously and was convinced that she could have been a great novelist. She stood, in Lyndon's mind, for the life of the word—preaching, teaching, and writing—and for the excellence thereof. Turning to politics amounted, for Johnson, to rejecting the world of speech in favor of the life of action.[31]

It is interesting to speculate what might have happened had LBJ made the other choice. In his brief career, Johnson was a splendid teacher; it is not hard to imagine him as a great evangelist; he clearly had intellect enough to have made a success of the life of the mind. In fact, I am convinced that he was deeply ambivalent about his choice of the life of action, and that he experienced it as an act of self-denial—rejecting an immediate identification with his mother's things in favor of pleasing her in a higher way. At one and the same time, Johnson was radically insensitive to intellectuals and easily wounded by them. As George Reedy points out, Johnson seemed blind or indifferent to the theoretical or scholarly work of intellectuals and, in a rather affrontive way, tried to enlist them in practical tasks like speech writing. The very excess of such incidents, however, speaks eloquently. In any other situation, Johnson would have seen the tactical value of appearing interested in another's pursuits, and his eagerness to draw intellectuals into practical affairs seems strikingly like an effort to reassure himself of the rightness of his own choice.[32]

In any case, Johnson adopted his father's profession, but he resolved to pursue it in his mother's way and for her ends, as a disciplined, self-denying pursuit of the opportunity to practice monumental benevolence. "I would finish college," he wrote; "I would build great power and gain high office. Mother would like that. I would succeed where her own father had failed. I would go to the capitol and talk about big ideas."[33]

Johnson learned the arts of politics from his father, but those arts, though useful, were insufficient for his ambition. "Politics is a science," he told a fellow student at San Marcos, "and if you work hard enough at it, you can be president."[34] Johnson's family reinforced his equation of self-denial and service with the pursuit of love, but Johnson himself appealed to political science as the high road to political success.

The science of politics, as Johnson understood it, begins with the proposition that "relations of power" rest on an implicit "contract" between leaders and led by which leaders agree to further the interests of their followers.[35] This is a Madisonian argument to the extent that it sees politics as intended to further the private interests of essentially private citizens. But Johnson's formulation emphasizes, in a rather un-Madisonian way, the different motives of leaders, who forgo their own interests for the sake of power, pursuing ends which are decisively public or political.

Despite this asymmetry, both leaders and followers naturally favor the creation of a large state endowed with great power. The large regime has more resources with which to satisfy private interests; it offers leaders more power and the chance for greater fame. Johnson's political science rejected the ancient view that political participation—sharing in ruling and in being ruled—is vital for human happiness and moral education. Where classical political thought had argued for the small state as a school for public virtue, Johnson scorned small units of government because they were "built around archaic horse-and-wagon conditions" and were unsuited for efficient administration.[36]

In one sense, Johnson's view appears to be elitist, since he substitutes a sharp distinction between leaders and led for the ideal of the citizen. But leaders exist to *serve,* not to rule. Johnson regretted that the people did not "take a keen and continuing interest in the art of governement," and he urged the teaching of the "art of statecraft," but as he saw it, the arts of government and statecraft amounted to public administration, not politics. Government is an essentially administrative task. Moral education is the job of society; goals and values are established in private life. The role of the public is spectatorial: the people should take an "interest" in the art of government, but they have no particular reason to practice it. As George Reedy argues, Johnson had little appreciation for the idea that the purposes of politics could be achieved through deliberation. He had even less room for the possibility that deliberation might *be* a purpose of politics. Citizens have a right and are needed to applaud the performance of their leaders (and vice versa), but not to share in governing itself.[37]

In Johnson's doctrine, elections were a winning of consent, constructing and renewing the bonds between leaders and followers. Since the hope of public esteem plays such a vital role in persuading leaders to take on the discipline of politics, elections are essential mechanisms of punishment and reward. Nevertheless, elections are at least a distraction from the real tasks of government. They are also dangerous, because contact with the public can be so gratifying or so wounding to political leaders. Certainly, Johnson experienced it in that way: he was inclined to interpret the reaction of any crowd entirely in terms of his own popularity, and he was exalted by the marks of public affection. "There was some form of vitalizing force in frenzied crowds," Reedy writes, "that drove him into a state of ecstasy."[38]

Such considerations led Johnson to favor less frequent elections, and he urged a four-year term for the House of Representatives and a president elected for a single, six-year term without the possibility of re-election.[39] In opposing re-eligibility, Johnson outdid even the Twenty-second Amendment in rejecting the argument of the Framers of the Constitution. In *The Federalist,* number 72, Hamilton argues that the chance of re-election encourages the president to pursue great aims and projects and reduces the temptation for the president to use his office for private gain. Johnson, by contrast, feared that re-eligibility inclines the president to forgo controversial programs and grand designs in order to further his chances for re-election.

Both Johnson and Hamilton assume that public opinion, at least in the short, electoral term, will be parochial and myopic. Johnson departs from Hamilton because of his judgment that the itch for public favor in the minds of political leaders is likely to crowd out virtually all other aims and motives. Hamilton worried that private motives might sway leaders unless checked by the hope of honor, but Johnson treats private aims as unworthy of concern, essentially beneath the Constitution's contempt. He appears to have considered that nest-feathering, for any serious political person, would be no more than an afterthought; a public figure who allowed himself or be ruled by private interests would be a trivial person whose crimes would amount to no more than petty nuisances in democratic life. The desire to be loved, on the other hand, was a ruling passion, capable of moving even the masterful to betray the people's true interests and their own hopes for greatness.[40]

Great achievements presume great power, "political capital" accumulated by the discipline of political self-denial. Johnson's version of "inner-worldly asceticism" demanded that he subordinate himself to his goal, and despite his lapses into drink or other sins of the flesh, Johnson was almost totally absorbed by his profession and his purpose.[41]

To superficial observers, Johnson seemed unprincipled; in fact, his opportunism was an act of will by which he "steeled himself to say and do almost anything to get more power," accepting humiliations for the sake of greater glory. He was capable of very brave political acts, after careful calculation, and he flattered himself that he had been as liberal as possible within the limits imposed by practicality and his own long-term goals.[42] Nevertheless, the dominant theme of Johnson's years of preparation and struggle was the subordination of self. Johnson held his own ambition in check; he courted and deferred to older patrons; he was patient; he bided his time, played by the rules and waited his turn. He had warm moments and knew great satisfactions, but the practice of politics, as Johnson experienced it during those years of anticipation, necessarily entailed frustration and inner rage.[43]

Governed and stimulated for so long by his own great expectations, Johnson, once he became president, abandoned the accumulation of power in favor of a kind of political extravagance. Old indignities made him doubly eager: "I've been kissing asses all my life," he said, "and I don't have to kiss them any more."[44]

There was a calculated side to Johnson's haste. As he explained, the Madisonian system gives the advantage to all those who wish to resist change; members of Congress have only a short time before the need for re-election compels them to defer to opinion; the limits on the president's tenure progressively limit his bargaining power.[45] These considerations, however, do not really account for Johnson's recklessness, his imprudent attempt to fight, simultaneously, against racism, poverty, and Vietnamese insurgency. Johnson yearned for the "fruits of victory," the end for which he had sought power: to do more good than any of his predecessors so that he could claim, as his *due,* the highest place in the affections of the people. Only the illusion of love without dependency made the discipline of power endurable; only new obstacles could preserve that illusion. Johnson, as Doris Kearns comments, was "as discontent in conquest as he was eager in pursuit."[46] He needed to pursue Nemesis in order to preserve his dream.

After John and Robert Kennedy were assassinated, Johnson reflected, they were accorded the "storybook image of great heroes who, because they were dead, could make anything they wanted happen."[47] Given so many advantages by birth and fortune, the Kennedys seemed to have won fame cheaply; their unchosen sacrifice has won them an undeserved reward. Johnson's decision not to seek re-election in 1968 was the ultimate gesture of political self-denial, a conscious, chosen surrender of power which put Johnson beyond any reward in the public's gift *except* love. It was the measure of his dignity and of his devotion.

Johnson's Political Science

Johnson's internal struggle to discipline and overcome his feelings of need and neglect, yearning and fury, made him highly sensitive to similar passions in the public at large. His sympathy for the poor was very real, and he understood that indignity can do moral damage in a way that material deprivation cannot. The small community in which Johnson grew up gave him a place and an identity, and when he left home to seek greater things, Johnson knew and retained the townsman's indignation at the indifference of the larger society.[48] Similarly, Johnson was at his best in translating legislation for civil rights into the language of personal dignity. "A man has a right not to be insulted in front of his children."[49]

There is no doubt that Johnson felt less empathy for the middle class Americans who suffer from more formless feelings of alienation.[50] Yet Johnson was acutely aware of, and played on, the need for dignity, love, and attention among even very powerful Americans.[51] He sensed the rage of mass society and he had a striking capacity to recognize and identify with injuries and indignities even if he had little or no experience of them.

> We'll never know how high a price we paid for unkindness and injustice inflicted on people—the Negroes, Mexicans and Jews—and everyone who really believes he has been discriminated against in any way is part of that great human price. And that cost exists where many people may not even think it does.[52]

I do not think one can explain LBJ's political problems on the ground that his program had become outdated in an "age of affluence and education."[53] Today, economic issues do not seem as passé as it was once fashionable to believe them to be. More important, the Johnson administration made real— and so far, almost the *only*—attempts to address the quality of life in America and to enlist public policy in the cause of beauty and community.[54] That those policies were imperfectly successful, at best, does not affect the nature of the administration's concern or the daring of its innovations. As in its support of racial equality, the Johnson administration gave its support—and in some cases, created—new movements for equality, I suspect that, had he felt the need, LBJ, supremely adaptable tactician that he was, could have accommodated himself to the political forces which were in so many ways his own creation.[55]

It is true that Americans at large did not feel a sense of "adventure" in Johnson's programs as they had with the New Deal. In part, that reflects the prior existence of the New Deal and the prosperity of Johnson's times.[56] But it also derives from the fact that Johnson did not seek to promote public excitement; he feared it. In retrospect, he regarded FDR's rhetoric—his attacks on business in particular—as dangerously divisive and demagogic.[57] Whatever one thinks of that judgment, Johnson's assessment of the American mass public had become deeply pessimistic, and it shaped the style and the substance of his administration.

Johnson's science of politics did envision a diminished sort of public spirit. As an audience, spectator-citizens still have an essential role: public attention and applause (and their contraries) set the limits of public life. Good citizenship, in these terms, is a just appreciation of rule. Like sports fans, good citizens must love the game as well as victory, and must recognize and honor good play even when it is performed by the opposing team.[58] Johnson's science remained basically Madisonian; He did not expect this devotion to the whole to outweigh or even equal the force of private interest, but he did hope that it would be strong enough to limit faction and to embolden leaders to strive for great things.

Even this species of public spirit, however, was passing from the American scene. It required that citizens have some minimal sense of personal importance and civic responsibility, some confidence that their concerns were heard and voiced in public councils. Above all, good citizenship depended on a personal bond between leaders and led.

Johnson was intensely aware that indignity and felt weakness drive human beings into a desperate, embittered defense of their private concerns. He knew at first hand the "desire for recognition," and his greatest political successes turned on lavishing attention and consideration on those whose support he sought to win. Being consulted and treated with deference, Johnson knew, gives a sense of personal significance and security. It encourages and permits human beings—leaders and citizens alike—to step beyond the confines of narrow self-interest into "self-interest rightly understood" and the limited magnanimity which, Johnson trusted, could be harmonized with the common good.[59] Johnson's Madisonian science told him that human beings were private by nature; his experience taught him that they were political animals.

Traditionally, American politics had been rooted in small communities in which individuals were relatively able to form personal bonds with their representatives. Those representatives, in turn, could be drawn toward the common good by the leaders of Congress and by the president. This, at least, was the sort of politics in which Johnson excelled and with which he felt morally comfortable. Yet Johnson recognized that the communities which were the foundation of traditional politics and civic spirit were passing away, undermined by change. Whatever his regrets, Johnson was devoted to progress and he accepted the irrelevance of the traditional small community in technological society.[60] The American public was becoming more and more massified, increasingly rootless, anonymous, and resentfully undignified: the "roots of hate" were on the way to ubiquity.[61]

Johnson had little hope that the more contemporary intermediate groups could close the gap between citizens and their government. In the first place, the connections between ruled and ruler had to be personal, tied to relationships in the flesh. The great interest groups were too large to practice anything except mass politics and would always be bound to the narrow self-interest of narrow constituencies. One could expect to find public spirit, now and again, among the *leaders* of such organizations, since they were lifted into positions of dignity and responsibility and (sometimes) were moved by the same public motives as political leaders themselves. The leader, however, had only a very limited ability to move or elevate the organization: Johnson admired George Meany, but he was not enamored of organized labor.[62]

Johnson was even more hostile to the media. The media act in a *public role,* speaking of public issues and concerns, but are tied to *private constituencies* (and Johnson suspected most journalists and media figures of being ruled by private motives). Television newspeople, especially, are compelled to practice mass politics by addressing, in necessarily simplified terms, the anxieties and passions of isolated individuals. And, in Johnson's view, the great majority of journalists, whatever their medium, were a kind of anomic, scrabbling mob; the only exceptions were the few who were elevated far enough to achieve public dignity and personal responsibility.[63]

Political parties might have commended themselves to Johnson as a way of re-creating, in a new era, some of the virtues of traditional American politics. Johnson, however, was suspicious of parties, in part because he had grown up with a one-party politics in which party was only a loose association of personal followings and economic factions.[64] He recognized the necessity of party, but he continued to see parties as intruders, imposing essentially narrower interests on the process of government.[65] Moreover, Johnson perceived that party structures tend to be dependent on the existing form of society. In this, he was correct, but he neglected the creative possibilities of party, the ability of partisanship and party organization to contribute to public spirit and hence, to civic renewal.[66] That he did not attempt the reconstruction of party politics in America is the most glaring institutional failure of his presidency.[67]

On the other hand, many of Johnson's programs—most notably, the underrated Community Action Programs—were at least intended to attempt a kind of social reconstruction, and one must presume that Johnson believed they had a reasonable chance of success. In fact, they achieved a good deal even on the limited scale which events permitted. But Johnson was bound to realize that the effects of such programs, even by the most optimistic account, would be felt only in the long term. They could make no significant dent on mass politics in Johnson's own time.[68]

Johnson had no confidence in his own ability to educate the mass public. Of course, LBJ did not rank with the great orators, but his rather tedious public style was an effect, much more than a cause, of his distaste for mass politics. Johnson, after all, had taught speech and debate, and he could be evangelically eloquent when he abandoned a prepared text.[69] He was at his best in speeches which involved an implicit or explicit attack on his audience, such as his addresses in the South on behalf of the Democratic ticket in 1960, and later, in support of civil rights. In such speeches, Johnson aften overwhelmed his audience with a rhetoric of controlled force, radiating menace even when the words apparently conciliated and suggesting a supreme indifference to the worst the audience could do.[70] Necessarily, this was a mode which could not be used very often, but Johnson felt at ease with it, I think, because such punitive rhetoric put a distance between him and his audience and protected him against his desire to curry favor and against the attendant temptation to demagogy.

The temptation and the danger were real enough. More often than he liked to remember, Johnson was carried away by his desire to please an audience and said outrageous things which he later regretted.[71] His ambition and his morality of self-denial commanded him to avoid such offenses. And mass politics made Johnson even more distrustful of inspiring eloquence. He recognized that the mass blurs individuality and lessens responsibility, and—in LBJ's imagining—an "aroused" citizenry came to seem indistinguishable from an inflamed mob, moved to unlimited goals and forcing its leaders to refuse all compromise.[72]

By contrast, he felt at ease with his very personal private oratory, the astonishing repertoire of techniques and tales he used, in private discussion, to further his determination to persuade at any cost. That private rhetoric served his own desire for ascendancy, but it also reflected his passion for bringing political leaders together, overcoming the barriers imposed by interpersonal rivalries and hostile constituencies. He did not fear eloquence in such face-to-face contexts because they *emphasized,* rather than effaced, the dignity and moral responsibility of individuals.[73] In public, by contrast, he felt compelled to a ponderous moderation, hoping to restrain public passions as he restricted himself.[74]

Repeatedly, Johnson spoke of his desire for unity, "the deepest wish of my heart," and his concern mirrored his doubt about the moral foundations of the regime.[75] Johnson sought consensus even though he realized that it could hamper effectiveness, since smaller majorities are often more cohesive and disciplined.[76] He was voicing the old, evangelical ideal of Union, the hope for a kind of fraternal covenant that would unite all Americans as Americans, transcending the loyalties of class and the claims of interest.[77] Johnson appealed, in this sense, to an ideal which is at least transpluralist if it is not antipluralist, made necessary by the strength of the forces working to divide America.[78]

Johnson was haunted by the suspicion that the country could not survive serious political disagreement. Political safety and unity, consequently, required Johnson to persuade Americans that his policies served the interest of virtually everyone. That necessity, in turn, impelled him to seek growth and expansion, since only growth would allow Johnson to advance the unfortunate without requiring material sacrifice. It commanded toughness in Vietnam because détente and arms limitation could be pursued only if there was no suggestion that America was "losing." Johnson's passion for unity tended to dictate his ends, reducing him from a great leader, an ingenious improviser.

Moreover, while growth makes it possible to reward the unfortunate without inflicting an *absolute* deprivation on the comfortable, any real gain for the excluded involves a *relative* loss for the privileged, and a corresponding decline in status. Any improvement in the condition of minorities or the poor—and especially, any moral improvement or increase of dignity—was bound to be experienced as a loss by the middle class. Unity could not be had by the promise that no one would lose: Johnson's goal commanded him to persuade the privileged to make sacrifices on behalf of the common good. Yet it was just such civic education that Johnson feared to attempt.

The limitations of Johnson's position were clear in Vietnam. He believed that the war was worth fighting—in order to resist aggression and to maintain American credibility—but that victory in Vietnam was not worth a total war. (On both counts, I thought then that he was correct, and I still do.) It was evident to Johnson, and to everyone else, that American opinion was the key to the war, since Hanoi could not hope to win on material terms.[79] Yet Johnson made no real effort to mobilize American opinion on behalf of a limited war in Vietnam.[80] He was persuaded that any effort to enlist the public would slide over into superpatriotism and lead to escalation.[81] As a result, he refused to mobilize reserve forces; he minimized the risks and the costs of the war in ways which helped to destroy his credibility at home; he held back from asking for even so mild a measure as an anti-inflationary tax increase.[82] He hoped, in other words, that American opinion would persist if the sacrifices asked of it were not too great.[83] At that, he might have succeeded but for the Tet offensive and the terrible blunder of the joint chiefs of staff in presenting an exaggeratedly dark picture of the military situation in the hope of forcing a partial mobilization.[84] Yet the public's despair over Tet, which the generals helped to magnify, was in many ways an artifact of Johnson's policy.

In one sense, he deserves our regard for his policy in Vietnam. Johnson kept the war within the restraints imposed by the objective, and he created a political climate which prevented his successors from escalating the war even if they chose. But in the end, the Vietnam War produced both the other results which Johnson had feared: a shameful peace and lacerating divisions within America itself.

Presidential Greatness

Perhaps Johnson was right: it may be that American opinion could not have been persuaded to make the necessary sacrifices in Vietnam without the fury of a war for total victory over a villified foe. Yet I wish he had trusted himself— and the rest of us—enough to have made the attempt. As passionate as LBJ was for the public's love, there were things he would not do to win its favor, as he proved over and over again. In truth, he was a much better human being, and potentially a better public educator, than he thought himself.

That he held back from the task of political education is to be doubly regretted because he was correct in judging that American political life was threatened by the indignities, loneliness, and indifference of mass politics. He was right to fear that privatism was becoming ungovernable and that the fabric of political unity might require reweaving. His own shortcomings are less excusable because he *was*, in so many ways, the last of the great presidents.

The disintegrative tendencies in American society and politics have grown stronger with the years, and none of Johnson's successors has made a serious attempt to confront those great problems in their present dimensions, let alone the monstrous scale of the future. American democracy, if it is not past saving, will need greatness at least and possibly virtues still more exalted. Johnson's most serious fault was not hubris, but the failure to put his great abilities to the most exacting test. All the more reason to accept Harry McPherson's verdict, "I would not have traded Johnson's vast hopes and intentions for another man's bookkeeping prudence."[85]

> Far from thinking that humility ought to be preached to our contemporaries, I would have endeavors made to give them a more enlarged idea of themselves and their kind. Humility is unwholesome to them; what they most want, in my opinion, is pride. I would willingly exchange several of our small virtues for this one vice.[86]

Notes

1. George Reedy, *Lyndon B. Johnson: A Memoir* (New York and Kansas City: Andres and McMeel, 1982), pp. 53, 158.

2. William Leuchtenburg is correct in arguing that there was a difference in the hostility felt toward LBJ and FDR, and as will be clear, I do not find it surprising that Roosevelt inspired more genuine and abiding love. (Leuchtenburg, *In the Shadow of FDR: Harry Truman to Ronald Reagan* (Ithaca, N.Y.: Cornell Univ. Press, 1983), p. 155). This does not, however, affect the relative likeness to which I refer. It is more than a little suggestive that it is Johnson who appears, under a portrait of Roosevelt, on the cover of Leuchtenburg's book.

3. LBJ resented this; as Reedy tells, he envied Herbert Lehman for being called "sincere," not realizing that the term was just this side of patronizing. (Reedy, *Johnson*, pp. 61-62) Obviously, it damns Ronald Reagan that he is so often referred to as "amiable."

4. Eric Goldman, *The Tragedy of Lyndon Johnson*, (New York: Knopf, 1969).

5. Leuchtenburg, *In the Shadow of FDR*, p. 142; see also p. 123.

6. *Ibid.*, p. 138. Given racism, to say nothing of issues which—like the inequality of the sexes—troubled Johnson less, there was and is a good deal to be said for such a diagnosis.

7. Harry McPherson, *A Political Education* (Boston: Little Brown, 1972), pp. 302-303.

8. Edmund Burke, *Reflections on the French Revolution,* Everyman Edition, (London: Dent, and New York: Dutton, 1955), p. 45.

9. G.K. Chesterton, *Charles Dickens: the Last of the Great Men* (New York: The Readers Club, 1942). This book, published by Dodd Mead in 1906, had a considerable influence on Orwell's wonderful essay, "Charles Dickens," (*Collected Essays, Journalism and Letters of George Orwell,* edited by Sonia Orwell and Ian Augus (New York: Harcourt Brace and World, 1968), vol. 1, pp. 413-460), and I connected both Chesterton's argument and Orwell's with the appreciation of the best qualities of political liberalism.

10. Leuchentenburg, *In the Shadow of FDR,* pp. 236-246.

11. Chesterton, *Dickens*, pp. 7-8.

12. *Ibid.*, p. 6; Plato, *Republic*, 334A.

13. Friedrich Nietzsche, *Beyond Good and Evil*, sect. 269. "The 'great men', as they are reverenced, are poor little fictions composed afterwards; in the world of historical values, spurious coinage *prevails*" (translated by Helen Zimmern).

14. Chesterton, *Dickens*, pp. 8, 11-12.

15. *Ibid.*, p. 8.

16. On the insufficiency of such tests, see Bruce Miroff, *Pragmatic Illusions: The Presidential Politics of John F. Kennedy* (New York: McKay, 1976).

17. Chesterton, *Dickens*, p. 7; see also Alexis de Tocqueville, *Democracy in America* (New York: Schocken, 1961), vol. 2, pp. 264-267. Hannah Arendt's insistence that antisemitism is an offense against common sense, in my view, is not the least of her claims to greatness. (*The Origins of Totalitarianism* (New York: Harcourt Brace, 1951), pp. 3-10.)

18. Paul Peterson and David Greenstone, "Racial Change and Citizen Participation," *A Decade of Federal Antipoverty Programs* edited by Robert Haveman (New York: Academic Press, 1977), pp. 269-270.

19. Burke's verdict on Cromwell's revolution seems appropriate to the turbulence of the Johnson years:

> These disturbers were not so much like men usurping power as asserting their natural place in society. Their rising was to illuminate and beautify the world. ... The hand that,

like a destroying angel, smote the country, communicated to it the force and energy under which it suffered. (*The French Revolution*, pp. 45–46).

20. Reedy, *Johnson*, pp. 32, 52, 72; McPherson, *A Political Education*, p. 98; William O. Douglas, *The Court Years, 1939–1975* (New York: Vintage, 1981), pp. 312, 333–336.

21. See the description of the young Johnson in Ronnie Dugger, *The Politician: the Life and Times of Lyndon Johnson* (New York: Norton, 1982), p. 171.

22. *Ibid.*, pp. 57, 204.

23. *Ibid.*, p. 89.

24. *Ecclesiastes* 9:11, 7.

25. Reedy, *Johnson*, p. 34; see also Doris Kearns, *Lyndon Johnson and the American Dream* (New York: Harper & Row, 1976), p. 21.

26. Thomas Hobbes, *Leviathan*, edited by C.B. Macpherson (Baltimore: Penquin, 1968), pp. 162–163.

27. Cited, Leuchtenburg, *In the Shadow of FDR*, p. 9.

28. As Ronnie Dugger points out, however, capitalism was acquiring a more favorable aura in the churches, which helps account for the disparity between Johnson's own views and the Texas opinion with which he was later forced to deal (*The Politician*, p. 57).

29. As Dugger indicates, Johnson saw preaching and politics as, to some extent, the only real alternatives in his life (*Ibid.*, p. 25).

30. *Ibid.*, pp. 57–59.

31. *Ibid.*, pp. 64, 74; Sam Houston Johnson, *My Brother Lyndon* (New York: Cowles, 1970), p. 8; on the choice of lives, see Reedy, *Johnson*, pp. 6, 7, 12. On Rebekah Johnson's character and convictions, see Dugger, *The Politician*, pp. 59–61, 64; Reedy, *Johnson*, pp. 33–34.

32. Reedy, *Johnson*, pp. 76–79.

33. Cited in Dugger, *The Politician*, p. 107. It is suggestive that Johnson thought of *talking* in connection with pleasing his mother by political success. Johnson's adherence to the Christian Church, his father's, in preference to his mother's Baptist Church, parallels his choice of politics as a career. It has a double significance because the Christian Church is less rigidly doctrinal than the Baptist Church and in that sense, less theologically intellectual and more practical in its view of faith.

34. Cited, Dugger, *The Politician*, p. 122.

35. Cited in Kearns, *Johnson and the American Dream*, p. 112.

36. Lyndon B. Johnson, *The Vantage Point: Perspectives of the Presidency, 1963–1969* (New York: Holt, Rinehart and Winston, 1971), p. 344.

37. *Ibid.*, p. 234; Reedy, *Johnson*, pp. 6, 7, 12, 81; McPherson, *A Political Education*, pp. 263–264.

38. Reedy, *Johnson*, pp. 5, 137.

39. *The Vantage Point*, p. 344.

40. Whether or not one accepts this argument, it amounts to a devastating critique of biographies which "expose" Johnson's private dealings; the defect of such works generally is that they interpret public men in terms of motives which are comprehensible to, and govern, private ones, but this source of popularity makes them radically misleading.

41. Reedy, *Johnson*, pp. x, 32, 51–52, 74, 156; his brother comments on Johnson's personal frugality and his preference for "baggy, ready-made suits from Sears Roebuck."

What first impressed Johnson about Walter Jenkins, apparently, was the fact that Jenkins had saved all of his pay when in military service. (*My Brother Lyndon*, pp. 63–65, 149). On the general point, see Richard Neustadt, *Presidential Power: The Politics of Leadership, with Reflections on Johnson and Nixon* (New York: Wiley, 1976), p. 31.

42. Dugger, *The Politician*, p. 307; see also pp. 205–217, 316–317, 343; Reedy, *Johnson*, p. xv; McPherson, *A Political Education*, p. 97; Kearns, *Johnson and the American Dream*, p. 134. Doubtless, of course, Johnson often compromised more than was truly necessary. (Dugger, *ibid.*, p. 292).

43. Kearns, *Johnson and the American Dream*, pp. 76, 91, 103, 105, 113, 173; Neustadt, *Presidential Power*, pp. 29–30; Dugger, *The Politician*, pp. 112, 200, 204, 264, 276, 346.

44. Cited, Reedy, *Johnson*, p. 138.

45. *The Vantage Point*, pp. 440–441; McPherson, *A Political Education*, p. 268; Jack Valenti, *A Very Human President* (New York: Norton, 1975), p. 144.

46. Kearns, *Johnson and the American Dream*, p. 134; certainly, Johnson knew or suspected that love cannot be had without dependency, but as his personal relationships testify, he continued to pursue it nevertheless. His celebrated amorousness was less specifically sexual than it was a desire to be loved and nurtured. In his flirtations, LBJ—like so many of us—manufactured a self tailored to the object of his affections, revealing part of himself and veritably oozing intimacies, but concealing himself in a more fundamental way. Such liaisons, for obvious reasons, were never really comforting. His bond to Mrs. Johnson, by contrast, was responsible for more of his real greatness than we are likely to realize. In fact, I suspect that Johnson "strayed" only because he feared the extent of his attachment to Mrs. Johnson and the dependence it implied. But this dependence was the source of heroic strength. In the same way, the president relied on and needed friends like Jenkins, Clark Clifford, and George Reedy, although he feared the egalitarian side of their friendship and periodically rejected and punished them for it. (See Garry Willis, "Singing 'Mammy' to Doris," *New York Review of Books*, June 24, 1976, 23:8; Reedy, *Johnson*, p. 36; Kearns, *Johnson and the American Dream*, pp. 8, 9, 26; McPherson, *A Political Education*, pp. 435–436).

47. Cited in Kearns, *Johnson and the American Dream*, p. 350.

48. Evidently, this contributed to his delight in outraging the complacently respectable and to his admiration for Huey Long, as well as to his general pattern of love and hatred for the elite (Reedy, *Johnson*, pp. 9, 23, 26, 39; Sam Johnson, *My Brother Lyndon*, p. 45; Kearns, *Johnson and the American Dream*, pp. xi, 5, 13, 42, 213).

49. Cited in George Will, *Statecraft as Soulcraft* (New York: Simon and Schuster, 1983), p. 87.

50. Reedy, *Johnson*, p. 9.

51. Consider, for example, his treatment of Harry Byrd (Reedy, *Johnson*, p. 88).

52. Kearns, *Johnson and the American Dream*, pp. 305–306; see also *The Vantage Point*, p. 167. Johnson's emphatic capacity to identify with the pain of others was, if anything, too strong; certainly, it sometimes led to rhetorical excess. (Dugger, *The Politician*, pp. 33–34).

53. Nor is it just to refer to traditional, working class Democratic loyalties as "blind urges." Theodore White's contempt for memory and allegiance is disreputable,

but then, one must consider the source. See *The Making of the President, 1968* (New York: Atheneum, 1969), p. 68.

54. McPherson, *A Political Education*, pp. 301–302; Johnson, after all, titled a chapter in his memoirs, "The Quality of Life"; *The Vantage Point*, pp. 322–346.

55. Franklin Roosevelt, after all, was a rather unwitting champion of organized labor, but he certainly became adroit in playing the role. See the chapter by Marc Landy, "FDR and John L. Lewis: The Lesson of Rivalry," in this book.

56. Leuchtenburg, *In the Shadow of FDR*, p. 155.

57. *Ibid.*, p. 147.

58. This view is similar to, but different from, the pluralist emphasis on the "rules of the game" since it is not the rules, but the game itself—and the things which make it beautiful—which inspire the knowledgeable fan. (Compare David Truman, *The Governmental Process*, (New York: Knopf, 1959), pp. 159, 463–467, 506–528.)

59. Kearns, *Johnson and the American Dream*, pp. 92, 120, 181, 184, 221–222; Reedy, *Johnson*, p. xii; Valenti, *A Very Human President*, pp. 178–179, 189, 200; *The Vantage Point*, pp. 448, 451.

60. *The Vantage Point*, pp. 343–344; Kearns, *Johnson and the American Dream*, pp. x, xi, 34, 36, 64.

61. *The Vantage Point*, pp. 29, 72, 79; Kearns, pp. 97, 113.

62. Joseph C. Goulden, *Meany* (New York: Atheneum, 1972), pp. 297–298, 336–403; Dugger, *The Politician*, pp. 197, 225–226, 230, 232, 287–294; see also Marc K. Landy, "The Political Imperative: George Meany's Strategy of Political Leadership," *Leadership in America*, edited by Peter Dennis Bathory (New York: Longmans, 1978, pp. 79–96.

63. Reedy, *Johnson*, pp. 59–69.

64. V.O. Key, *Southern Politics* (New York: Random House, 1949), pp. 254–276, 298–311.

65. David Broder, *The Party's Over* (New York: Harper & Row, 1977), pp. 76–77; *The Vantage Point*, p. 433; Kearns, *Johnson and the American Dream*, pp. 155, 244.

66. For example, see Joel Silbey, *The Shrine of Party* Pittsburgh: Univ. of Pittsburgh Press, 1967).

67. Gerald M. Pomper, ed., *Party Renewal in America* (New York: Praeger, 1981).

68. David Price, "Community, 'Mediating Structures' and Public Policy," *Soundings 62* (1979): 369–394, especially pp. 382–385.

69. Kearns, *Johnson and the American Dream*, p. 69; Dugger, *The Politician*, pp. 123–129; Valenti, *A Very Human President*, p. 206.

70. Theodore White, *The Making of the President, 1960* (New York: Artheneum, 1961), pp. 132–133; *The Vantage Point*, p. 109; Valenti, *A Very Human President*, p. 208.

71. Reedy, *Johnson*, pp. 12, 18, 45–46; McPherson, *A Political Education*, pp. 106, 107; Dugger, *The Politician*, pp. 297, 371; speaking to please was an old habit; he apparently gave speeches to his college dates in order to impress them (*My Brother Lyndon*, p. 28).

72. *The Vantage Point*, 158, 451; Kearns, pp. *Johnson and the American Dream*, pp. 92, 109, 128, 142, 154, 244.

73. McPherson, *A Political Education*, p. 172; Kearns, *Johnson and the American Dream*, p. x, 122, 127, 225; Valenti, *A Very Human President*, pp. 188–189, 193, 199; Reedy, *Johnson*, p. xii.

74. Kearns, *Ibid.*, pp. 14, 128, 150, 154–155, 354–356.

75. *The Vantage Point,* pp. 30–31, 95, 110, 427.

76. *The Vantage Point,* pp. 27, 35.

77. Kearns, *Johnson and the American Dream,* pp. 156–157; on the evangelical ideal, see Alan Heimert, *Religion and the American Mind* (Cambridge, Mass.: Harvard Univ. Press, 1966).

78. For a similar view, see Robert Bellah, *The Broken Covenant* (New York: Seabury, 1975).

79. Herbert Y. Schandler, *The Unmaking of a President: Lyndon Johnson and Vietnam* (Princeton, N.J.: Princeton Univ. Press, 1977), pp. 52–53; Leslie Gelb, "The Essential Domino: American Opinion and Vietnam," *Foreign Affairs 50* (1972): 459–475.

80. Phil G. Goulding, *Confirm or Deny* (New York: Harper & Row, 1970), pp. 81–82; Col. Harry Summers, *On Strategy: The Vietnam War in Context* (Carlisle, Pa.: U.S. Army War College, 1981), p. 8; he made a halfhearted effort after Tet, but by then it was far too late. (Schandler, *The Unmaking of a President,* pp. 248–249; McPherson, *A Political Education,* pp. 393–394; Don Oberdorfer, *Tet* (Garden City, N.Y.: Doubleday, 1971), pp. 294–295).

81. Kearns, *Johnson and the American Dream,* pp. 142, 252–253, 282, 338; Summers, *On Strategy,* p. 8; Valenti, *A Very Human President,* pp. 300, 354–355.

82. Schandler, *The Unmaking of a President,* pp. 20, 22, 39, 56; Summers, *On Strategy,* pp. 14–15; Kearns, *Johnson and the American Dream,* pp. 296, 302.

83. Schandler, *The Unmaking of a President,* p. 56.

84. *Ibid.,* pp. 66–67, 79, 82, 99–101, 110–111, 115–116, 183–184, 199–202, 210–211, 327–328.

85. McPherson, *A Political Education,* pp. 302–303.

86. *Democracy in America,* vol. 2, p. 297.

20

Comments on Part VI

Harry C. McPherson, Jr.

I want to commend Professor McWilliams for a really interesting chapter. I hope it will be one of many serious looks at Lyndon Johnson as something other than a fellow who used to yell in the Taj Mahal and embarrass the United States, or who had an outsized cowboy idea of what we could do in Vietnam and who got us all into a lot of grief. It's a serious chapter and one that very much repaid my rereading.

When I think of the word *greatness,* I think of excellence, and I think of the George Will column commenting that there are really only two institutions of excellence in America: the Baltimore Orioles and the telephone company; Will said that the government is fiddling around with the second one, so it may be that the Orioles will be the only institution of excellence left.[1] Lyndon Johnson may not be the last of the great presidents; there may be others. But he is to me the last of the really interesting ones. Since Johnson, the others have simply just not been as interesting.

Professor McWilliams says that Johnson did neglect or scorn public speech. Particularly for somebody who wrote speeches for him, like me or John Roche, that was a particularly gruesome fact. When you wrote something that was spectacular and when you said it in your own mind and felt so wonderful about it that you were practically singing it, and then you would hear it read—it was painful. Professor McWilliams' description is perfect: Johnson converted into angry vehemence something that was meant to be conciliatory. He could not keep the emphasis from falling like stones out of a sack on the street.

And then you would see him with a small group, and there was nobody as good. I first saw him in this way in 1957, at a breakfast in Abilene, Texas, with a bunch of rural electrificaiton cooperative people. Johnson electrified his district in more ways than one. In the tenth congressional district of Texas he brought in electricity by persuading FDR to help him out. So these were his people—farmers and others who were involved in the REA districts. They came in one morning when we were on a tour of West Texas to get some support for his politics and they had breakfast with him. We waited for him a long time. He came down; he was grumpy about something, as usual, and he had two or three bowls of cream of wheat. I remember he listened to these farmers and REA people talking as he ate cream of wheat, and then he started talking while still eating. It was a loud, slurping kind of performance. But as he got into it, it went on for about forty-five minutes and I don't think I've ever heard a better political talk. He was talking to about thirty or forty people, most of them standing around the room as he finished his breakfast. He talked about their stake in a better economy and lower interest rates and he said, "You know who people like us have got to tie up with are people like Walter Reuther and the auto workers."

He began in a way that was not really as exciting or popular as William Jennings Bryan might have been or someone else in the 1960s. But in an extremely persuasive and telling way, he was able to make these people see what kinship they had, and how much of a common purpose they had, with workers and labor unions. Labor unions were not the thing that most Texas farmers were willing to tie up with. He talked about legislation then current. He talked about the Eisenhower administration and about George Humphrey, secretary of the treasury, and tight money policies generally. He was funny, and as he really got rolling and as his blood got going, he was just terrific.

He was essentially an operator among representatives, not a public persuader. He was at his best operating with representatives of other groups—political representatives, business representatives, representatives of civil rights groups. He could go to a place and speak to 1,000 blacks and he would be rather nervous, even though he was responsible for getting the 1957, 1960, 1964, 1965, and 1968 Civil Rights Acts through—they were all his and Martin Luther King's products. But he was his best talking to a room full of people like Roy Wilkins and Whitney Young. He would not have been worth a hoot talking to a Chamber of Commerce convention. He really had nothing in common with Chamber of Commerce conventions, but he was terrific talking with a half dozen or a dozen business leaders—the head of U.S. Steel, Henry Ford, people like that. And he was an inspiring teacher with them. He made them feel awful if they weren't willing to make some jobs available to hire some people in the slums. He fired them up. Walter Haus of Levi Strauss became so fired up by LBJ's talk about the responsibility of business to hire blacks that he went back out to California and he hired twelve people and put them on his own payroll to go out and teach black businessmen the principle of accounting, inventory control, and so on. He just thought that's what he ought to do. He would come back from Washington and write a letter to Johnson which said, "I've done that—is that enough?" LBJ was at his best at such inspiration.

Johnson's main line of operation, of course, was down Pennsylvania Avenue between the White House and Congress. I described it in my book as the armature of the dynamo of government. Johnson was excellent on that street, the fifteen blocks or so between the White House and the Congress. He was not so good at dealing with the public in the mass. This is a particular problem when you're thinking about 200 million people, and you're trying to sense what their politics are; where they are. The American president is not like a banana republic dictator or maybe even the president of the French Republic.

John Roche would say that the American president has almost no intelligence network in this country. He has a bunch of regional offices of Housing and Urban Development, Health and Human Services, Medicare, and the Internal Revenue Service around, but he doesn't really have an intelligence network that gets back to him with a sense of what's going on except among politicians. The point Professor McWilliams made about Johnson's shortcomings as a party politican is quite true and quite unfortunate. One of the sad things about our current political condition is the weakness of our political parties; we pay for it every week. Presidents lack an intelligence–gathering network that is devoted to them but also devoted to telling them the truth.

Some presidents compensate for this lack with intuition or particular skill in speaking and communicating. Johnson did not compensate for it with anything really. He was not a great communicator through today's method of communication, television. He was in fact grim. He came on like a Methodist bishop. He sincerely attempted to sound just as nice and simple and cards-on-the-table as could be, and everybody thought: That's not real. In fact it was *not* real. He *was* an operator. When he had just worked out a fantastic compromise by trading off all kinds of things in the back room, he would come out and put on a face of benign soporific sanctimony, and everybody would say, "Holy Moses! That can't be true!"

It's impossible to think of his presidency absent the events and the environment that surrounded him. He came into office a Texan mistrusted by most of the northern liberal elements of the Democratic party. The city bosses thought he was pretty fine. Many of them were his friends from way back. But he knew that he had to earn his way into the favor of the main parts of the Democratic party: blacks, Jews, the elements that have made up the Roosevelt coalition for a long time. So he had worked hard at that and it was one of the driving forces, along with his profound sense of trying to rectify the wrongs of many years, that caused him to be the great civil rights president he was. That was one environmental circumstance. Another was obviously the Vietnam War.

A third was the long-building pressure for equal rights, for justice for Negro Americans which exploded in Johnson's time. This occurred appropriately and bravely in the marches in the South and in the sit-ins that finally resulted in the civil rights legislation, and excessively and inappropriately in the riots in the cities. The riots had a devastating effect on the coalition that was necessary to put through the liberal legislation of the 1960s. When black Americans began burning down the inner cities, the Johnson administration, representing black Americans as their administration, caring for them, tried to respond in ways that were helpful. The turmoil, the absolute tempest of language and emotion, that this stirred up in black Americans, in labor unions, in the Archie Bunkers, and all the rest of them who had supported a lot of the basic legislation of the great society—Medicare, education, and the rest of it—had a fractionating effect. It really hit the coalition like a hammer and broke it.

I remember in 1968 talking with Richard Scammon, the wise man and pollster. I asked, "How does Johnson strengthen his position as a civil libertarian?" Scammon said,

> If I were you I'd get him photographed with a man in blue, get him photographed with a policeman. Because what the democratic voter wants is a guy who will get social justice done but will also make sure that the streets are okay to walk on and that nobody's going to burn them down.[1]

And finally, the baby boom produced a gigantic cohort, as the sociologists would call it: the young with young attitudes, the Beatles; left politics; people taking over colleges. John Roche went back from the White House to Brandeis and found himself surrounded by it at every turn. This created an atmosphere, both among the young and among their parents. People remember that parents were wearing the open shirts with the chains and other youthful garb; they remember the slogan "Don't trust anybody over 30." All of that created a very troublesome situation for a man who, despite his distaste for a lot of the Chamber of Commerce types, was still kind of an institutionalist, who sort of believed in the fundamental institutions of the society and didn't really think that they ought to get shoved over the side simply because somebody nineteen years old with a bullhorn said they should be.

Note

1. Harry McPherson. *A Political Education* (Boston: Little, Brown, 1972), pp. 377–378.

21
Comments on Part VI

John P. Roche

At the moment I'm involved in teaching Roman law, and this may influence my view. It thus seems to me that Professor McWilliams has done a remarkable job of transforming Lyndon Johnson from a Roman to a Greek. That is, if we can say that Arthur Schlesinger deified Robert Kennedy, I think Professor McWilliams has reified LBJ.

Indeed, if Johnson had not died some years before the cordless phone, he undoubtedly would have taken one with him to the grave. I can hear him now calling Harry McPherson or me and saying, "What's that professor saying about me?" I think the McWilliams chapter is a singular exercise in bringing out, at quite an abstract level of analysis, a number of aspects of the Johnson administration that are underestimated, or sometimes deliberately distorted. If I had to analyze Johnson, the first thing I would challenge is the common notion that he was some kind of an unprincipled megalomaniac. In fact, he was a man who went up and down like a yo-yo, torn by conflicting principles and interests. Johnson needed an ear; he had to talk. People, when he started screaming in their presence, thought that he was screaming at them. Harry McPherson and I, who were a couple of the "ears," realized that he was actually screaming at the cosmos in our presence. For example, after one of those infamous press conferences, I observed to one of my friends in the White House that I thought the president came over like a stuffed moose. A couple of days later he collared me and said, "I understand you said I looked like a stuffed moose." I said, "Yeah." He said, "That's what Lady Bird thinks."

Johnson, like Hubert Humphrey, was born without an ironic chromosome. If you happen to come from my cultural background, you tend to be a bit ironic on occasion. For example, right after he had his operation and showed his scar to a number of reporters, I was out to lunch with my friend, Mel Elfin, the Washington bureau chief, from now to eternity I take it, of *Newsweek*. Mel said to me, "Why the hell did Johnson show his scar?" I said, "Mel, one thing that we should really be happy about is that he wasn't operated on for hemorrhoids." The next week "Periscope," a *Newsweek* feature, appeared with that particular quote. I hadn't left the house that morning (Johnson got the first copy; I think the ink was still wet) when he called me at home as I was getting

---

I did not have the opportunity to read Mr. McWilliams' chapter in advance of its delivery at the symposium.

ready to come to the office. I picked up the phone and this mournful voice said, "Johnny, you know some times you're really not very funny," and he hung up. That was that; no verbal vitriol, no keel-hauling. He knew I had him figured right.

Johnson was a profound believer in the doctrine of original sin, although he would certainly not have articulated it in that fashion. He started with the assumption that basically there is a good bit of the sinner in all of us, including himself. One day I was in the Oval Office on some business (I think it was in 1967), and he was sitting there with a yellow pad with a whole list of things on it. The phone rang and it was Secretary McNamara. Johnson said, "Now, Bob, you do need a nuclear frigate ... no, Bob, you *do* need another nuclear frigate and the ideal place that they're just ready to build it right now is in Baton Rouge, that's in Louisiana you know." He motioned to me to pick up the phone on the dead button, and there was Bob McNamara explaining how his cost benefit computers had all said he didn't need another nuclear frigate. And the president said, "Bob, you *do* need another nuclear frigate and you just *go right ahead* and get one, and Baton Rouge is just the place."

> He hung up and looked at me and said, You know, Johnny, your liberal friends would have said that I was just immoral, but you know why we're going to have a nice brand new nuclear frigate? Because, [and excuse my vulgarity] when there was a cloture vote on the Voting Rights bill, old [Senator] Allen Ellender didn't vote. If he had, it would have taken two liberal votes to take him out. He just happened to go take a piss at that point and, as a consequence, we got cloture.

Then he asked, "Which do your liberal friends think is more important, voting rights or a nuclear frigate?" That's a good question.

Another time, somebody had just written that he had been the "dictator of the Senate." He said, "Dictator? [as Majority Leader] I was no dictator of the Senate." He wheeled on me and asked, "Do you know why I had that power? I did all the work for them. Senators are lazy; most wouldn't roll over in bed for the Second Coming. I did their work for them and now they're screaming I was a dictator."

I don't think he ever read the tenth or fifty-first *Federalist* papers, by Madison, or the ninth, by Hamilton, but he believed that the essence of politics was decisions and not conclusions. During the Middle Eastern war in 1967, the State Department decided that the president didn't really know enough about the Middle East to do an intelligent job of deciding what to do. So a State Department representative called me and asked if he could send over a couple of briefers, one to brief the president on the history of Zionism, and the other to brief him on Arab Nationalism. I talked to the president about it, and so, on the appointed day, two foreign service officers appeared with excellent briefings.

After they finished, he thanked them very much. (By the way, he absorbed it all in his mental computer. It was incredible. He did not do research, but he listened and he picked things up that way.) Then he turned to the two foreign service officers and he said,

> Now, gentlemen, I'd like to ask you a question. You told me a great deal about Arab Nationalism and I appreciate it, and you told me a great deal about Zionism, and I appreciate it. Right now Nasser has the Strait of Tiran blockaded. What does your history tell me to do?

The two State Department officers passed, went back to the Department, and said they'd been bullied! This, of course, is characteristic, because most State Department professionals are like scholars or researchers writing M.A. or Ph.D. dissertations. Johnson had to make a decision, to take positive action. He approached politics from that point of view.

One of the key differences between Ronald Reagan and Lyndon Johnson, both of whom are outsiders in terms of the so-called Northeastern Establishment, is that Ronald Reagan really doesn't give a damn what the boys from Harvard with the pigs on their ties, or with the skull and bones on their ties from Yale think about. Reagan couldn't care less. Where he comes from, they have spurs and Adam Smith on their neckties. Johnson did care. He lived in the shadow of Jack Kennedy and then Bobby. He was conviced that not a sparrow fell in politics without the intervention of Robert F. Kennedy. I tried to work him out of that. In his biography of Kennedy, Arthur Schlesinger, Jr. quoted a couple of my memos. He thought they were pretty awful, but when I reread them I thought they were pretty good. (Everyone to his own memos!) Johnson always wanted the "Establishment's" favor.

What you are seeing in 1984 is the triumph of the jacquerie with Ronald Reagan. The country's self-styled natural leaders are not getting called upon. It's the same thing that is happening with Margaret Thatcher. Hardly a day goes by without an Etonian being defenestrated from the Cabinet Room in 10 Downing Street. Out they come and bounce on the street; it's outrageous you know, *no* Etonians in the cabinet? They had a virtual Tory monopoly and now Maggie's bringing in the jacquerie. In France, they're protected because any cleanup of the top bureaucrats is being handled by other top bureaucrats— "Enarques"—so I think we can anticipate no severe changes in the structure of the French bureaucracy. But LBJ had this inferiority complex toward what the Rockefellers thought about him, what the intellectuals thought about him. I kept trying to get him to fire disloyal political appointees, mostly "Jacobites" rallying around the "Old Pretender," Bobby. He couldn't do it. They had a jinx on him—in fact, a self-inflicted jinx.

A basic part of Johnson's character was a very elemental loyalty to those he felt merited it. It could come out in a very eccentric way. For example, he did not attend Churchill's funeral. Why? He claimed to have a cold, but he did not have a cold. The reason he did not attend Churchill's funeral was that Churchill did not come to FDR's funeral. This led to a terrific brouhaha about Hubert, who wanted to go. LBJ was mad at Hubert about something at that point; he used to say that the way to get confidential material out around Washington was "telephone, telegraph, or tell Hubert." At any rate, Chief Justice Warren was sent to the funeral.

This kind of loyalty lived on with him. And it went along with his suspicion of mass politics. He wanted to know all the players. He wanted to have a feel for them, literally. Once I was watching him in the Oval Office meeting with Lee Quan Ju, Prime Minister of Singapore. By the time they finished a fascinating talk (it was supposed to be fifteen minutes, and I think it ran over an hour; the Joint Chiefs of Staff were sitting in the Cabinet Room waiting and there was a line around the block). Johnson practically had "Harry Lee" by the knee. (When you had that huge hand grabbing your knee, you really knew it.) He wanted to know all the individual players, and believed that politics was founded on private relationships.

He also accepted as given that circumstances altered the application of principles. This is a proposition which those of us raised in the Irish political tradition can understand. It is illustrated by the story of the Irish farmer who lines up his seven sons one morning, and said, "All right, who pushed the outhouse into the Shannon." Not one of them said a word.

> Now let me tell you a little story, [he said]. Once upon a time the Americans had a grand president, he was the father of his country, George Washington. In fact, we even have him on a Free State stamp. You know, one day George went out in a bad mood, and chopped down his Da's cherry tree. And that night his Da said, "George, who chopped down me cherry tree?" George said, "Da, I cannot tell a lie, I did it." Because George was so well behaved and so honest and showed such integrity, his Da did not punish him. Now, who pushed the outhouse into the Shannon?

Sean, the oldest son said, "Da, I did." At which point the old man took off his belt, and laid on, started walloping him. The second son, Seamus said, "Da, don't, you just told us about George Washington and how his Da didn't punish him when he told the truth." His father stopped laying it on and said, "Seamus, George Washington's Da wasn't sitting in the cherry tree." Circumstances invariably alter the applicaion of principles!

Lyndon Johnson had a tropism for inside politics. He looked on the Senate as the ultimate political universe. He would make a deal; it worked. The troops delivered. But when he got into the open politics of the presidency, he found himself out of his depth. In the Senate he could say to Senator X, "You miss this vote and everything will work out all right, and don't say I suggested it. Say somebody else did." These guys would go off and mind their own business and it would not hit the press. But the minute you start, in effect, trying to operate private politics in the presidency, you develop what is called a credibility problem. You are now dealing with structural forces, the media particularly.

To end up on a critical note, I would say that the most difficult aspect of Johnson's character was his lack of a sense of limits. The Greek word *telos* has two meanings: both purpose and limit. Johnson lacked that sense of limits. I recall a press conference of his in 1967. Bill Moyers earlier had come up with the idea of putting a Band-Aid over the red light of the camera so Johnson wouldn't know when he was on, but he still froze, hanging on to that podium. Finally on November 17, 1967, we got a throat mike on him and he walked back and forth and was spectacular. He called up and said, "How did I do? What do you think? How did I do?" I said, "Oh, I thought you did an absolutely superb job. Now for God's sake, don't do seventeen more in the next three days." That would be his manic custom. If a walk with reporters around the White House grounds worked beautifully one day, he would hold five more the next—at which point, all the reporters would be off to their foot doctors, complaining.

But the one redeeming dimension of it was that he knew he lacked this sense of limits. One minute he would be pounding his chest as King of the Hill; a few minutes later he would ask, almost like a child, "Why did I do that stupid thing?"

Part VII
Nixon

22

The Nixon Presidency

John J. Rhodes

I have been asked to discuss the presidency of Richard Nixon. I am glad to try, but first I must define the yardstick I am using in measuring this man and his stewardship.

Many people have tried to formulate a job description for the president of the United States. It isn't easy. There is no such thing as on-the-job training. The individual who succeeds to the presidency must take whatever baggage he already possesses and try to grow into the job.

The presidency of the United States is undoubtedly the toughest job in the world. Not only does the president have the personal responsibility for executing the laws passed by the Congress, he is also the person responsible for assessing the state of the union and recommending legislation which appears to be necessary for the welfare of the nation. The president and vice president are the only two people elected by all of the people of the United States. The president is, therefore, the undoubted and unchallenged leader of the nation. Since our nation is the strongest one in the Free World, this makes him in effect the leader of the Free World. The capability of the person who fills that position is extremely important. Its requirements are awesome indeed.

A prime requisite for a president is a thorough knowledge of history. I happen to believe profoundly in the truism "the past is prologue." Unless the president is well aware of situations which have occurred in the history of the world in general and this country in particular, he will likely be overwhelmed by some of the problems that he faces. He will also be tempted to reinvent the wheel on too many occasions instead of following paths which had succeeded in the past.

The president must also have a thorough knowledge of the contemporary world, and a sound basis in geopolitics. He needs to know the scenery on the stage upon which he will perform. He also needs to know the other members of the cast, who, like himself, are heads of state.

The president must have an understanding of both the domestic and world economies. As the leader of the strongest nation in the Free World he bears a large share of the responsibility for keeping a stable economy capable of producing the necessities required for the health and happiness of its people. The interplay of the forces of supply and demand, the intricacies of the international monetary system, and the needs and aspirations of the nations of the world are worthy of his concentrated study.

The system of alliances and understandings around the world, and the hopes and fears of the people and leaders of the various nations are items of indispensable knowledge to one who must be concerned with world politics.

The president must have the ability to communicate. The greatest ideas are of no value unless they are expressed in such a way that they can be understood and appraised by the leaders and the people of the world.

A president must have at least the personal attributes, which I list without reference to the order of priority:

1. An economic and political philosophy
2. A liking for his fellow man
3. The ability to make decisions promptly
4. Personal integrity
5. Belief in a Supreme Being
6. A dash of humility
7. A lot of self-confidence

A president must have, or he must very quickly acquire, a deep knowledge of the three branches of government and the way each impinges upon the other. Equally important is a knowledge of the framework of the various state governments and the particular problems and assets of each state. The last but by no means least attribute of a successful president is a well-developed sense of humor. His failures will be many. His vexations will be frequent. The people and the news media will frequently misjudge him, and he will feel that they are being unfair. Unless he is able to keep his eye on the big picture, and put the lesser annoyances which he must endure in their proper places, he will not only not be able to do a good job, he will loathe every minute of his incumbency.

Measuring the Richard Nixon who was elected president in 1968 against this job description, you come to the conclusion that this man was as well prepared for the presidency as any person in our country's history. He had served in the House and the Senate, and for eight years as vice president of the United States. If there had been a presidential training school, he would have graduated cum laude. He certainly had a fine knowledge of history, the contemporary world, and geopolitics. He was never a great student of the domestic economy or the world economy, but he certainly understood the interplay of international politics and geopolitics, as well as any man could. He and Henry Kissinger made a superb team in the conduct of foreign policy because each had a basic understanding of the world and its problems, and the kind of treatment needed to further the interest of the United States of America while dealing with other nations.

Richard Nixon certainly had the ability to communicate. He was a forceful and convincing speaker. He spoke without notes, but certainly not without preparation. In fact, I was in his hotel room on an occasion prior to his election to the presidency, when he was writing a speech on a yellow pad. I asked him if he had the means of having it typed and he said "Oh no, I don't want to type it. In fact, I'll probably tear it up after I memorize it."

His personal attributes would give him a mixed score. He certainly had a philosophy and the ability to make decisions. There is grave doubt as to whether or not he really liked his fellow man, and, in the latter days of his administration, his personal integrity was subject to question. As for humility, I doubt that he could even spell the word. He gave the impression of being supremely self-confident. However, I am told that some psychologists might come to the conclusion that the ego displayed came from a deep-seated feeling of inferiority. I am not making that judgment, but I do advance the possibility that persons more qualified than I in psychology have done so.

While I would not really say that President Nixon had a well-developed sense of humor, he certainly did have a sense of humor. One personal instance bears out this analysis. At a leadership meeting when I was chairman of the Republican Policy Committee, there was a question as to whether the Congress would take a certain action before adjourning for a long recess. I said:

> Mr. President, if Congress does not act, I suggest very strongly that you call the Congress back into Special Session for the purpose of completing this legislation. If you do this, I would also like to request protection from the Secret Service, because my own colleagues will probably try to assassinate me for what I have just said.

I went back to my office and within one hour my secretary told me that Mr. Smith, a Secret Service man, was outside and wanted to talk to me. He came into my private office and said "President Nixon has told me to be at your disposal and protect your life." I said, "Is this the way President Nixon tells me he will call the Congress back into Special Session?" The gentleman said, "I don't know, Sir, but he told me to stay with you until I was dismissed." I said, "You're dismissed now, and tell the President that I get his message."

Richard Nixon was elected president in 1968 over Hubert Humphrey by a margin not much larger than the one by which John Kennedy had defeated him in 1960. Both houses of Congress were dominated by the Democratic party. President Nixon was never popular with Democrats. He was extremely partisan, and had, in the Jerry Voorhees and Helen Gahagan Douglas campaigns, been accused of being not only partisan but unfair. His personality could be very brusque, and very brash. In some ways he was easy to dislike, and many Democrats found those ways.

Thus, he came in with an uncertain mandate, and with many members of the congressional majority prepared to dislike him. This was not an enviable position, to put it mildly.

Also, President Nixon inherited the most unpopular war in our history. When he took office, we had over one-half million Americans in Vietnam. We had suffered casualties which saddened and sickened most of the American population. Our reasons for being in the war were never explained adequately by either the Kennedy administration or the Johnson administration and, therefore, our people were making sacrifices that they did not want to make and did not understand.

During the 1968 campaign, Nixon said that he had a way to end the war. He never elaborated on this until after he became president. Then it became apparent that he truly did want to end the war but not with the loss of South Vietnam to the Communists. His secretary of defense, Melvin R. Laird, was the author of the Vietnamization program. The concept was to build up the capabilities of the South Vietnamese army and air force so that the United States could withdraw its forces and South Vietnam could defend itself from incursions from the predatory North Vietnamese.

Unfortunately, intervening events made it impossible to complete the process of Vietnamization successfully. The "sixties' generation" mainly were disenchanted with the war. It is true that most of the members of that generation went along loyally and served in the armed forces when drafted, but many of that generation and other Americans too, demonstrated against the war. In many instances, those demonstrations turned into full-fledged riots. Draft dodging and desertion were common. The situation at home was not good, to say the least.

Although Richard Nixon was supposed to have been a "tough guy," those demonstrations and the fervor of the opposition to the Vietnam war disturbed him deeply. They also encouraged the North Vietnamese and made it more difficult to have meaningful negotiations for peace between the belligerents.

Even so, by the end of 1972, things were going our way. The full-fledged attack of the North Vietnamese in a conventional manner employing many divisions, which occurred in late 1972, was turned back, largely by the South Vietnamese. The bombing which took place in December of 1972 and January of 1973 practically decimated the ability of North Vietnam to support the war. It was then that the North Vietnamese finally agreed to meaningful negotiations, and the treaty which purported to end the Vietnam War was signed in 1973.

As we know, the Vietnam War was not thus concluded. The South Vietnamese held the North Vietnamese at bay for almost two years, with the help which we gave them. However, in the end, the South Vietnamese were overrun by a cunning, resourceful enemy who refused to play by the rules we thought they had agreed to.

The final blow to South Vietnam came when the House of Representatives refused to adopt an emergency authorization and appropriation of $300 million, asked for by President Ford, to bolster the South Vietnamese forces, which were in danger of being overrun. The morale of the South Vietnamese was shattered. They were confronted by an enemy who was freshly supplied by Russia, freshly manned, and whose infrastructure had been rebuilt. Their own infrastructure was a shambles. They were short of ammunition, fuel, transportation, aircraft, and most of the munitions of war. The final debacle was certain and foreseeable.

It is easy to second guess Nixon's conduct of the Vietnam War. As previously mentioned, he felt deeply the divisions in the nation which sprang from American involvement in Vietnam. Perhaps this caused him to start withdrawing increments of American troops, probably sooner than he should have. I can certainly understand the political desirability of "bringing the boys home." However, withdrawal of Americans at that time, with Vietnamization still a dream and North Vietnamese troops still on the soil of South Vietnam, gave the wrong signal to everyone. It encouraged the North Vietnamese, discouraged the South Vietnamese, and did not help the domestic situation very much.

There were times when the North Vietnamese army was almost completely committed in South Vietnam. Hindsight indicates that an Inchon-type landing in North Vietnam at that time promised great success in disorganizing and perhaps overrunning the logistical rear of the North Vietnamese army. Had we been committed to winning that war, we would have found this opportunity to be irresistible.

Many of us felt that it was a mistake for the United States to have involved itself so deeply in Vietnam. However, since we were there, and so deeply mired in that struggle, it may have been that the best way out was to do everything necessary for the conquest of North Vietnam. After that, Vietnamization could have proceeded full speed, with almost 100 percent assurance of success. This would have taken longer American involvement, but in the final analysis, we may have had success instead of failure and perhaps would have shortened the war considerably.

However, by the time this opportunity occurred, the United States had been led to anticipate an end to American involvement in this unpopular war. Even a president who had been recently elected by an overwhelming majority might have found trouble maintaining popular support for an escalation. The mold had already been set, and we now know that the course to eventual loss of South Vietnam was then irreversible.

Had President Nixon's mandate in 1968 been greater, he might well have taken a more aggressive course in Vietnam—one calculated to bring victory. Vietnamization was a gamble which might well have worked had the support of the American people for our effort in that part of the world not waned so rapidly. As it turned out, Vietnamization took at least four years, and then, because of the failure of American public support, failed. Perhaps President Nixon should have realized that the time it would take for Vietnamization was probably not available to him considering the rapidity with which American support for the war was disappearing. Then he would have had only two alternatives: (1) cut and run, getting our people out as fast as possible, or (2) adopt a strategy calculated to win the war.

I do not fault his choice of the Vietnamization strategy, considering the situation which confronted him. I only regret that under the circumstance it was not possible to have followed a course which would have saved the people of Indochina from the agony they have suffered.

The tragic sequence of events we call "Watergate" must be dealt with. The most destructive phase of Watergate was the weakening of the American presidency just at a time when a strong president could have completed the work of Vietnamization and ensured the survival of a Democratic regime in Indochina. Instead of that, as the capabilities of our allies decreased, the Soviet Union rebuilt North Vietnam, resupplied its army, and enabled it to break the solemn obligations of the Treaty of Paris. The War Powers Act, obviously aimed at the already wounded President Nixon, cast further doubts upon American capabilities or desires to insist upon the performance of obligations undertaken under the Treaty of Paris. There was no longer any doubt that whatever North Vietnam did, we no longer had the will to intervene.

I do not intend to go into a long dissertation on Watergate. Suffice it to say that in my opinion, the combination of the unpopular Vietnam War and the overreaction of Richard Nixon to leaks of information from the White House probably were the root causes of the events which finally led to the resignation of a president of the United States.

I was well aware that the Nixon White House leaked like a sieve. On at least three occasions after meetings of the Republican leadership in the Cabinet Room, Jack Anderson quoted verbatim conservations which took place at those meetings. He quoted me several times, and always did so with absolute accuracy. It was enough to disturb anyone, and I certainly have no fault to find with the desire of President Nixon to discover the source of those leaks. Nonetheless, the formation of the "plumbers" was a classic bit of overkill. It was never properly controlled, and at last lurched into the chaos which not only brought down Richard Nixon, but damaged the Republican party almost beyond repair.

One of Richard Nixon's more noble attributes is loyalty to his friends. This virtue probably caused him to refrain from taking the actions which he should have taken as soon as Watergate broke, since many of those most intimately involved in the whole matter were close associates of the president.

I think every president should read Machiavelli's *The Prince*. The theme which runs through the entire work is "The Prince Must Survive." Others are expendable, but the prince and, in this case the presidency, must survive. Nixon's loyalty to his friends kept him from taking the action which any chief of state should have taken in order to protect not only the presidency, but the Republic itself.

It has always been a source of wonderment to me that the Nixon tapes were not destroyed. I know of no theory which adequately explains this. The best explanation I have heard is that both Bob Haldeman and Richard Nixon felt that the executive privilege would keep them from ever having to give up the tapes and that they could "stonewall it" to the end. What a price to pay for an extended ego trip, which those tapes represented!

The domestic policy of the Nixon administration deserves comment. Although Nixon thought of himself as a conservative, some of his domestic proposals were more to the liking of liberals than they were to members of his own party. The Family Assistance Plan which was crafted by Daniel Patrick Moynihan was in many ways a good plan. It would have been terribly expensive in the early years, but it at least had a chance of getting many people back to work and off of the welfare rolls. I supported it, as did Gerald Ford and many others whose conservative credentials were impeccable. However, the plan failed because of lack of sufficient congressional support, even from traditional liberals.

Nixon proposed a plan to reorganize the executive branch which had a great deal of promise. The underlying idea was to reduce the number of people who reported to a single boss. The government would have been divided into four superdepartments each comprising part of the present departmental structures of the government. The Democratic party-dominated Congress would have no part of this plan.

In fact, the Democrats made it very difficult for President Nixon to do much of anything toward cutting the size of the government. In his budgets he requested changes which would have saved money and undertook unilaterally to impound funds in areas which he thought could be cut. The Impoundment Act severely limited the power of the president to refuse to spend funds appropriated by the Congress. The federal government is still suffering from this ill-considered piece of legislation. Future students of government may well look with favor on the economic policies Richard Nixon tried to adopt. Because Watergate and Vietnam have overshadowed so much of the Nixon domestic program, the jury will be out for many years.

As previously stated, in Richard Nixon you saw a man who was on paper better prepared for the presidency than practically any man in our history. On the other side of the coin are events, some of which were caused by the president and his staff and some of which were not, which combined to flaw the entire administration. You also see personal traits of character, and unexpected shortcomings of performance on the part of the president himself, which contributed mightily to the downfall of the Nixon administration.

It was not easy for some members of Congress, including this one, to decide for impeachment. Unfortunately, quite a few of my colleagues had such a personal dislike for Nixon that they would have voted for even harsher treatment. Those of us who had worked with the president and respected his capabilities came to several conclusions: (1) The words of the president taken from his own tapes amounted to flagrant obstruction of justice, (2) the president's support in the country was irreversibly low, and (3) leaving him in office would have ensured a crippled presidency until 1977. We had to conclude that removing him would be more likely to strengthen the country.

We are fortunate that Gerald Ford came in, healed a lot of wounds, and restored integrity and respect to the presidency. The Republic survived another harsh test, but only after paying a horrible price. The full cost of this sad episode is still undetermined, and only future generations will be truly able to assess its cost in treasure, broken lives, loss of world esteem, and lowered national self-respect.

The bottom line is that this is still a great country—probably the greatest in history—because a great people have willed it to be so. They still do.

23
Comments on Part VII

Hedley W. Donovan

O ne of the most striking things in Congressman Rhodes's fine chapter is his list of desirable attributes for a president, which are all essentially qualities of character or the heart. These are more important than any specific past career pattern. Congressman Rhodes has pointed out that, on paper, Nixon was as well qualified as any president of the twentieth century, and it is interesting that the runner up would be Lyndon Johnson, whose past career pattern was quite similar. Johnson had been a federal bureaucrat briefly in the National Youth Administration (NYA) in Roosevelt's day. Nixon, though he didn't brag much about it, was in the Office of Price Administration (OPA) for the first year or so of World War II. They both served in the navy; they both served in the House of Representatives, went on to the Senate after the war; and both served as vice president. Nixon, in the interval between his 1960 run and his 1968 successful run, traveled very widely in the world on his private law business, which he very skillfully combined with political probings—I don't mean on his own behalf—which strengthened his own grasp of world affairs. So when he was elected in 1968, to judge by his formal biography up to that point, he could have had reasonable expectations for a very successful presidency. But I think his lack of some of the qualities that John Rhodes listed was indeed his ultimate undoing. The same might have been said about the undoing of Lyndon Johnson in a somewhat different fashion, but still his was essentially another broken presidency.

I would make a side bet with Congressman Rhodes that Nixon has read Machiavelli at least once. More to the point, Nixon was a big Disraeli fan, and he urged many of his associates to read a then quite recent biography of Disraeli by Robert Blake. He loved it when journalists or others in any way compared him with Disraeli. Elliot Richardson, who knew Nixon very well, having served him as secretary of defense, secretary of health, education, and welfare, and as attorney general, gave a talk at the University of Virginia not long ago on the Nixon presidency. From this point about Disraeli, Richardson has evolved what he considers to be the definitive explanation for Nixon's resignation from office. Blake's biography of Disraeli probably is the best biography of Disraeli that is ever going to be written, but the reader puts it down with the sense that this extraordinary, exotic, even bizarre creature remains elusive. How the dandy, the satirist, the Jew, the alien even, could ever have become leader of the

Conservative party, chancellor of the exchequer, prime minister, and favorite of Queen Victoria still remains a mystery. Now it seems reasonable to assume that Nixon put down the Disraeli volume with the same thought. When the time came, therefore, when it was the obvious move in self-preservation to destroy the tapes, he could not do it. The tapes were going to be the indispensable tool whereby his biographers would gain the insights denied to Blake in accounting for the career of Disraeli.

Richardson had an opportunity at a dinner sometime after Watergate to put this theory to Blake the author, now Lord Blake. "Lord Blake, do you realize that you're probably responsible for the resignation of Richard Nixon?" Blake looked at him blankly. Richardon said "No, I'm quite serious," and then gave this explanation. By the time he got through, Blake looked quite shaken.

John Kennedy was a great admirer or Lord Melbourne and impressed upon his White House staff the importance of reading David Cecil's biography of Melbourne, which was then current. I never heard Jimmy Carter identify his favorite nineteenth-century British prime minister and I doubt Reagan spends a lot of time on the point. I should specify my credentials for talking about Nixon because, although they are spread over a good many years, I have had some acquaintance with him for about thirty years. I think I first interviewed him as an editor just about thirty years ago just after he had become vice president. I saw him again last winter for a very fascinating two or three-hour conversation, partly about the Reagan presidency and partly about his views on foreign policy, some of which are reflected in his new book. Over the years in between I may have seen him on average once or twice a year, not counting a rather long gap starting in 1973 when *Time* magazine published an editorial (the first editorial in its history) urging him to resign.

Along with some members of *Time's* Washington Bureau, I was to have lunch with Alexander Haig, then Nixon's chief of staff, on the same day we were to publish this editorial urging Nixon to depart. I did not want any leak of our editorial, but on the Sunday evening before the Monday that the editorial was to be published, the same Monday we were to have the lunch, I asked one of my colleagues in the Washington Bureau to notify Haig that there was going to be something in *Time* the next morning that would distress him and perhaps would distress the president, and, if he wanted to cancel our lunch, I would understand. In his soldierly way, he came to lunch. When he arrived, looking a little bleak, I asked, "Well, what did you think of it?" and he said, "It's like getting up in the morning and getting hit in the face with a cold fish." Then I asked if the president had seen the editorial. And he said, "I think you can assume he has." That was as far as we got with that.

I was interested in John Rhodes's formulation of the bind that many members of the Congress would have been in if they had to choose between Agnew and Nixon. Nixon himself occasionally used to refer to Agnew as his insurance policy, not without reason. I happened to see Elliot Richardson shortly after he had brought down Agnew and then had himself resigned in the famous Saturday Night Massacre. I was congratulating Richardson (this would have been about December 1973) for finally making it possible for the impeachment or resignation of Nixon to take place which nobody in good conscience could have advocated as long as Agnew was vice president. Well, Richardson, though out of office, was still very much in Republican politics and not without thoughts about a further career, so he accepted my compliments without comment. But the Justice Department easing of Agnew out of office was what made it possible for congressmen and others to contemplate impeachment, or, failing that, resignation.

It is interesting to speculate whether Nixon, in history or even in his own lifetime may be somewhat better regarded than he was the day he resigned. We have all seen the revisionism applied to Eisenhower's benefit in recent years. A president once very lowly regarded, particularly by academics and intellectuals, is now generally rated as quite a successful president, particularly in view of what has transpired since. Truman began being upgraded almost as soon as he left office. He was at a very low ebb in the public opinion polls during his last year, or year and a half, as president, but began rising quite rapidly.

As to Nixon, my own speculation is that he will be slightly better regarded in the future than he was in 1973–74; but not spectacularly so. He has got two or three things working for him; one is simply the process of getting older, appearing in pictures with some white in his hair or with his very attractive children and grandchildren. It is hard even for the most addicted Nixon haters to feel quite as bitter as they might have ten or twelve years ago. By the time somebody gets to be seventy-five, eighty, or eighty-five, it gets harder to hate him. Herbert Hoover was thoroughly reviled and despised on the day he left office, being very widely blamed for the Depression. Partly just by living to be ninety, he came to a grand old man. He wrote quite pleasant memoirs, and made stout Republican speeches at Republican gatherings, and finally inspired a good deal of affection. Well, without suggesting any disrespect to Hoover or Nixon, I wonder how we would feel about Adolf Hitler if he were still alive. He'd be in his midnineties; we might see a photo of him puttering around a garden in a prison compound somewhere, Eva perhaps at his side. It probably would not be possible to hate him quite as much as we did. But time will do something for him.

Aging will do something for Nixon, but more important is a greater general appreciation of his foreign policy achievements. In his books, he has concentrated almost entirely on foreign policy, analyzing current problems but also reminding us, not too subtly, of his own accomplishments. We will not linger over how much was his accomplishment and how much was Kissinger's but, in one way or another, they were a very effective team. Richard Nixon certainly does not want us to forget that; nor does Henry Kissinger, from his somewhat different perspective. When we see Nixon appearing on the Op-Ed Page of the *New York Times,* of all places, perhaps once a year, it's really quite startling.

Nixon's reputation will also be helped—this is perhaps an unpleasant reflection of human nature—by the somewhat disagreeable and disillusioning revelations about other presidents. The revelation of the full extent of the Kennedy tapings does not justify by any means what Nixon did, but it makes it seem a little less horrendous. Presumably there is no evidence of obstruction of justice coming out of the Kennedy tapes, but there definitely was eavesdropping. Even the sainted Franklin Roosevelt had some tapes running for a while. The tremendous biographical assaults that are being conducted against Lyndon Johnson, are, in a perverse way, perhaps slightly beneficial to Nixon's reputation. So I speculate he will look a bit better today than he did ten years ago.

The dynamite still to be exploded, I do not know how much dynamite there is, is that the great bulk of his tapes have not yet been heard. Assuming there are no further illegalities disclosed, there's still a strong probability of pretty unpleasant episodes and passages that may offset much, if not all, of what might be a modest improvement in his place in history.

24
Comments on Part VII

Robert Scigliano

Congressman Rhodes has in his chapter answered one question that was in my mind, and perhaps in Richard Nixon's mind, too, at one point: how he regarded Nixon. In his *Memoirs,* Nixon discusses his last meeting with congressional leaders, in which he informed them he was going to resign his office. Mike Mansfield did not react; Hugh Scott seemed friendly and sympathetic; and Nixon says of Rhodes that he was his usual pleasant self, and noncommittal. I think Mr. Rhodes has clarified his position in his chapter. I was impressed with its presentation because it reflects considerable thought by Mr. Rhodes on President Nixon, and it attempts to be fair to him and to the record. The assessment is clearly a favorable one overall. My task is made more difficult because I find myself in close agreement with Rhodes both with respect to the favorable aspects of Nixon and those not so favorable.

With regard to Nixon's preparation for the presidency, I would emphasize his own views. He states that he decided in the 1940s that foreign affairs were to be the area of his major concern and, incidentally, that his first opinions of the Soviet Union were favorable ones. According to him, he was pro-Russian during World War II—well, that may have been the case. He says that Churchill's speech at Fulton, Missouri in the spring of 1946 at first irritated him, for he thought Churchill had gone too far in criticizing an ally; but the speech did have a delayed influence on him.

I have read most of Nixon's *Memoirs,* which are not easy reading, and also his book, *The Real War.* It's interesting that Nixon should have written three books since leaving the presidency—these volumes and a new work, *The Real Peace*—because they bear on what he said to Henry Kissinger on his last night in office as they were walking toward the White House. There are two accounts. Nixon's account is that Kissinger said, "Mr. Nixon, you are going to be remembered as a great President." Kissinger's recollection is that he said, "Mr. President, you are going to be remembered for the major achievements of your Presidency." There is a certain difference there, but, in any case, they are in agreement that Nixon's response, which Kissinger says he repeated many times, was, "It all depends, Henry, on what they write about me." Well, it seems to me that Nixon has taken steps to ensure that the writing will include his point of view by doing a good deal of it himself: his *Memoirs* alone run to about 1,100 pages, and he may not have reached the end. I have the impression that much of the *Memoirs* was not written so much for readers such as ourselves—one doesn't want to plow through all that discussion of Watergate—but that Nixon is laying out his case for historians and political scientists in the future. He is putting his case before a future public.

Nixon thought that the Vietnam War was extremely important. In his view, it was not his war, as it was in progress when he came into office, and yet, as he put it, he couldn't "bug out" of it. He was fearful that the results could be disastrous for the United States if we left in dishonor. In one place he said he told Kissinger that we might not survive the political effects. That might have been an exaggeration, but, at least, he was convinced that the results would be dangerous. I think his view on Vietnam explains his determination to bring the United States out of the war as well as he could. Whether he could have done anything else than to "Vietnamize" the war, I don't know, considering the situation at home at the time. I do think that the domestic benefits of that policy were somewhat greater than Congressman Rhodes does. At any rate, Nixon believed that we had to fight the war to what he hoped would be an honorable conclusion. I agree with Mr. Rhodes that Congress acted dishonorably in the years following the January 1973 ceasefire, and that the North Vietnamese, in their own way, did too. Of course, they looked on the matter a little differently. They saw that the presidency was being cut up, that Congress was denying arms to America's ally in South Vietnam, and that President Thieu had to fight a poor man's war. Thus they decided the time was ripe for another invasion, and carried it off in early 1975.

Let me take up something that Mr. Rhodes did not discuss, Nixon's relationship with Kissinger. I'm not an expert on Kissinger, but I am impressed in reading Nixon's *Memoirs,* and also those of Kissinger, which are even more lengthy, that on big questions Nixon was probably right and Kissinger was not right, as events have shown. One difference between them was Kissinger's attachment to negotiations and Nixon's suspicion of negotiations. For example, Nixon would argue with Kissinger that the North Vietnamese were not going to negotiate seriously until there was something in it for them. There was something in it for them only in late 1972, when they found they had achieved what military success they could through their invasion of that spring and then was the time to negotiate seriously. Kissinger was always much more optimistic than Nixon as to what negotiations with the North Vietnamese could accomplish, and, during the 1972 invasion, that was connected perhaps to Kissinger's optimism that he could get the Soviet Union to put the brakes on North Vietnam. In fact, Kissinger thought the Soviets were doing their best to restrain the North Vietnamese. Nixon's view was that the USSR was using its intimations of assistance in order to stall us, in order to keep us from taking strong action against the North Vietnamese invasion, and that the tactic had succeeded because we did not take such action for over a month after the invasion had begun. The Soviet Union would say, yes, go into these next meetings with the North Vietnamese; they're going to tell you surprising things. Nixon's understanding of Soviet policy was clearer than Kissinger's.

My final comment concerns Nixon's responsibility for the collapse of Vietnam and the serious situation in which the United States—the West—has found itself since then. Our failure there has, it seems to me, encouraged the Soviet Union to become more bold. After having pursued their ends rather cautiously, the Soviets have shown boldness in Africa and the Middle East and the Far East—for example, in obtaining what amounts to a naval base in Communist Vietnam. Nixon bears a responsibility for the invasion of South Vietnam in 1975 and the aftermath, for his terrible blunder. I agree with Mr. Rhodes that a good part of the blunder probably was caused by a desire to defend his friends (up to a point). But I don't think one needs to read Machiavelli, as Rhodes recommends, to learn that a politician cannot stand by friends who do him wrong. There might have been other reasons for Nixon's conduct; for example, extreme partisanship might have played a part, in that Nixon saw his enemies go after those around him and didn't want to satisfy them.

If Mr. Nixon must bear responsibility for the weakening of the presidency and the events which have followed, so do his enemies. They drove him from one cover to another, farther into a corner from which he tried to escape with lies and evasions, and they kept working on the American people until the people came to believe that there must be a great fire behind the smoke of what I consider to have been the relatively minor incidents of Watergate. Nixon made the incidents serious by his lies and thus made it impossible for him to stay in office, but those who did the driving bear some of the responsibility for subsequent events as well.

25
Comments on Part VII

David Manwaring

A large part of Nixon's problem with Watergate flowed from serious personality difficulties. He could not do the smallest misdeed without it looking like a felony when he did it and tried to explain it. Try to imagine Ronald Reagan, Reaganomics and all, sitting in the White House in 1973 and having this stuff start rolling in; him holding the press conferences, his releasing this partial transcript. There never would have been a resignation. He is such a nice man. I speak as a frustrated Democrat. Reagan could be out there raping nuns on the Boston College "dust bowl" and, when the smoke cleared, people would be saying "My gosh, doesn't he act young at his age."

Nixon could get the same result, or worse, by telling an off-color joke at the table. One has to sympathize with the man in some ways—not many, of course. I still speak as a charter member of the I Hate Nixon Club. I was not in at the very ground floor, but I date back to before I could vote and before I was a Democrat. But I want to give a certain amount of grudging admiration to Nixon as president, especially before Watergate. He was one of the very most capable and hard-working people ever to occupy the White House. His foreign policy achievements have been oft referred to. He was a pioneer in the modern attempt to recapture control of the executive branch, most of which has been effectively out of presidential control for a large number of years. In the face of consecutive Democratic Congresses, he wielded very extensive domestic power.

What excites me as a constitutional lawyer is that Nixon's clout was wielded not as a political manager, not as a negotiator or wheeler-dealer like, say, Johnson, but specifically as an independent actor wielding a variety of grants of presidential discretion Congress had incautiously parted with in previous terms to more congenial occupants of the White House. He protected these discretionary powers with the veto power because he did have the votes to prevent an override. He invoked, and played to the hilt, the independent powers that the presidency occupies separately from Congress. He pushed all of these to such a degree as to force at least to a partial resolution, a lot of constitutional ambiguities which have been lying around since the founding. One need only run off a short list beginning with impoundment.

Roosevelt impounded funds; Truman impounded funds; Eisenhower impounded funds. But these were usually isolated instances and a self-defense against a Congress which had exhalted the deals of some subordinate over the president's policy. Nixon looked at this and said that is a *power*—and he used it to effectively repeal whole ongoing programs, by withholding all their money. As a result, he wound up in court, where he lost a lot, and he also provoked the congressional statute covering the impoundment of funds and regulating same.

Certainly he was not the broadest user of executive privilege. After all, there was a point at which President Truman put the personnel files of the entire executive branch off limits to Congress. But he probably went further in using executive privilege in specific self-defense against investigations of his own wrongdoings, thereby provoking a Supreme Court test which, as you know, was fatal to his own career. His use of his power as commander in chief to send troops off to shoot at people was not unprecedented. That had been going on for a very long time, but he was really the first person to keep troops in the field for over a year, a couple of years, in the teeth of substantial congressional opposition. There are no Supreme Court tests of wars, but Congress did pass the War Powers Act. He attempted to exploit the president's powers as commander in chief for various domestic purposes, including surveillance, prosecution of dissidents like Dr. Spock, and clamping down on the Pentagon Papers. This provoked a series of court cases, all of which he lost, but in most of which he gained substantial recognition for a certain degree of presidential power. And finally you have, of course, wire tapping, the plumbers, the dirty tricks, and the rest.

Not one thing charged in the Watergate investigation, up to and including coverups and perjury, had not been committed by previous presidents. The thing that brought Nixon down, aside from the personality flaws I have already mentioned, was that previous presidents only did this now and then, one at a time. They did not make a business of it, as was being done in 1972. It is a matter of magnitude that produces the different reaction.

In this regard I suppose I have to quibble with Professor Scigliano about the responsiblity of Nixon's pursuers for the harm done the presidency. There is something to this but it is a much more debatable question than it appears to be. I refer you to the problem we have here in the Boston area. We are, after all, the car-theft capital of the world. Somebody steals a car; the police spot the car; the police wave him over and the guy takes off at eighty miles an hour; the police chase him and eventually have a very messy crash. You get all kinds of complaints. Should the police be engaging in high-speed chases? Look at the harm it does. But after all, where does the responsibility really lie? Nobody put a gun to the car thief's head and said, "Take off at eighty miles an hour." He made the choice. The police are basically doing what they should be doing. And, I think, some of the analogy carries over here. The tricks, the cover-up, the lying—these were *choices* made by a man with more honorable alternatives.

Selected Bibliography

The following books and articles have been chosen on the basis of their superior quality from among the vast number of writings about the presidency in general and the specific topics covered in this volume.

General Works on the Presidency

Besette, Joseph, and Geoffrey Tullis, eds. *The Presidency in the Constitutional Order.* Louisiana State Univ. Press, 1981.

Corwin, Edward S. *The President: Office and Powers, 1787-1957.* New York: New York Univ. Press, 1957.

Cronin, Thomas. *The State of the Presidency.* Boston: Little, Brown, 1982.

Laski, Harold J. *The American Presidency.* New York: Harper & Brothers, 1940.

Neustadt, Richard. *Presidential Power.* New York: Wiley and Sons, 1960.

Pious, Richard M. *The American Presidency.* New York: Basic Books, 1979.

Polsby, Nelson, and Aaron Wildavsky. *Presidenial Elections.* New York: Charles Scribner and Sons, 1975.

Rossiter, Clinton. *The American Presidency.* New York: Harcourt Brace and World, 1956.

Thach, Charles. *Creation of the Presidency, 1775-89.* Baltimore: Johns Hopkins Univ. Press, 1922).

Tugwell, Rexford. *The Enlargement of the Presidency.* Garden City, N.Y.: Doubleday, 1960.

White, Leonard D. *A Study in Administrative History: The Federalists, The Jacksonians, The Republican Era,* 4 vols. New York: Crowell Collier and Macmillan, 1947-1958.

The Institutionalized Presidency

A New Regulatory Framework: Report on Selected Independent Regulatory Agencies [Ash Council]. Washington, D.C.: U.S. Government Printing Office, 1971.

Anderson, Patrick. *The President's Men.* Garden City, N.Y.: Doubleday, 1968.

Baade, Hans W., and Norman C. Thomas, eds. *The Institutionalized Presidency.* Oceana, 1972.

Berman, Larry. *The Office of Management and Budget and the President. 1921-79.* Princeton, N.J.: Princeton Univ. Press, 1979.

Clarke, Keith C., and Laurence J. Legere, eds. *The President and the Management of National Security.* New York: Praeger, 1969.

Cronin, Thomas E., and Sanford D. Greenberg, eds. *The Presidential Advisory System.* New York: Harper & Row, 1969.

Cronin, Thomas E., and Rexford G. Tugwell, eds. *The Presidency Reappraised.* New York: Praeger, 1974.

Heclo, Hugh, and Lester M. Salamon, eds. *The Illusion of Presidential Government.* Boulder, Colo.: Westview Press, 1981.

Hess, Stephen. *Organizing the Presidency.* Washington, D.C.: Brookings Institute, 1976.

Hobbs, Edward H. *Behind the President.* Public Affairs Press, 1954.

Hoxie, R. Gordon, ed. *The White House: Organization and Operations.* Center for the Study of the Presidency, 1971.

Jackson, Henry M. *Commission on Government Operations: The National Security Council.* New York: Praeger, 1965.

The Rhetorical Presidency

Bessette, Joseph; James Ceaser; Glenn Thurow; and Jeffrey Tulis. "The Rise of the Rhetorical Presidency." *Presidential Studies Quarterly* (Spring 1981): 233-251.

Cornwell, Elmer. *Presidential Leadership of Public Opinion.* Bloomington: Indiana Univ. Press, 1965.

Reedy, George. *Twilight of the Presidency.* New York: World, 1975.

Thurow, Glenn, and Jeffrey Wallin, eds. *Rhetoric and American Statesmanship.* Carolina Academic Press, 1984.

Franklin D. Roosevelt

Alsop, Joseph. *FDR: A Centenary Remembrance 1882-1945.* New York: Viking, 1982.

Alsop, Joseph, and Robert Kintner. *The Men around the President.* Garden City, N.Y.: Doubleday, Doran, 1939.

Burns, James MacGregor. *The Lion and the Fox.* New York: Harcourt, Brace, 1956.

———. *Roosevelt: Soldier of Freedom.* New York: Harcourt, Brace, 1971.

Divine, Robert. *The Illusion of Neutrality.* Chicago: Univ. of Chicago Press, 1962.

Freidel, Frank. *Franklin D. Roosevelt: The Apprenticeship; The Ordeal; The Triumph; Launching the New Deal.* 4 vols. Boston: Little, Brown, 1952-1974.

Goldman, Eric. *Rendezvous with Destiny.* New York: Knopf, 1952.

Leuchtenburg, William E. *Franklin D. Roosevelt and the New Deal* New York: Harper & Row, 1963.

Moley, Raymond. *After Seven Years.* New York: Harper & Brothers, 1939.

Schlesinger, Arthur M., Jr. *The Age of Roosevelt: The Crisis of the Old Order; The Coming of the New Deal: The Politics of Upheaval.* 3 vols. Boston: Houghton Mifflin, 1957, 1958, 1960.

Tugwell, Rexford G. *The Democratic Roosevelt.* Garden City, N.Y.: Doubleday, 1957.

Dwight D. Eisenhower

Adams, Sherman. *Firsthand Report: The Story of the Eisenhower Administration.* Harper, 1961.

Albertson, Dean. *Eisenhower as President.* Hill and Wang, 1963.

Alexander, Charles C. *Holding the Line: The Eisenhower Era.* Bloomington: Indiana Univ. Press, 1975.

Divine, Robert A. *Eisenhower and the Cold War.* London: Oxford Univ. Press, 1981.

Donovan, Robert E. *Eisenhower, The Inside Story.* New York: Harper & Brothers, 1965.

Ewald, William B. *Eisenhower the President: Crucial Days, 1951–1960.* Englewood Cliffs, N.J.: Prentice-Hall, 1981.

Greenstein, Fred I. *The Hidden-Hand Presidency: Eisenhower as Leader.* New York: 1982.

Hughes, Emmet John. *The Ordeal of Power.* New York: Dell, 1962.

Kempton, Murray. *America Comes of Middle Age.* Boston: Little, Brown, 1963.

Lyon, Peter. *Eisenhower: Portrait of the Hero.* Boston: Little, Brown, 1974.

Rostow, W.W. *Europe after Stalin: Eisenhower's Three Decisions of March 11, 1953.* Austin, Univ. of Texas Press, 1982).

Lyndon B. Johnson

Blissett, Marlan, and Emmette S. Redford. *Organizing the Executive Branch: The Johnson Presidency.* Chicago: Univ. of Chicago Press, 1981.

Caro, Robert A. *The Path of Power: The Years of Lyndon Johnson.* New York: Knopf, 1982.

Divine, Robert A., ed. *Exploring the Johnson Years.* Austin: Univ. of Texas Press, 1981.

Evans, Rowland, and Robert Novak. *Lyndon B. Johnson: The Exercise of Power.* New York: New American Library, 1966.

Ginzberg, Eli, and Robert M. Solow, eds. *The Great Society: Lessons for the Future.* New York: Basic Books, 1974.

Goldman, Eric F. *The Tragedy of Lyndon Johnson.* New York: Knopf, 1969.

Graff, Henry F. *The Tuesday Cabinet: Deliberation and Decision on Peace and War under Lyndon B. Johnson.* Englewood Cliffs, N.J.: Prentice-Hall, 1970.

Kearns, Doris. *Lyndon Johnson and the American Dream.* New York: Harper & Row, 1975.

McPherson, Harry C. *A Political Education.* Boston: Atlantic-Little, Brown, 1972.

McWilliams, Wilson C. "Lyndon Johnson and the Politics of Mass Society." In *Leadership in America,* edited by Peter Dennis Bathory. (Longman, 1978, pp. 177–194.

Reedy, George E. *Lyndon B. Johnson: A Memoir.* New York: Andrews and McMeel, 1982.

Roche, John P. *Sentenced to Life.* New York: Macmillan, 1974.

Rulon, Philip R. *The Compassionate Samaritan: The Life of Lyndon Baines Johnson.* Nelson-Hall, 1981.

Schandler, Herbert Y. *The Unmaking of a President: Lyndon Johnson and Vietnam.* Princeton, N.J.: Princeton Univ. Press, 1977.

Richard M. Nixon

Brodie, Fawn M. *Richard Nixon, The Shaping of His Character.* New York: Norton, 1981.

Burke, Vincent J., and Vee Burke. *Nixon's Good Deed: Welfare Reform.* New York: Columbia University Press, 1974.

Evans, Rowland, and Robert Novak. *Nixon in the White House: The Frustration of Power.* New York: Random House, 1971.

Kissinger, Henry. *White House Years.* Boston: Little, Brown, 1979.

———. *Years of Upheaval.* Boston: Little, Brown, 1982.

Nathan, Richard P. *The Administrative Presidency.* New York: Wiley, 1983.

———. *The Plot That Failed: Nixon and the Administratie Presidency.* New York: John Wiley and Sons, 1975.

Safire, William. *Before the Fall.* Garden City, N.Y.: Doubleday, 1975.

Silk, Leonard. *Nixonomics.* New York: Praeger, 1972.

White, Theodore H. *Breach of Faith: The Fall of Richard Nixon.* New York: Atheneum, 1975.

Wills, Garry. *Nixon Agonistes.* Boston: Houghton Mifflin, 1970).

Ronald Reagan

Cannon, Lou. *Reagan.* New York: Putnam, 1982.

Evans, Rowland, and Robert Novak. *The Reagan Revolution.* New York: Dutton, 1981.

Greenstein, Fred I. *The Reagan Presidency: An Early Assessment.* Baltimore: Johns Hopkins, 1983.

Greider, William. *The Education of David Stockman and Other Americans.* New York: Dutton, 1982.

Haig, Alexander M. *Caveat: Realism, Reagan, and Foreign Policy.* New York: Macmillan, 1984.

Nathan, Richard P. *The Administrative Presidency.* New York: Wiley, 1983.

Ornstein, Norman J., ed. *President and Congress: Assessing Reagan's First Year.* Washington, D.C.: American Enterprise Institute, 1982.

Smith, Hedrick, et al. *Reagan the Man, the President.* New York: Pergamon, 1981.

Index

About the Contributors

Samuel H. Beer, Eaton Professor of Government, Emeritus, Harvard University, was the first holder of the Thomas P. O'Neill, Jr., Chair in American Politics at Boston College. He is the author of many books, among them *Britain Against Itself* (1982), *The State and the Poor* (1970), and (with Adam Ulam) *Patterns of Government* (1958).

Richard Bolling represented the Fifth Missouri Congressional District from 1949 until his retirement from the Congress in 1983. From 1979 to 1983 he was Chairman of the House Rules Committee. In 1983 he was the Thomas P. O'Neill, Jr., Professor of American Politics at Boston College, and is the author of *House Out of Order* (1965), *Power in the House* (1968), and (with John Bowles) *America's Competitive Edge* (1982).

Lou Cannon worked for local newspapers and for the Ridder chain in California from 1961 to 1972, when he joined the *Washington Post.* Since then he has been a White House correspondent for the *Post,* and from 1977 to 1980 was the head of the *Post's* West Coast Bureau. He is the author of four books, including *Jesse and Ronnie: A Political Odyssey* (1969) and *Reagan* (1982).

James W. Ceaser is a member of the Woodrow Wilson Department of Government and Foreign Affairs at the University of Virginia. He is the author of *Reforming the Reforms: A Critical Analysis of the Presidential Selection Process* (1982) and *Presidential Selection: Theory and Development* (1979).

Thomas E. Cronin is a member of the department of political science at The Colorado College, and the author of the *The State of the Presidency* (1982) and *The Presidential Advisory System* (1969). He is co-editor (with Rexford Tugwell) of *The Presidency Reappraised* (1974).

Kenneth S. Davis is a freelance writer and the author of *Soldier of Democracy: A Biography of Dwight Eisenhower* (1949). He has also written *The Politics of*

Honor: A Biography of Adlai E. Stevenson (1967) and *FDR: The Beckoning of Destiny* (1972).

Hedley Donovan is the former editor-in-chief of *Time,* Inc. He was senior advisor to President Jimmy Carter from 1979 to 1980, and is presently a fellow of government at the John F. Kennedy School of Government at Harvard University.

Robert J. Donovan is the author of *Eisenhower: The Inside Story* (1956), *The Future of the Republican Party* (1964), and *Tumultuous Years: The Presidency of Harry S. Truman, 1949–1953* (1982). He was, before his retirement, an associate editor and national columnist at the *Los Angeles Times.*

James M. Fallows is the Washington Editor of *The Atlantic Monthly* and the author of *National Defense* (1980). From 1977 to 1978 he was chief speechwriter for President Jimmy Carter.

Katharine Ferguson is a former White House correspondent for National Public Radio, and producer of "All Things Considered." She now reports on foreign policy for NPR.

Barney Frank represents the Fourth Massachusetts Congressional District in the U. S. House of Representatives. He was first elected to Congress in 1980, following three terms in the Massachusetts legislature.

Fred I. Greenstein is director of the Woodrow Wilson School Leadership and Presidency Studies Program at Princeton University. He is the author of *The Hidden-Hand Presidency: Eisenhower as a Leader* (1982), *The Reagan Presidency: An Early Appraisal,* and *Children and Politics* (1965), among others.

Irwin "Tubby" Harrison is co-founder of the polling and political consulting firm of Harrison-Goldberg in Boston, and does polling for national, state, and local candidates as well as for the *Boston Globe.*

Hugh Heclo is a member of the department of government at Harvard University, and is a former senior fellow at the Brookings Institution. He is the author of *A Government of Strangers: Executive Politics in Washington* (1977) and coauthor of *The Illusion of Presidential Government* (1981) and *Comparative Public Policy* (1978).

Harry C. McPherson, Jr., is an attorney with the firm of Verner, Liipfert, Bernhard and McPherson, in Washington, D.C. From 1964 to 1969 he was a special counsel to President Lyndon Johnson. Before coming to the White House he was deputy under secretary of the army for international affairs (1963), and assistant secretary of state for educational and cultural affairs. His memoir of government service, *A Political Education,* was published in 1972.

Wilson C. McWilliams is a member of the department of political science at Rutgers University, and the author of *The Idea of Fraternity in America* (1973).

David Manwaring is a member of the department of political science at Boston College, and the author of *Render unto Caesar* (1962).

Richard E. Neustadt is the Lucius N. Littauer Professor of Public Administration at the John F. Kennedy School of Government, Harvard University. He served as consultant to the president under Presidents Kennedy and Johnson. Among his books are *Presidential Power* (1960), which received the Woodrow Wilson Foundation Award, and *Alliance Politics* (1970). He is a fellow of the American Academy of Arts and Sciences.

Edward F. Prichard, Jr., is an attorney with the firm of Wyatt, Tarrant, and Combs in Lexington, Kentucky. He was a member of the Roosevelt administration, and served in the Department of the Treasury in the 1930s and 1940s.

George E. Reedy was the special assistant to Vice President Lyndon Johnson from 1961 to 1963, and President Johnson's press secretary from 1964 to 1965. Prior to serving in the White House, he was a member of several congressional committee staffs and a congressional correspondent for United Press International. He is the author of *Lyndon Johnson: A Memoir* (1982) and *The Twilight of the Presidency* (1970).

John J. Rhodes represented the First Arizona Congressional District in the United States House of Representatives from 1955 until his retirement in 1981. From 1973 to 1981. From 1973 to 1981 he was the minority leader of the House of Representatives.

John P. Roche is Henry Luce Professor of Civilization and Foreign Affairs, Fletcher School of Law and Diplomacy. He was a special consultant to President Lyndon B. Johnson from 1966 to 1968. He is the author of *Political Legitimacy,* (1979), *American Nationality—1607-1978: An Overview* (1980), and *Sentenced to Life* (1974).

Robert Scigliano is a member of the department of political science at Boston College. He is the author of *South Vietnam: Nation under Stress* (1963), *The Supreme Court and the Presidency* (1971), and is coauthor of *Representation* (1981).

Geoffrey C. Ward is a former editor of *American Heritage* and is the author of *Before the Trumpet: Young Franklin Roosevelt* (1985).

About the Editor

Marc Landy is an associate professor of political science at Boston College and a lecturer in political science at the Harvard School of Public Health. He is the author of a book, *The Politics of Environmental Regulation: Controlling Kentucky Surface Mining* (1975) and coeditor (with Dennis Hale) of *The Nature of Politics: Selected Essays of Bertrand de Jouvenel* (1985). His articles and reviews on the subjects of political leadership, the presidency, and public policy have appeared in such publications as *World Politics, Society, The Chronicle of Higher Education, Worldview* and *The FDR Encyclopedia.* He is a graduate of Oberlin College and received his Ph.D. from Harvard University.